Michael Thumann

# Revenge
How Putin Created the Most Menacing Regime in the World

Michael Thumann

# REVENGE

How Putin Created the Most Menacing Regime
in the World

**Bibliografische Information der Deutschen Nationalbibliothek**
Die Deutsche Nationalbibliothek verzeichnet diese Publikation in der Deutschen Nationalbibliografie; detaillierte bibliografische Daten sind im Internet über http://dnb.d-nb.de abrufbar.

**Bibliographic information published by the Deutsche Nationalbibliothek**
Die Deutsche Nationalbibliothek lists this publication in the Deutsche Nationalbibliografie; detailed bibliographic data are available in the Internet at http://dnb.d-nb.de.

Cover photo: ID 242050777 | Russia War Ukraine © Rokas Tenys | Dreamstime.com

The Original German-language version was published in 2023:
Michael Thumann: *Revanche. Wie Putin das bedrohlichste Regime der Welt geschaffen hat.*
© Verlag C.H.Beck oHG, München 2023

Copy-editing by Academic Consulting Services, Oxford

ISBN-13: 978-3-8382-1903-5
© *ibidem*-Verlag, Hannover • Stuttgart 2024
Alle Rechte vorbehalten

Das Werk einschließlich aller seiner Teile ist urheberrechtlich geschützt. Jede Verwertung außerhalb der engen Grenzen des Urheberrechtsgesetzes ist ohne Zustimmung des Verlages unzulässig und strafbar. Dies gilt insbesondere für Vervielfältigungen, Übersetzungen, Mikroverfilmungen und elektronische Speicherformen sowie die Einspeicherung und Verarbeitung in elektronischen Systemen.

All rights reserved. No part of this publication may be reproduced, stored in or introduced into a retrieval system, or transmitted, in any form, or by any means (electronical, mechanical, photocopying, recording or otherwise) without the prior written permission of the publisher. Any person who does any unauthorized act in relation to this publication may be liable to criminal prosecution and civil claims for damages.

Printed in the EU

# Table of Contents

Foreword by Fiona Hill..................................................................7

Attack.
Russia is out for revenge..........................................................15

Misguided.
How German politicians helped Putin......................................23

Gallery of Ancestors.
Why the 1991 putschists have won today................................47

Exercises in Democracy.
The hopes of the 1990s............................................................59

Rogue Republic.
The Chechen model..................................................................77

Nationalists by choice.
Putin's good friends in the world..............................................93

Information War.
How the Russians are incited..................................................107

The Putin Archipelago.
Russia's system of penal camps..............................................123

Elections Without Choice.
Descent into dictatorship.......................................................137

Executor of History.
Putin's abuse of the past .......................................................149

Special Operation.
How to wipe out Ukraine........................................................167

Planet Putin.
Russia seals itself off..............................................................191

Empire of Fear.
The mobilization of the people........................................................217

Rebels—resistance from the right ...................................................231

Holy War.
Putin's Revenge on the West ............................................................245

Triumph or Armageddon.
His endgame ......................................................................................265

Further Reading ................................................................................279

Thanks................................................................................................289

# Foreword

The Vladimir Putin that Michael Thumann describes in this book is a radical nationalist and a revolutionary. He is the Russian ruler who, since he returned to the presidency in 2012 after a single term as Prime Minister, has been bent on overturning the European and international orders that have prevailed since the end of the Cold War. In the name of "revenge," Putin has revolted against the 1990s when the Soviet Union collapsed, leaving the United States the lone superpower astride the world stage. Putin has invaded Ukraine and unleashed the largest land war in Europe since World War II to boost Russia's diminished position in the region. And, Putin has upended the security and foreign policy calculations of countries well outside the European arena.

    For Vladimir Putin, the dissolution of the USSR was not the end of the Communist system; it was the disintegration of the historic, imperial Russian state. Other large former Soviet republics, like Ukraine and Kazakhstan, may have seen this as a liberation and the chance to build a new country, but for Russia it was a catastrophe. Putin saw the Soviet collapse as marking the loss of territories that Russia had seized over centuries and of Moscow's geopolitical influence. Since first annexing Crimea from Ukraine in 2014, Putin has returned to the kinds of imperial obsessions that the last Soviet president, Mikhail Gorbachev, and first Russian president, Boris Yeltsin, seemed to cast aside. Putin has returned to the "ash heap" of Russia's history to gather up the pieces and shape a monument to its present. In launching a full-scale invasion of Ukraine in 2022, Putin has made it clear that *his* version of Russia's past is now the only acceptable foundation for Russia's future.

As Michael Thumann notes, Putin claims that the invasion and war in Ukraine was imposed on him. He and Russia had no choice but to react to Western actions and to a long succession of events dating back to the 1990s, including the expansion of NATO, and US decisions to intervene in the Balkan conflicts, invade Iraq, recognize Kosovo, or interfere in Libya. Everything he has done, Putin says, is in response to the US—every action must have a swift and severe counteraction. Putin is simply mounting an offensive defense of Russian interests. In fact, as Michael makes clear, Russia is in many respects reacting to itself, to Putin and the Kremlin's interpretations and often misinterpretation of events.

The West—the US and Europe—certainly made many mistakes along the way, particularly in not fully grasping the import of Putin's perspectives on world affairs; but the West also had limited impact on Russia's internal political development. Russia is not a small or peripheral state. Vladimir Putin has been in power for a very long time—a quarter of a century by 2024. The progress and regression of this country that spans eleven time zones is largely independent of the West—and so are the decisions of its ruler. Vladimir Putin, alone and with full sovereignty over his own actions, chose to attack Ukraine in February 2022. Well before taking this decision, Putin also chose to wage a hybrid war against the West, including interfering in the 2016 US presidential election. Putin did this, because, in his view, America was weak. The time was ripe for his own actions.

After this book was completed, Vladimir Putin seemed to have reached peak political strength. At home, in March 2024, he re-legitimized his reign with 88% of the vote in the Russian presidential election—his highest ever result since 2000. Putin's only real political competitor, Alexei Navalny, died in a Siberian prison camp exactly a month before Russians went to the ballot box. Other presidential "contenders" were either marginalized or marginal figures, largely unknown inside or outside Russia. In the 2024 election, Putin was essentially re-anointed as a modern Tsar, and seemingly set on course for a six-year term that would take him out to 2030. He also had the possibility to "run" for yet another term after that, which would see him in office until 2036.

By 2030, Putin will have outlasted all elected Western leaders, he will also overtake Soviet leader Josef Stalin, who was in office 30 years (from 1922-1952). By 2036, Vladimir Putin will have reigned (as president and also prime minister) longer than formidable Empress Catherine the Great, who ruled Russia for 34 years (from 1762-1796). He will still fall short of Tsars Peter the Great, Ivan the Great, and Ivan the Terrible, who each had more than four decades on the Russian throne. Nonetheless, as Michael makes clear, Putin views himself as a historic figure at home and abroad. Based on his political permanence as Russia's dominant leader of the first quarter of the 21$^{st}$ Century, and his dramatic deeds, Putin believes he deserves his place in Russia's pantheon of the "greats."

Abroad, Putin's obsession with restoring Russia's great power position, and ending "American dominance" once and for all, has surfaced in every foreign policy move he made after invading Ukraine. As Michael writes, Putin views the US as the puppet master behind global developments. He sees himself leading an international coalition of disaffected states opposed to the West and US hegemony. In this regard, Putin and Russia benefit from the fact that, as an imperial power, the expanding Russian state did not take territories in Latin or South America or Africa and establish colonies there. Russia is subsequently given a "pass" by major regional states like Brazil and South Africa that other European powers and the United States are not accorded.

Putin has capitalized on this by seeking to cement Russia's role as a leader of what he deems the "global majority" (or what we also might call the global community beyond the US and the transatlantic alliance) in a contemporary revolt against Western colonial imperialism. The irony, of course, as Michael details in the book, is that Russia has a long history of brutal conquest and colonial wars in parts of Europe and Asia. Russia wrested Ukrainian lands from the Polish, Swedish, and Ottoman empires. It annexed land in the Caucasus from the Ottomans and Persians, and in the far east from China. Russia clashed with the British Empire in Central Asia and the northern reaches of the Indian subcontinent and fought a war with Japan over the Korean peninsula.

Russia subjugated the peoples it incorporated with just as much violence and disregard for their rights as any other European colonial power. And it retained imperial subjects and territories long after other empires disintegrated. Indeed, Putin rode into power on the wave of the Chechen wars of the 1990s–2000s, when Moscow viciously suppressed the North Caucasus republic of Chechnya's efforts to secede from the Russian Federation. Russia's invasion of Ukraine is nothing other than an imperial landgrab to retake a former colony. Nonetheless since February 2022, Ukraine's efforts to make common cause with other colonized peoples and states that received their independence after the two world wars of the 20th Century have failed to get traction. Putin's version of Russia's globally "blameless" history and the legacy of Western misdeeds has proved too potent.

On October 7, 2023—on Putin's 71st birthday no less—a new, exploitable opportunity to turn the tide of world affairs against the US and Western imperialism emerged in the Middle East. Hamas attacked Israel, and Israel launched a devastating counterattack in Gaza. This dramatic series of events brought three sets of conflicts where both the US and Russia are protagonists together in sharp relief: in Ukraine, in the Middle East, and in the Indo-Pacific, where mounting tensions between the US and China raise the specter of new cold and hot wars. And it also joined the wars in Ukraine and Gaza in unexpected ways as an anti-US axis of sorts began to form from Europe to the Middle East to Asia, among Russia, China, Iran, and North Korea.

On the sidelines of the Beijing Olympics in early February 2022, Putin seemed to secure Chinese President Xi's acquiescence in his decision to invade Ukraine. China had no prior disputes with Ukraine. Nor did Iran and North Korea, which stepped into the Ukraine war as arms suppliers to compensate for Russian shortages of drones and ammunition. What attracted Beijing, Tehran, and Pyongyang to Moscow's attack on Kyiv were Putin's assertions in 2022–2024 that Russia was fighting against the US, NATO, and the West in Ukraine. Putin presented his war in Ukraine as a *proxy* war with the US. He offered an opportunity for China, Iran, and North Korea to thwart US policy in their own regions. Assisting Russia in Ukraine, and watching the US become increasingly embroiled and even potentially bogged down in the largest European land war since World War II, was an attractive means of signaling displeasure with US actions elsewhere.

With these other countries now in the mix, Putin's decision to invade Ukraine and to focus his efforts on undermining the United States at every possible turn took post-Soviet Russian foreign policy in new directions. In the Middle East, Iran's support for Russia, and its hostility toward both the US and Israel, encouraged Moscow to rupture previously cordial relations with Israel. Prior to October 7, Russia had, in some respects, been a strong supporter of Israel's regional position; but after October 7 Putin made a choice between Iran and Israel in the Middle East. In Asia, Putin similarly threw in his lot with China and North Korea—in the latter case noticeably changing Moscow's longstanding post-Soviet policy of keeping Pyongyang and its mercurial leaders at arm's length.

By 2024, Putin's war in Ukraine had become a pivotal test for the European and international security systems. A Ukrainian capitulation to Russia and Putin's demands would not bring a lasting peace to Europe. It would mark the evident success of the Kremlin's nuclear bullying that Michael describes in this book and the fulfillment of Putin's determination to change borders by force. A failed state in Ukraine would invite increased Russian coercive attention toward other former Soviet and Eastern bloc countries and bring more instability. The rupture of the post-Cold War European security order would mean the lack of European diplomatic bandwidth to deal with the war in Gaza and other conflicts in the Middle East and Africa, as well as a dearth of development funding as European countries dashed to build-up their militaries and even a European nuclear deterrent.

Putin's depiction of the war in Ukraine as a war with the US and NATO, also meant that Ukraine's potential defeat would highlight the weakness of the Western alliance and the failure of its security institutions. Russia would be emboldened, but so would Iran and North Korea, and also China, to act in other arenas. Indeed, outside the transatlantic alliance—as Putin seemed to peak in his political power after March 2024—many countries already believed that Putin had won his war, and Ukraine and the West had lost. Russia appeared poised to dominate Eastern Europe again, and project power against the United States. Pessimistic Western rhetoric ahead of European parliamentary and US presidential elections on top of Russian propaganda helped to consolidate this view.

In the first half of 2024, as this book moved to publication, relations between the US and Europe also shifted. European leaders seriously began considering the prospects for reducing their heavy security reliance on the US and stepping up defence production to match Russia's rearmament efforts. Europe's military posture and defense capacity beyond the NATO had not deterred Russia from moving against Ukraine in 2022. The key challenge was how to show European military as well as political resolve to shift Russia's calculations—as well as the rest of the world's—so they would not count Europe down and out as a global security player.

In sum, Putin's revolt against the 1990s has returned Russia to its traditional role of threatening its European neighbors. The last great European land empire has bitten back, with a vengeance.

April 2024<br>
Fiona Hill

# Attack

## Russia is out for revenge

The day Vladimir Putin mobilized his people for war, I met an old Moscow friend. We went to a café near the Cathedral of Christ the Savior, where many young people usually gathered. It was almost empty on September 21, 2022, and only women sat at the sparsely occupied tables.

»The men are probably hiding at home in case the field hunters come,« my friend speculated. He didn't feel safe either. Although in his late 40s, he had served in the army and was not allowed to leave the country. He told me about his son, who was 31 and had a secure job in Moscow in administration. Unmarried and without children, he was a prime candidate for the front.

»We talk on the phone every few hours, and I urge him to leave.« The son fought back, believing none of this concerned him. The war, the draft, the front, death or the penal camp if he retreated or went into captivity voluntarily, all that had nothing to do with his life. His father saw it differently. It was only a matter of time, he said. »If they need more soldiers, they'll come for all of us.«

That's why he so carefully planned his son's departure. Never talking about it, only writing or texting, buying flights with return tickets to show at the border to cover the escape to Istanbul. He persistently tried to convince his son. He begged him, nagged him, yelled at him, »Go!« It tore his heart apart. Two days after our meeting, my friend called me. His son had just flown out to Turkey. He didn't know if he would ever see him again.

It was the right decision. The Russian ruler had brought the war from Ukraine to his own people in September 2022. Young people like my friend's son have been mobilized from the streets since the end of September. Draft orders were delivered by the janitor, the pizza delivery person, the electricity meter reader, and the neighborhood police officer. In Moscow, buses drove through the city to pick up anyone reporting to the front. Anyone who protested against the war was sent to the front in handcuffs. I talked and texted day and night with friends and acquaintances about border crossings, about the children, about asylum applications, and about life in the West. Many of them left, until the end of September 2022 when Russia largely closed its borders to its citizens of military age.

War returned to Europe in 2022. It is the biggest quake since World War II and has profoundly changed the lives of Europeans. And we are only at the beginning. Putin's criminal war of aggression has robbed tens of thousands of Ukrainians of their lives and ripped the roofs off the heads of millions who were turned into refugees. The European continent has plunged into a protracted social and economic crisis, and no one knows when or where it will end. Rapid demonetization and a crisis of scarcity have shaken many countries, including those in the Global South. Humankind will have to bear the consequences of this war for years to come. The causes do not lie in geopolitical power rivalries or storms of capitalist speculation. One man, his regime, and his supporters are to blame. They invaded a neighboring country not for need or distress but with imperial intentions and terrible consequences for the whole world.

Vladimir Putin was a narrow-faced and almost-shy head of government when I met him for a first interview at the end of 1999. He seemed awkward and angular in his movements, and he spoke a very awkward Russian riddled with bureaucratic formulas. At the time, he acted as if he wanted to build good relations with the West. He spoke of democracy, cooperation, and the joint fight against terrorism. Even then, I didn't really believe him. I thought he was an authoritarian secret-service man who rang in his term of office with a brutal war against Chechnya. I would never have guessed that I was meeting a man who, a good 20 years later, would threaten the entire world with nuclear catastrophe from his bunker.

In this respect, Putin surprised us all. The real question is »who realized that the man was not to be trusted and when?« The timing is highly political. After all, Western credulity, cronyism, and a huge leap of faith are what made Vladimir Putin great. Former US President George W. Bush's error in 2001 is often cited: »I looked the man in the eye. I found him to be very straightforward and trustworthy.[. . .] I was able to get a sense of his soul«. So, too, is the clean bill-of-health proclaimed by former Chancellor Gerhard Schröder, who in 2004 called Putin a »flawless democrat.« Schröder repeated this several times years later, by which time the ex-chancellor had long since become an oligarch in Russian corporations. But many of his party friends in the SPD also refused to see what was so obvious about the Kremlin ruler long after the annexation of Crimea in 2014. People in the other German parties, in the FDP, the CDU/CSU, even in the Greens, were also happy to be deceived by Putin—not to mention the leftists and the AfD, who openly took sides with Russia and its president. The Germans talked themselves into believing the man. When Ukraine was invaded, those who trusted were suddenly surprised. German politicians, German businesspeople, and German representatives of associations were »severely shocked« and »disappointed.« They said, »We could have never expected!« Why not? Putin's invasion of Ukraine is a war that began back in 2014 with the annexation of Crimea. All they had to do was look and listen.

The illusions of Western politicians and businesspeople have helped Vladimir Putin threaten the world to the extent that he has today. Germany stubbornly capped its defense budget until 2021 but increased its gas dependence on Russia from 38 percent in 2012 to 55 percent in 2021. The rationale, already false at the time, was that Russia had always been a reliable supplier. Putin has had years of good fortune in international relations because many believed him. Because many underestimated him. Because many thought that were one to talk to him diligently and hold him in high esteem, he would be ready for any form of partnership. Two errors helped Putin in particular: the assumption that he was actually a good man even if easy to provoke and the fear that everything would be much worse in Russia should he leave. But could things be worse?

When Russian troops invaded Ukraine in the early morning of February 24, I was asleep in my Moscow apartment. The editors of *Zeit Online* rang me out of bed at half past five in the morning. Before I even had my first tea, I wrote the lead story. It warned that this war was not a local affair between Russia and Ukraine but a threat to all of Europe. A few hours later, the first reactions came in. One reader protested that this was a matter between two former Soviet republics. Why would I scare everyone and claim that »we« were also threatened? A few weeks later, an indignant reader wrote to me: »Putin is not waging war against us, he is only reacting to the Western sanctions.« Months later, I read in the letters: »Putin was only reacting to our arms deliveries to Ukraine with the threats against Germany. NATO had provoked Russia.« Again with the exculpatory arguments. Again with the insinuation of harmlessness.

Again with a gross underestimation of Putin.

That is why I am writing this book. Ukraine is still the theater of hot war as I write these lines, but the hybrid great war is, more broadly, targeting us. Putin wants to bury liberal democracy. He is attacking Europe's way of life, its security, and its economic foundations. He wants to use a gas embargo to destroy Germany's industrial base. He wants control over the continent. This attack is all the more dangerous because Russia is part of Europe. Former President of Russia and current Deputy Chair of the Russian Security Council Dmitri

Medvedev exposed the Russian view of European civilization when he shouted to the Baltics and ultimately to all Europeans: »That you are in freedom is not your merit, but our failure.« An unrestrainedly imperial and belligerent Russia has become a threat to all of Europe and the world. This book recounts the unstoppable radicalization of one man, his regime, and Europe's largest country.

Three basic ideas guide my analyses and reports. First, Vladimir Putin is taking revenge. The Russian ruler sees the disintegration of the Soviet Union and the shrunken Russian nation-state not as a liberation but as a catastrophe. His war is an attempt to turn back time: Putin is leading a revolt against the 1990s, the opening of his country, Russia's polyphony, power-sharing with the republics, disarmament treaties with the West. He has returned to an imperial obsession that the last Soviet president, Mikhail Gorbachev, had ended. The war against Ukraine is »Russia's armed response to the fall of the Berlin Wall«—this is how Italian philosopher and publicist Angelo Bolaffi tried to answer the question about the deeper reasons of the historical caesura of February 24, 2022. But here it should be added: The war is the reaction of those nationalists and Soviet imperialists who, even then, believed that the GDR citizens and the non-Russian peoples of Eastern Europe should not have been released from eternal Soviet captivity in 1990. Putin is leading these imperialists today—against the Russians who saw the end of the Reich and the 1990s as liberation. Putin has been out for revenge for the past three decades.

Second, Russia is not reacting to us. It is reacting to itself. The search for a sense of meaning and what we did wrong that is popular in the West is pointless when it comes to interpreting Russia. The West undoubtedly made mistakes, from Iraq to Afghanistan, but these had little impact on Russia's political development. Nevertheless, the opinion that conditions in Russia and the actions of its ruler depend on what the West does or does not do has become entrenched among part of the German public. From my perspective as a correspondent and temporary Muscovite, this is an intolerable arrogance. Indeed, this view assumes that Russia, a world power, is dependent on the West for its internal development or shapes its policies as a reaction to the West. Russia is not a small state. The progress and regression of this country that spans eleven time zones is largely independent of the West—and so are the decisions of its ruler. Vladimir Putin, alone and in full sovereignty, chose to attack Ukraine; he chose to wage a hybrid war against the West because, in his view, the time was ripe, and the West was about to go under. People should stop belittling him by constantly implying that he is only acting in response to larger, more important powers. He is self-sufficient.

The same applies to the attempt to constantly see Russia through the prism of Western history. There are many attempts, to explain Russian actions via Western history. This is especially true of the frequent comparison of the Russian war of aggression on Ukraine with the German war of extermination in Eastern Europe up to 1945. These are all observations by people who have never lived in this country and who lack an appreciation of the tsarist and Soviet legacy that has never been overcome in its monstrosity and that shapes all Russian society, but above all its ruling elite. What is unfolding in Ukraine, with all its horrors, crimes, destruction, looting, chaotic warfare, and indiscipline, is not the return of the Third Reich. It is a continuation of a colonial, imperial, and Soviet tradition, a precarious historical amorphousness that comes from within.

Third, Putin's rise is a variant of the radical new nationalism that dominates many countries in our era. In Turkey, Hungary, and China, new nationalism dominates; in France and Brazil, it is the strongest opposition force; in the United States, it was in power from 2016 to 2020 and may return in 2024. Putin proves that new nationalism leads to war and that state stabilization by hook or crook leads to dictatorship. The maximum tolerated dose of authoritarian nationalism is zero. Authoritarian violence at home will eventually turn into violence abroad if the nationalists are not forced out of government in time. Auto-aggression turns into aggression against neighbors. Every voter must think carefully about what they are doing on election day. There is no protest vote, as some AfD voters believe, only a mandate or empowerment vote. Those who unleash the new nationalism must know there is no going back. There is no such thing as a little nationalism or a little hatred. Nationalism is a total program. Russia offers a cautionary model for the whole world. At the end of the pluralistic, semi-democratic 1990s, an exhausted majority in the country believed that a little stabilization might not hurt. In the Putin Pact, they traded their freedom for ephemeral prosperity. Many Russians undervalued their democratic achievements after the fall of the Soviet dictatorship. After his rise to power, Putin brought the media to heel, expanded the secret services, and manipulated and falsified elections. Nevertheless, millions of people voted for Putin again and again, after his repressive return to power in 2012, after the invasion of Ukraine in 2014, and after the bombing of Aleppo in 2016. Putin's loyal voters legitimized him and made themselves complicit in their country's fall into a totalitarian dictatorship and in unleashing a war that is now coming back to bite the Russian people.

This book traces the main stages on the way to this war and looks ahead to what comes next. First, I describe the German illusions about Russia and their consequences, without which the Russian 1990s and Putin's thirst for revenge cannot be understood: the failed coup of the secret services and imperialists in 1991, the laborious attempts at democracy, and the Chechen war. After that, I devote myself to an in-depth analysis of the Putin system: his nationalist ideology, the propaganda army, his archipelago of penal camps and the repressive apparatus, and Russia's slide into dictatorship. The third part of the book describes the country at war. It discusses how Putin invaded Ukraine and on what grounds, how he sealed off his country from the world and reality and mobilized his people, how he unleashed the holy, great war against the West and used the atomic bomb as a threat. With this war, he initiated the last, extended phase of his rule.

Under Vladimir Putin, Russia, the largest European country, is leaving Europe. Once again, an Iron Curtain is being lowered across the continent. When I travel to this country, I am repeatedly stopped at the airport. The border guard holds my passport and makes long phone calls to his superiors. A man in a dark suit, probably a secret service agent, picks me up and leads me into a basement room. There is a desk, an old mattress with springs, broken chairs, and dust in the corners. I must answer questions: Where do you live? What do you think about the military operation? What are your plans in Russia? I answer curtly and ask myself: Will I even get into the country? Will I get in on the next trip? And will I get out again?

Russia is closing its borders against the world. Most of my Russian friends and acquaintances now live abroad. In September 2022, those who felt directly threatened by the mobilization left. This book is also a farewell to a Russia in which I once liked to live, which was very welcoming to me. And which no longer exists today under this regime.

# Misguided

## How German politicians helped Putin

The scene gave many German correspondents in Moscow an uneasy feeling at the time: Gerhard Schröder and Vladimir Putin standing close together in Moscow's Cathedral of the Redeemer at the Orthodox Christmas celebrations in January 2001. The chancellor and the president, the former Juso chairman and the former head of the secret service, the social democrat, and the security bureaucrat. An incongruous group at first glance. The politicians had their black coats neatly buttoned up to the knot of their ties and were led by the Orthodox patriarch through the gold-covered cathedral on the banks of the Moskva. An oversized structure, Stalin had it blown up, and an ambitious Moscow mayor with family ties to the construction industry had it rebuilt in the 1990s. The chancellor and the president lit candles and whispered in each other's ears as the patriarch wished them »Merry Christmas« in German. The next day, the two and their wives sat in a red sleigh and crisscrossed the snow-covered Kolomenskoye park, once the tsar's residence in Moscow. This was the beginning of a scandalous friendship that years later would lead Schröder to the supervisory boards of Russian energy companies and Germany to its fateful dependence on Siberian gas fields.

I was surprised by the warmth of the visit at that time.

I had also seen Schröder on his first visit to Russia in November 1998. I waited for him for hours in the library of the Hotel Kempinski because he was still discussing Bonn issues with his delegation. At that time, he was late everywhere in Moscow and conveyed a general attitude of, »I'm not particularly interested in anything here. Above all, I don't want to go to the sauna!« (His predecessor in office, Helmut Kohl, had enjoyed this ritual with President Boris Yeltsin). But with Putin, Schröder was a changed man. The atheist Schröder was converted in the cathedral of salvation. He fell not only for Putin as a person, but also for an idealized vision of Russia that he henceforth defended against any criticism of the regime. He later adopted two Russian children. Twenty years later, after Russia's second invasion of Ukraine, Schröder broke not with Putin but with his party, the SPD, which distanced itself from him. He blew the whistle on Germany and stood by Russia. Schröder is a particularly blatant example of German Putinophilia but only one example among many.

In thirty years of reporting on Russia, I have met many of Putin's supporters in Germany. They saw him as a realistic man with whom one could do business, the German in the Kremlin, the approachable president, a young, sober politician who seemed so very different from the Yeltsins, Brezhnevs, and Khrushchevs before him. German politicians, managers, and journalists, even in my own newspaper, *Die Zeit*, were quite taken with the man. During my visits to Hamburg, senior editors encouraged me to look on the bright side, if possible. The editor and former chancellor Helmut Schmidt said nothing; he always let me write what I wanted. But in the *Zeit* political conference, over menthol cigarettes and cookies, he declared: »Putin has a realistic picture of the world.« He said that we had to work with him and that he was an opportunity for Germany.

Many Germans saw it the same way. In September 2001, Putin gave a speech in the Bundestag, partly in German, that took the hearts of some of my compatriots by storm. Industrialists hoped to reach personal agreements with Putin and overcome the uncertainties of the 1990s. Politicians, businesspeople, and foundation representatives in Moscow were taken in by Putin. The head of the Friedrich Ebert Foundation in Moscow, Peter W. Schulze, tried to convince me in heated discussions that Putin was pursuing an »authoritarian path to democracy.« The new president was met with an enormous amount of understanding among the German elites. What is more, there was a willingness to ignore or persistently excuse his darker side. Blame was laid elsewhere: with the Americans, with the West, with NATO. In this way, they helped Putin expand his influence in the West. At that time, I got the impression that many German politicians and managers wanted things to work out with Putin, no matter the cost. It became even more expensive than they thought.

In many cases, the desire to establish good relations with Russia at all costs was not based on any particular insight or closeness to Russia but on three main motivations. The starting point was often fundamental criticism of America and unease among Germans who saw themselves at the mercy of US dominance, especially in times of American wars and interventions. Russia was seen by some German politicians and their voters as a geopolitical deterrent. They valued Russia as a counterweight to »US imperialism,« »Wall Street capitalism,« NATO's eastward expansion, and liberalism. Second, some Germans were attracted to Russia because they attributed a sense of depth and truthfulness, a genuineness that had been lost in the superficial West, to Russians. This was a very effective stereotype. Third, German industrialists not only saw Russia as a market as early as the 20th century, but also as an alternative source of raw material to American and British oil supplies. These links between German energy companies and Russian state monopolists continued from the 1970s onward. Some even associated this with a crude idea of geopolitical power multiplication: Moscow and Berlin could reorder the world with Russian raw materials and German technology.

None of this is new. Schröder had his forerunners, for example, in the 1922 government of the center politician Joseph Wirth, when the Chancellor of the Reich signed the Treaty of Rapallo. This agreement deserves a closer look because it is where the stage was set for the whole drama of an ill-considered intertwining with Russia. Rapallo is a lesson that hardly anyone in Germany wanted to remember after Putin came to power. Or, if one could speak with Karl Marx: The construction of the Nord Stream 2 pipeline was the repetition of history as farce. The Rapallo Treaty and the Nord Stream projects were based on a shared misconception: Russia and Germany were bound by higher interests more important than good or untroubled relations with the states of East–Central Europe and the West. Both the 1922 treaty and the construction of the pipelines against the opposition of many EU countries placed Berlin under general suspicion of collaboration with an authoritarian regime that was difficult to shake off and burdened German foreign policy for many years to come. Both events merit a comparative examination.

The Treaty of Rapallo and its consequences mark a German tradition that extends to the present, as we shall see. Its roots lie in the Prussian–Russian alliance that led to the partition of Poland in the 18th century and sought to contain the consequences of the revolutions since 1789 in the first half of the 19th century. In 1922, the main issues were military cooperation, oil supplies, and dreams of an economic alliance beyond the West. Thus, the German Reich—internationally isolated after World War I and burdened by reparations, inflation, coups, and assassinations—wanted to find its way back onto the world stage with the help of Russia, similarly isolated and devastated by revolution and civil war.

The industrialist and foreign-minister Walther Rathenau was a contradictory and tragic figure who signed the German–Soviet Treaty of Rapallo more than 100 years ago. Tragic because he actually wanted to prevent the agreement onto which he affixed his name. While the *Völkisch* nationalists in the German Reich condemned the rapprochement with Bolshevik Russia, German leftists and conservatives celebrated Rapallo as a triumph over the liberal-capitalist West. The treaty became a symbol of Germany's seesaw policy, praised by Soviet propaganda, condemned in England, demonized in France, and signed by a pro-Western German foreign minister.

What amazes me most about Rapallo in retrospect is why a liberal foreign minister, of all people, signed the treaty.

This question leads us back to the Italian port city of Genoa, where at a conference held in April 1922, Great Britain wanted to negotiate a new economic order and, to this end, correct some of the provisions of the Paris Suburb Treaties that had ended the First World War in 1919/20. The delegations lodged like monarchs in the city's many palace hotels: the British took up quarters in the hilltop Villa d'Albertis, the French held court in the Savoy Hotel, the Germans had booked an all-inclusive stay in the more modest Eden Hotel, and the Bolshevik negotiators resided in the Imperiale Palace Hotel in Rapallo, 30 kilometers from Genoa, like the tsar's family at a spa. On April 10, the negotiations began in the medieval Palazzo San Giorgio at the port of Genoa. The reporter Harry Graf Kessler later recalled: »Imposing barriers, military chains in field gray; patrolling cavalry; white-gloved, red-bosomed royal guardians around the perimeter of the palazzo leading to the potted plants and red stair runners of the old bank palace decked out in courtly pomp.« Under the high ceilings of the palace's grand Renaissance vault, the heads of 34 states sat at green tables surrounded by white antique statues on black marble tiles.

British Prime Minister Lloyd George was the leading figure. He campaigned for free world trade, disarmament, and the »detoxification of the world.« He wanted to get the German economy going again and build up Soviet Russia at the same time with an international financial consortium. The French foreign minister, however, insisted on all the reparations that his country had imposed on Germany at Versailles. German Chancellor Joseph Wirth sought to ease the burden of debt.

Germany was plunged into a permanent crisis. Wirth even feared an increase in reparations after Genoa. According to Article 116 of the

Treaty of Versailles, Russia could have joined the reparations demands against Germany, and France encouraged Russia to do just that. The Moscow delegation was led by the brilliant Foreign Minister Georgy Chicherin, who spoke not only French but also perfect German. He was pursuing a very specific goal. Moscow wanted Berlin to waive prewar loans and privatization debts, as well as a most-favored-nation clause that would facilitate trade. Above all, however, it wanted to keep the Germans out of all capitalist alliances against Soviet Russia, including the international consortium, condemned as »imperialist,« that the British were planning. Soviet government emissaries had already negotiated with the Germans in the months before about a corresponding agreement, but Chicherin's initiative threatened to fail in Genoa. The liberal and industrialist Walther Rathenau, who had been appointed Germany's foreign minister at the beginning of 1922, was about as accessible to Chicherin as Annalena Baerbock with her »feminist foreign policy« was to her Russian counterpart Sergei Lavrov in 2021.

Rathenau had many connections to the West; he knew Lloyd George well. At Genoa, like Wirth, he hoped for debt relief and a loan for Germany. He shied away from a separate agreement with Russia, however. He considered the preliminary negotiations with Moscow »unforgivable.« Nor did he like the extensive, secret German–Russian cooperation in the military, armaments, and raw materials, about which he had learned only shortly before the conference. On this, he was alone. Army chief of the Reichswehr, General Hans von Seeckt, German industry, and the chancellor all pushed for a special German–Russian agreement. And they were thus part of a tradition of German Ostpolitik that sought to close ranks with Russia to bypass, divide up, or neutralize East-Central Europe.

The Soviets' closest ally in Rathenau's ministry was top diplomat Ago Freiherr von Maltzan, the gray eminence of Weimar Ostpolitik: Maltzan kept in touch with the Russians and strategically prepared the political rapprochement. Maltzan interposed himself between Lloyd George and Rathenau. Maltzan cultivated the connection to the Reichswehr and the oil industry. Maltzan (together with Chancellor Wirth) wanted to bust the »Ring of Versailles.« His most important tasks in April were to prevent Foreign Minister Rathenau from putting the brakes on German–Russian rapprochement at all costs and to dampen the influence of the Social Democratic Reich President Friedrich Ebert, who also thought little of an overly friendly relationship with Soviet Russia. Therefore, in the first days of the Genoa Conference, Maltzan tried to seal off his boss, Rathenau, and control the flow of information.

The discussions centered on Article 116 of the Treaty of Versailles. Rathenau, too, feared that the British and the French might persuade the Russians to demand reparations from Germany. Chicherin had been spotted outside Lloyd George's Villa d'Albertis (Maltzan sprinkled such news in well-measured doses). »Like an animal tamer whom his beast would not obey,« a German politician recounted, he had paced up and down in front of the Eden Hotel. Most of what we know about the proceedings at Rapallo, however, comes from Maltzan's own lore. Rathenau died before he could write it down, and Wirth left only a few glimpses. From Maltzan's perspective, the events unfolded as follows:

It was Easter Sunday, April 16, 1922, when Maltzan called on Rathenau at about 2:30 a.m. and told him that the Russians had called and were ready to negotiate.

»They bring me my death sentence?« asked Rathenau. He sensed a plot and said he wanted to speak to Lloyd George.

»Impossible!« returned Maltzan. He was not prepared for such a »betrayal of Chicherin.« Shortly thereafter, Wirth also entered Rathenau's suite. The foreign minister, in his pajamas, had to let Maltzan and the chancellor talk to him. Their main argument was that the alleged negotiations between Chicherin and the British were to the disadvantage of the German Reich. Early in the morning, Rathenau gave in: »Le vin est tiré, il faut le boire« (»The wine is uncorked, now you have to drink it").

On the morning of Easter Sunday, the German delegation left for Rapallo to meet with the Russians at the Imperiale Palace Hotel. Shortly before 7 p.m., they signed the treaty. It sealed the establishment of diplomatic relations, the renunciation of reparation claims and old claims, trade on a most-favored-nation basis, and far-reaching economic cooperation.

The treaty »hit like a bomb,« Chancellor Wirth later wrote. That was putting it mildly. Lloyd George had cried out »like the monster bull of Uri« as British hopes for a new European economic order were devastated with the establishment of diplomatic relations between Berlin and Moscow. What is more, the treaty was regarded in the West as an expression of German unreliability and disloyalty. The Soviets's plan to blow up the »capitalist ideas« of Genoa had succeeded. And Rathenau's attempts to prevent military-political agreements by shaping the treaty failed. What was not in the treaty was later added in the new environment of warmed German–Soviet Russian relations. In the years that followed, the Rapallo Treaty became a diplomatic shell for a series of secret agreements and cooperative ventures. Reichswehr Chief von Seeckt expanded clandestine military cooperation and circumvented the Versailles provisions. In Russia, German pilots practiced in Lipetsk and German tank drivers in Kazan. German chemists experimented with warfare agents near the Volga river. German technology went to Russia, and Russian oil flowed back. The young Soviet Russia helped the Reichswehr to build up its power, and, in return, Berlin brought the Bolsheviks out of international isolation.

Hitler, an opponent of the Rapallo Treaty, later brutally exploited all this to partition Poland and East-Central Europe with Stalin in 1939—before invading the Soviet Union himself two years later. The prelude to the Hitler–Stalin Pact belongs to the inglorious tradition of

German–Russian policy against East-Central Europe. Rapallo was nothing but a stage in the long German–Russian cooperation at the expense of third parties. Rathenau did not live to see any of this. He was shot by right-wing extremists in Berlin-Grunewald a few weeks after signing the treaty.

Strangely enough, Germany learned little from the history of the ill-fated treaty. After the German war of annihilation against the Soviet Union was lost, the Rapallo Treaty was praised in the GDR as a precursor to socialist brotherhood. In the Federal Republic, conservative historians interpreted it as a piece of realpolitik that had been appropriate given French pressure on Germany in the early 1920s. Ostpolitik under SPD chancellors Willy Brandt and Helmut Schmidt also followed a strong realism in the 1970s. In contrast to Rapallo, however, this policy proved to be a stroke of luck because it was based on different assumptions. The Federal Republic was firmly anchored in the Western alliance. Its Ostpolitik took up the American signals of détente of the 1960s and was mainly coordinated with its Western allies. Brandt's historic »insight into the necessity« of treaties with Moscow, Warsaw, and the GDR leadership paved the way for the 1975 Helsinki Conference, where the Western states effectively recognized the Soviet sphere of influence in exchange for the maintenance of inter-state security standards and respect for human rights. In the future, dissidents in Eastern Europe could also invoke these rights, and this was an opportunity to change the situation in Soviet-dominated Eastern Europe. The Polish, Hungarian, and East German dissidents who brought down the communist regimes at the end of the 1980s relied on this. Ostpolitik contributed significantly to overcoming the division of Europe.

The importance of having resisted these concessions to the Soviet Union was, unfortunately, completely forgotten in the so-called »second phase of Ostpolitik.« The former mastermind of Ostpolitik, Egon Bahr, and other social democrats stood for a progressive aberration of Ostpolitik, which had been so successful in the 1970s. When shipyard workers in Gdansk revolted against the Communist Party in the early 1980s, German social democrats wanted first and foremost to save »stability.« They considered Polish martial law regrettable but necessary. At »round tables« with the SED leadership in the 1980s, SPD politicians like Egon Bahr chatted away the fundamental differences between democracy and dictatorship. They fed the stabilization needs of the communist rulers instead of exposing their contradictions and human rights violations. In the end, that's what the outraged people themselves did when Soviet-dominated Eastern Europe was rocked by uprisings and national movements in the late 1980s. Old Bahr was later one of the main proponents of close collaboration with Putin's Russia at the expense of relations with the United States.

After reunification in the 1990s, Germans discovered a sympathy for the national impulses and democratic demands of the peoples of East-Central Europe that was uncharacteristic of them in the past. The German governments of the 1990s supported democratic developments in the region. This was true not only for the Christian Democrat Helmut Kohl, but also for the Red-Green government of Schröder from 1998 onward. They made great efforts to bring Poland, Hungary, the Czech Republic, Slovakia, the Baltic states, and other countries of East-Central Europe into the EU and NATO. At the same time, Russia was at least not excluded by the NATO–Russia Founding Act and the expansion of the G7 group to include Moscow and numerous other agreements. Nevertheless, the West missed an opportunity to bind Russia a little more firmly to itself during the era of halfway-democratically minded President Boris Yeltsin.

As is well known, Schröder made an attempt, but somewhere along the way, during the eventful sleigh ride with Putin in January 2001, he lost the compass that indicates the appropriate path between solidarity with East-Central European allies and cooperation with Russia. It was Schröder, after all, who continued the traditional German–Russian cooperation at the expense of East-Central Europe and drew out the entangled line from the Polish partitions of the 18th century via Rapallo to the construction of the Nord Stream pipelines. The pipeline under the Baltic Sea was a Russian idea, which Putin had brought to Schröder's attention and which Schröder signed and sealed at the end of his term in office in 2005. While still chancellor, he pushed through a loan guarantee from the state-owned Hermes insurers for the first pipeline. Gazprom and European companies, including Germany's BASF and the new E.ON group created by the Schröder government, were to build and finance the pipeline. Schröder had previously used a trick to get E.ON into a dominant position in the market. First Viag and Veba merged in 2000, then the new E.ON company took over the gas supplier Ruhrgas, which already controlled 60 percent of the German gas market. The Cartel Office rightly objected to the takeover, but the Schröder government coldly pushed through the takeover of Ruhrgas with ministerial approval. A giant emerged that later allied itself with the Russian giant Gazprom. Both companies were key financiers of the Nord Stream project. In December 2005, barely two weeks after his dismissal as Chancellor, Schröder took up a new post as head of the supervisory board of the newly founded Nord Stream AG. Here it was again, the idea that German technology and Russian raw materials can change the world, that Russia and Germany have special interests that are beyond Western influence and should not be disturbed by objections from Poles or Balts.

The construction of the two Nord Stream pipelines is an inglorious chapter that severely tainted Germany's relationship with its immediate neighbors and damaged its credibility in the long term. The German natural gas industry, like parts of German industry in the 1920s, has become greedily and blindly intertwined with Russia. From the beginning of the construction of the first pipeline in 2005, the project was met with outrage and protests from East-Central European governments that felt bypassed by the Baltic Sea pipe. Nevertheless, Russian, German, and other European companies continued to build the pipeline. Germany allowed it to go online, and the irritation in the EU and Brussels was great. It was therefore completely incomprehensible that a second pipeline could be built at all, in the face of the painful disputes with allies over Nord Stream 1 and the associated loss of trust. As in the Rapallo case, I would like to take a closer look at this German error in dealing with Russia.

The debacle began barely six weeks after Putin's annexation of Crimea in March 2014, when Schröder celebrated his 70th birthday in St Petersburg. Putin and Gazprom CEO Alexei Miller attended the opulent gala at the Yusupov Palace. The party in the historic, magnificent rooms on the Moyka River was paid for by Nord Stream AG, and the plan for a new double pipe under the Baltic Sea, called Nord Stream 2, was discussed. It was Putin's project to further weaken Ukraine after the attacks on Crimea and the Donbas and to make Germany an accomplice.

In a luxury hotel in Vladivostok, high-ranking Energy managers and Russian bureaucrats, among them Miller of Gazprom and representatives of the German corporations E.ON and BASF, met on September 4, 2015, one-and-a-half years later. In the often-windy city on the Pacific, a deal of the century was concluded that day. Miller reached an agreement with German, Dutch, and French companies on the new pipe, through which up to 55 billion cubic meters of gas per year were to flow from Russia to Germany—in addition to the 55 billion cubic meters flowing through Nord Stream 1. This was a volume to match the total capacity of the pipelines that ran through Ukraine. The deal turned into a nightmare for the German government. NordStream 2 worsened the strained relationship between Germany and Poland, pilloried Berlin in the EU, infuriated the US, and put Chancellor Angela Merkel in a bind. The German government tried to wriggle out of the debacle by claiming for a long time that the geopolitical project was purely economics.

Six weeks after the meeting in Vladivostok, on October 28, 2015, the German vice-chancellor and economics minister Sigmar Gabriel flew to Moscow. Putin took an unusually long time meeting with him. They spoke for almost two hours at the Novo-Orgaryovo state dacha, with Miller also sitting at the table. Gabriel was the key man in Berlin for the Nord Streamers. He served as a modern Ago von Maltzan, the Schröder-backed executor of Rohrpallo. In 2014 and 2015, the economics minister waved through the sale of Germany's largest gas storage facilities and natural gas infrastructure to Gazprom. He lobbied for German, not European, authorities to be responsible for Nord-Stream 2 in Brussels and European capitals. This was important because the German government wanted the pipeline, whereas the EU Commission rejected it.

The ensuing dispute resembled what happened over Nord Stream 1, when the Commission and the East-Central Europeans criticized the pipeline. Only in 2015, the political circumstances had changed radically. The Russian intervention in eastern Ukraine and the annexation of Crimea had shaken Europe. The EU wanted less dependence on Russian gas supplies. On November 30, 2015, economics ministers from Poland, Hungary, Romania, Latvia, Estonia, Lithuania, and Slovakia wrote a three-page letter to the EU Commission. They railed against Nord Stream 2: the planned pipeline would take transit fees away from Ukraine and increase the EU's dependence on Russia. Two weeks later, the European Parliament joined in the criticism, and the EU Commission distanced itself from the project.

Angela Merkel knew all this when she traveled to Brussels for the EU summit on December 17, 2015. In addition to the refugee crisis, the heads of government also discussed Nord Stream 2. Merkel should have taken a stand then at the latest. The Nord Stream 2 company had begun to apply for permits. The first components were already being stored near St Petersburg. But Merkel was reluctant to commit herself. In the chancellor's office, her advisors fought over a unified line.

Foreign Policy Advisor Christoph Heusgen was against it, whereas Economic Advisor Lars-Henrik Röller was in favor. Above all, the chancellor did not want to risk a permanent dispute with the SPD and its vice-chancellor, Sigmar Gabriel. In Brussels, she made the excuse that »it was an economic project first,« though the political dispute had long been simmering.

Merkel's maneuvering enabled her predecessor, Schröder, to push ahead with the pipeline project. He was entered in the Handelsregister of the Swiss canton of Zug as president of the board of directors of the Nord Stream 2 company in July 2016. In February 2017, he introduced Gazprom CEO Miller to the new, SPD-affiliated economics minister, Brigitte Zypries, in Berlin. Gabriel became the foreign minister, and he maintained close contact with Russia in his new post. On June 2, 2017, Vladimir Putin invited Gabriel to a one-on-one meeting in St Petersburg that was followed by a private dinner at Constantine Palace, Putin's St Petersburg residence. At the table, once again, sat Gerhard Schröder. It was a matter of letting the opposition to Nord Stream 2 run into the void. Gabriel explained his policy in retrospect in an interview in May 2022: »We believed that Russia would behave as reliably in terms of energy supply as the old Soviet Union. [...] This experience was seamlessly transferred to Russia and Putin. That was a miscalculation.«

In the EU, the fronts hardened. Resistance was strongest in the eastern EU countries, which were particularly dependent on Russian gas supplies and were now building LNG terminals on their coasts to be able to import liquefied gas from the US. But their attempts to use EU law to prevent the Gazprom pipeline failed. At first. The most dangerous attack against Nord-Stream 2, however, came not from Warsaw or Brussels, but from Washington. On June 13, 2017, the US Senate passed sanctions against the »Adversaries of America,« and Russia was at the top of the list. In Section 232, »Sanctions against Russian Pipelines,« the Senate gave the US president a selection of measures to punish the pipeline's builders that could also impact German companies as financiers and partners. Europe fell apart. While the Polish government unabashedly encouraged Washington to take this step, the German foreign minister condemned the US Senate's embargo. Gabriel accused the US of pursuing its own economic interests with sanctions that violate international law.

But opposition to Nord Stream 2 was also gathering in Berlin. The Greens and environmental groups criticized the project, and the Nature and Biodiversity Conservation Union of Germany filed a lawsuit. German authorities then stepped up the pace. On January 31, 2018, the Stralsund Mining Authority quickly issued a permit for the construction and operation of the pipeline in the German coastal sea. This was followed by permits from Sweden and Finland, through whose territorial waters the pipe was to run. Only Denmark refused permission, but that could not stop Nord Stream 2. The planners shifted the route without further ado and bypassed Danish territorial waters.

Faced with mounting pressure, Merkel went on the offensive for a diplomatic repair mission in April 2018. When Ukrainian President Petro Poroshenko called on her in Berlin on April 10, 2018, she stood next to him in a high hall of the Chancellor's Office and explained that Nord-Stream 2 was probably not an exclusively »economic project« after all and acknowledged that »there are also political factors to consider.« Poroshenko smiled sweetly. Merkel then tried to oblige the Russians to guarantee that their gas would be delivered to Western Europe both through the Baltic Sea and through Ukraine in the future: »Without a perspective on how the transit through Ukraine will continue,« Nord Stream 2 would not be possible. In fact, Merkel's government managed to broker a deal between Moscow and Kyiv to extend gas deliveries through Ukraine until 2024. None of that was enough to appease opponents.

On July 11, 2018, US President Donald Trump had breakfast with Secretary General Jens Stoltenberg at NATO headquarters in Brussels.

Trump attacked Berlin head-on: »Germany is Russia's prisoner.« He said it gets as much as 70-percent of its energy from Russia, and now the pipeline is coming. That was not true—at the time, about half of Germany's gas and oil imports still came from Russia. The NATO summit became a demonstration of disunity. Thus, Nord Stream 2—amplified by Trump's megaphone—damaged both NATO and the EU. It was hard to imagine a balanced, joint-EU response to the planned US punitive measures against European energy companies. Interests were too opposed, and the mistrust that the grand coalition and Schröder had fomented between neighbors was too great. Finally, in 2019, Merkel's staunch ally, Emmanuel Macron, also gave in and switched to the camp of the pipeline critics. Germany's Russia policy had made it easy for two populist nationalists, Putin and Trump, to divide the EU The pipeline construction continued on completely unscathed.

It took nothing less than a war to stop Nord-Stream 2. The pipeline was completed while the grand coalition was still in power; in the end, only one formality was missing: certification by the Federal Network Agency and the EU authorities. In the first weeks under Chancellor Olaf Scholz, Gazprom pumped the pipeline to capacity to supply Germany at the end of 2021. At the same time, Putin had more than 100,000 troops deployed on Ukraine's borders in preparation for an invasion of its neighbor. Foreign political pressure to call off the project grew. But Scholz defended Nord Stream 2 in the best Social Democratic manner. Even as finance minister in the Merkel government, he had held up the prospect of building a German liquefied-natural-gas terminal so the Americans would give up their opposition to the pipeline. Scholz was already chancellor on Feb. 10, 2022, when Gerhard Schröder was given the opportunity to consult with SPD foreign policy experts and Russia about the pipeline. For weeks, the head of Germany's government stuck to his line of keeping the fate of the pipeline in the dark, voicing no threat, no warning, no forecast. »Strategic ambiguity« is what the chancellor's office called this last German about-face to save an impossible, overdue project. It was only two days before the Russian invasion of Ukraine that Scholz finally pulled the plug and declared the suspension of the certification process. It was the twelfth hour.

Germany had long since lost its sovereignty and freedom of action. Since Schröder's sleigh ride, Germany's dependence on Russian energy resources, for oil, for coal, and for gas, had grown with each passing year. I consulted the yearly figures from the Federal Ministry of Economics, and I found that the statistics on gas imports from Russia have not been published since 2016. At that time, the order of magnitude was 40-percent. In response to my inquiries, the Ministry informed me that the authorities could no longer publish this data for »reasons of commercial secrecy.« In other words, out of consideration for the secrets of Gazprom and its associated German energy companies.

This was followed by a six-year statistical blind-flight, at the end of which Russia's share of Germany's total gas imports had risen to over 55-percent. This is why the German government was trapped after the Russian invasion of Ukraine. Although they could quickly dispense with coal and later also oil from Russia, previous federal governments and the German gas industry had done a great job with natural gas. Germany could not break away from Russia without enormous costs, and Berlin was attached to Gazprom's pipeline. Worse still, Germany's largest gas company, which had become deeply intertwined with Russia against its better judgment, collapsed at the very moment when everything depended on it.

This was the successor company to E.ON, which had bypassed the Cartel Office and been merged by Chancellor Schröder. Meanwhile, the natural gas operations had been spun off and sold under the Uniper name. Uniper was Germany's largest utility and was suffering from Gazprom's breach of contract in 2022. Putin instructed his state-owned company first to curb and then to stop deliveries through Nord Stream 1 to Germany. In September 2022, attacks destroyed three of the four strands of Nord Stream pipelines. The remaining gas flowed to the surface of the Baltic Sea and eventually into the atmosphere. The blind interdependence of the past 20 years was taking its revenge. Because Gazprom stopped supplying, Uniper had to buy gas at the highest prices on the international market—and collapsed. The German government invested billions of euros of taxpayer money and became a shareholder in Uniper to save the German supply. This was as inevitable as it was outrageous. Uniper—and until 2016, its predecessor E.ON—was a main agent for Germany's dependence on Putin's politically controlled gas supplies. This group, like BASF for that matter, had deliberately and systematically intertwined with Russia. Uniper was choking on bad decisions of the past.

E.ON/Uniper obtained most of its gas from Russia and could not get enough of it. More and more new supply contracts and, finally, participation in Siberian gas fields increased the dependence of Germany's largest energy company on Russia. To make matters worse, over the past 20 years, E.ON has ignored or even prevented alternatives to Russia's gas supplies. In the 2000s E.ON promised to build a German liquefied-natural-gas terminal in Wilhelmshaven. Everyone thought the project was on track and Germany would get its terminal, but the company delayed construction for years before burying the project in 2008. In 2020, the successor company Uniper once again rejected plans for an LNG terminal because demand was too low. It was not worth it, they said. But if it had an LNG terminal and supply contracts with Qatar and the US in 2022, Uniper would probably not have needed to be rescued by the state.

They also avoided other options as much as possible. In the 2000s, the European Commission promoted the Nabucco project, a pipeline that would bring gas from the Caspian Sea to Europe via Turkey, i.e., bypassing Russia. E.ON Ruhrgas CEO Burckhard Bergmann said in 2008 that he saw »serious problems in the implementation«—where would the gas come from? In Germany, such assessments from natural gas leaders destroyed the project's reputation. But for the Nord Stream pipelines, people were happy to throw money into a bottomless chasm.

And the company had been warned. There are many interviews from between 2008 to 2022 in which E.ON managers played down critical questions from journalists and experts about Russia's weaponization of natural gas supplies. E.ON Ruhrgas CEO Bernard Reutersberg called Gazprom »an extremely reliable supplier« in 2008. After Putin's 2014 invasion of Ukraine, E.ON CEO Johannes Teyssen said that »Russia has no interest« in using gas as a weapon because it lives off exports and that »the Russians could decide not to make money, which is very unlikely.« As recently as January 2022, Uniper CEO Klaus-Dieter Maubach made a similar claim: gas from Russia has been »absolutely reliable for 50 years.«

The opposite was true. During his conflicts with pro-Western government leaders in Ukraine between 2004 and 2014, Putin repeatedly ordered Gazprom to cut the flow of gas. Gazprom also extorted East-Central and Southeast European states with exorbitant prices. And in 2021, Gazprom leached German gas storage facilities, leaving Germany vulnerable. Gas is a political raw material and not a commodity in Russia.

Uniper (formerly E.ON) is not absolved by the fact that its German competitor, Wintershall, under the umbrella of BASF, threw itself into the arms of Gazprom in much the same way. Wintershall participated in Nord Stream 1 and 2 and bought into Siberian gas fields. Wintershall even sold all its German gas-storage facilities to Gazprom, with the blessing of SPD Economics Minister Sigmar Gabriel. That was in 2015, after Putin's 2014 invasion of Ukraine! There were many warnings about these gas deals with Putin, but the gas industry did not want to hear them.

With Uniper, an energy strategy that was as corrupt as it was misguided collapsed. And with Putin's war, Ostpolitik failed in its umpteenth new edition. Twenty years of understanding, mediation, and sympathy had all been to no avail. After two decades of countless conferences, summits, and talks, German politics stood naked, betrayed by Putin, and ashamed of itself. »We were wrong!« was the most frequently uttered sentence of the German political elite after the invasion. There was, however, often no reflection on why it came to this. A committee of inquiry to examine this total failure and name the names is lacking. Three German policy approaches failed fundamentally: the logic of economic interdependence, the misperception of Putin's Russia, and the know-it-all attitude from the moral high ground.

Since I started at *Die Zeit* in 1992, I have heard Helmut Schmidt say time and again in editorial conferences: »Those who trade with each other do not wage wars against each other.« This was an ironclad tenet of German foreign policy that guided generations of politicians in Bonn and Berlin. And for a long time, it was difficult to refute. While other countries were sending armies and weapons out, the Germans were supplying machines, luxury cars, and other high-tech products to the world. And also some weapons—but these hardly weighed in on the foreign-trade balance sheet. Oil and gas came to Germany from Russia at affordable prices. Germans networked and relied on the fact that mutual dependence would nip any desire for conflict in the bud, since the damage to themselves would have been so great. That went well for a long time. But not with Vladimir Putin after his return to the presidency in 2012. German politicians and gasmen believed that they were dealing with a man who would make rational decisions and for whom economic advantage was more important than nationalistic dreams. Was Putin not a »quasi-German«? The Germans missed the tipping point in 2012. Putin became a prime example of an authoritarian ruler for whom the economy counted little when it came to expanding his power. Since 2012, at the latest since 2014, he has mainly made decisions against the economic interests of his own country. Security first! The entanglement eventually became Germany's undoing because German politicians and energy managers did not want to hear these truths. Things had gone too well before.

In principle, it was not wrong to talk to the man. The now-sharply criticized idea of a »modernization partnership« with Russia during Dmitry Medvedev's brief presidency from 2008 to 2012 was at least worth trying. There is plenty of hypocrisy in the EU. The East-Central European states that criticize Berlin for its past Russia policy had their own entanglement scandals with Moscow. Countries like Poland, Bulgaria, Latvia, and Finland allowed Russia a similarly high share of their gas imports as Germany—or higher. Poland's right-wing nationalist government collaborated with nationalist Viktor Orbán against the EU for many years, thereby helping the man into the position from which he watered down EU sanctions against Russia and blocked an oil embargo. Yet EU sanctions and the 2015 Minsk ceasefire were supposed to prevent Russia from overrunning and completely capturing a then-virtually-defenseless Ukraine. Negotiation and mediation are not crimes, as some suggest today. The »peace process« of Minsk, a victorious peace in favor of Russia, was painful and humiliating for Ukraine, but it gave the country seven important years to strengthen and defend itself. The countless attempts that German politicians made to reach out to Moscow made liars of all those who claimed on German talk shows that there had not been enough talk. No one has conferred with Putin more than the Germans, except perhaps Turkish President Recep Tayyip Erdoğan.

The attempt itself was not the fault. It was the failure to take stock of one's own actions, the inability to recognize that talking was leading nowhere after a certain point, and the lack of will to prepare for the failure of talking by better equipping the Bundeswehr and diversifying energy sources. German politicians and economic leaders had two decades. They overlooked the true character of the Russian regime and ignored Russia's internal changes and the metamorphoses of Putin in power. Above all, they overlooked how Putin's Russia was not the victorious, saturated Soviet Union, but an increasingly revanchist state bent on revenge for 1991. In an interview after the outbreak of war in 2022, a key player in eastern policy, Sigmar Gabriel, admitted that »we underestimated the ambitions of the Russian president in the period from 2007 onward, or rather overestimated our experience in dealing with the Soviet Union and with Russia.«

It was much worse: the Germans thought they understood Russia best, and that was probably their biggest misunderstanding. I observed how German participants at European conferences explained to East-Central European representatives from their high-horse of moral grandeur how to deal with Russia. Moreover, the Germans felt free of anti-Russian resentment, which they suspected was a consequence of Soviet rule not only among Poles, Balts, and Czechs, but especially among Ukrainians. The history of Eastern European states independent of Russia was all too often ignored. In Ukraine, some Germans saw not much more than a curious variation of Russia and, in any case, a country in Moscow's sphere. This became apparent just after the 2014 invasion. My former editor, Helmut Schmidt, even denied the country its state tradition. Out of this doubt, even after Putin's invasion of Ukraine in 2022, some German politicians and intellectuals were ready to concede significant parts of Ukraine to the Kremlin ruler, if only the weapons would be silent. Many Germans considered themselves particularly purified because their country had spent more than half a century coming to terms with its past of an unprecedented war of extermination. To other European states, German politicians and diplomats occasionally let it be known that they simply understood Russia better. In retrospect, Gabriel very aptly describes it as an »arrogance.« It is precisely this attitude that gave rise to the Nord Stream Project in duplicate. The Germans thought they knew that Putin would never use gas as a weapon, although he had been doing just that to neighbors since the 2000s, in stark contrast to the Soviet Union. The know-it-alls in Berlin knew very little.

Thus, in the end, Germany's Ostpolitik failed in a mixture of arrogance, illusions, and a fair amount of corruption in pipeline construction. All this together helped Vladimir Putin become what he is today.

# Gallery of Ancestors

## Why the 1991 putschists have won today

There is a tunnel on my way to the *Zeit* office in Moscow. At this underpass in the Arbat district, three unarmed demonstrators were crushed by a Russian armed forces tank in 1991. Today, a small stele with the names of those killed stands there on a traffic island between the tunnel opening and the car lane, where no pedestrian can notice it. I passed by the crossing on my bicycle every day for more than a year without noticing the stele relegated to the edge. Even my Moscow friends did not know about the small monument, until I happened to read about it on the Internet. They all know about the big store at the Arbat tunnel, with its displays of tank posters, military hats, and uniforms. It is a Russian army surplus store.

The memory of the tank attack and the coup by the Soviet old guard against the last president of the Soviet Union, Mikhail Gorbachev, is suppressed in Putin's Russia today. In many other countries, a coup and its victims would be the occasion for a day of remembrance, an annual parliamentary session, or similar commemorative rituals. In Russia, silence reigns. For Putin, the coup is a complicated event because it was instigated by his former superiors in the intelligence service. He has ordered collective oblivion. It is too confusing and painful for him that at that in 1991 like-minded people revolted against the president, which for him is actually treason. The putschists wanted a Russia that would resemble the one of today. Their failure was a resounding defeat of the Soviet security services, in which Putin himself rose, and a defeat for the Soviet state apparatus. It was a defeat that opened a decade of freedom and opportunity for Russia. Suddenly, everything was possible: free travel abroad, free elections, democratization, and an end to the Russian curse of having to sacrifice personal lives for the country's expansion. The failure of the coup fueled the independence of the smaller Soviet republics and Russia's awakening at the same time. At that time, Russia freed itself from the shackles of the socialist–imperial Soviet Union and got a chance to become a normal nation-state. Putin has taken revenge on many who stood for this development. He does not want to remember the suppression of this deplorable coup. And that is precisely why it must be discussed at this point. The 1991 rebellion is key to understanding Putin and his security apparatus.

Mikhail Gorbachev was in Crimea when his close associates met on August 17, 1991. At 2 p.m., they gathered in a gray, granite building in southwestern Moscow, in the library of the KGB secret service with an adjoining sauna and swimming pool. The prime minister, the KGB chief, the defense minister, the head of the Security Council—Gorbachev's best people—got together and complained. They complained about the uprisings at the periphery of the empire, the loss of control of the Communist Party, and the disintegration of the armed forces. They also complained about President Gorbachev, who could no longer be relied upon and who thought only of himself. They complained that they would be dismissed as soon as the Soviet Union received a new Union treaty. When they had complained enough, they decided on a coup d'état.

With the August 1991 coup, the conspirators wanted to save the Soviet Union and themselves. The empire was more important to them than socialism and the Soviet people. But in the end, they destroyed the greatest country on earth. They thought they were fighting Gorbachev, who had lost power and empire. In fact, they were the ones who drove the non-Russian republics out of the Union with their backward somersault. And they drove a wedge between the Soviet power and the Russian Federation. During the coup, a far more dangerous opponent than Gorbachev emerged: Boris Yeltsin. The Russian president, in turn, had to take one of the putschists especially seriously: Vladimir Kryuchkov, the head of the powerful KGB secret service, Putin's cadre school. One hardly sees Kryuchkov in photographs from back then, yet the coup was actually a duel between these two men. Yeltsin and Kryuchkov fought a duel over Russia's path that has only been decided today—and in Putin's favor.

Vladimir Kryuchkov, the host in the KGB library on August 17, was well prepared that day. He persuaded Vice-President Gennady Yanayev to sign numerous emergency decrees, including the release of Gorbachev from his duties and the transfer of power to Yanayev and the State Emergency Committee (GKTschP). Minister of Defense Dmitry Yazov was equally important. He ordered the 2nd Guards »Taman« Motor Rifle Division and the 4th Guards »Kantemirovskaya« Tank Division to march on Moscow at 4 a.m. on August 19. Kryuchkov ordered KGB Group Alpha to the vicinity of the village of Arkhangelskoye, where Boris Yeltsin's dacha was located. The KGB chief slept barely more than an hour that night. He still saw Gorbachev as his opponent, not Yeltsin. At dawn on August 19, he declared to the KGB leadership that Gorbachev's hated perestroika was finally over. At 6 a.m., radio stations announced the emergency decrees. This was followed by excerpts from Tchaikovsky's *Swan Lake*, usually played only at the death of a Soviet leader. Gorbachev listened to the suite in Crimea on his portable radio, then his last link to the outside world.

»Dad, get up, a coup!« Boris Yeltsin was awakened early by his daughter, Tatyana, as *Swan Lake* played on the radio.

Tatyana, her sister Yelena, and Yeltsin's wife, Naina, stood before him. Ten minutes later, his bodyguard stormed into the room. Shortly thereafter, Yeltsin sat with his closest associates to draft an »appeal to the citizens of Russia.« It called on Russians to reject the »unlawful« Emergency Committee. His daughters diligently typed everything up on the typewriter. Yeltsin was surprised at how amateurishly the putschists proceeded. The telephone and fax worked, and his team sent the appeal to the agencies. Soon after, Yeltsin became restless; he wanted to go to Moscow. But how? His dacha in Arkhangelskoye was about 25 kilometers from the urban center, and armed KGB troops lurked in between. He simply did not know whether he would get through their lines, alive and free. But he was not deterred. At 9 a.m., Yeltsin got into his Chaika limousine. His bodyguard sat beside him with a submachine gun on his knees. What happened was hardly expected: Group Alpha let them drive by—Yeltsin was not yet their enemy.

Boris Yeltsin and Vladimir Kryuchkov came from the same elite caste of the Soviet state, the nomenklatura. In everything else, they differed. Yeltsin was 60 years old at the time, whereas Kryuchkov was seven years older. Yeltsin was a civil engineer; Kryuchkov was a lawyer. Yeltsin was regarded as a powerful, charismatic politician, a leader. Kryuchkov was considered a persistent bureaucrat, hardly noticeable outside the apparatus. The one earned a reputation as a political rebel, and the other was an obedient home service soldier. Yeltsin made his career in the Communist Party, rising from the leadership in Sverdlovsk on the Urals to party leader in Moscow then to the post of president of the Russian constituent republic. Kryuchkov first went into the diplomatic service and then took the KGB bull ride to the top. He followed his mentor, Yuri Andropov, the former head of the KGB and general secretary of the CPSU between 1982 and 1984.

Andropov is widely forgotten in the West, and those who do remember him think of him as one of the old men at the head of the Soviet state who ruled briefly in the early 1980s and bequeathed power to the next old man. But in Russian intelligence circles, Andropov was and is a cult figure. It was not only Kryuchkov who admired him, but also the young Vladimir Putin, who also made a career in the KGB. Andropov led those cadres in the early 1980s who wanted to cautiously reform and modernize the Soviet Union while fiercely defending its place in the world. The empire was to remain at all costs, but socialist stagnation was to be overcome. These cadres disliked the whole direction under Andropov's successors, Gorbachev and Yeltsin: opening to the West, political diversity, freedom of expression, growing independence of the Soviet republics. They would like today much better: Under Putin, the country is sharply separating itself from the West, eliminating political competition at home, increasing pressure on the former Soviet republics, and trying to force Ukraine back into the empire with a war of aggression. The two distinct paths of Russian politics in the modern era available in August 1991 were Westernization and liberalization or the Russian special path and authoritarianism.

Boris Yeltsin arrived in central Moscow shortly before 10 a.m. He jumped out of the Chaika limousine and barricaded himself in his seat of government, the Russian White House on the Moskva River, not far from the Kyiv train station. He discussed the matter with his companions, talked on the phone, and drummed his fingers on the table. After an agonizing hour, he realized that he could not win holed up in an office. Outside his window, he saw a tank, around which stood people who showed no fear of the panzer and the mounted machine guns. At that moment, Yeltsin realized that he belonged right there, on the street.

»I climbed onto the tank and straightened up,« he later wrote in his memoirs. »Here everything was clear; I felt completely at one with the people surrounding me.« Then he pulled out the sheet with the call-to-action his daughters had typed and read it. He condemned the »reactionary committee,« called for a general strike, saw the applauding people, greeted the commander of the tank, and looked into the eyes of the soldiers. He won the moment that became the eternal symbol of resistance to the coup. It was a memorable image that made Yeltsin the hero and carried him through the difficult 1990s. The first Russian president undoubtedly had his best moments in times of extreme distress. »Suddenly you feel a push and know the game is on, and you can go on the offensive,« he wrote in his memoirs.

Kryuchkov was not prepared for this stubborn survival mentality. Inwardly, he regretted not having arrested Yeltsin right away. The Russian president, leading the resistance in the White House, now brazenly called him. He asked the KGB chief on the phone: »Do you really not see what you are doing? People are throwing themselves in front of the tanks. There could be victims at any moment.«

Kryuchkov replied: »No, there will be no casualties. This is a purely peaceful operation without live ammunition. We just want to establish order.«

Yeltsin wanted to contradict, but Kryuchkov interrupted him: »All the unrest is coming from you, from the leadership of Russia. According to our information, people are calm, and life is normal.

The coup plotters ordered the closure of the liberal media and newspapers and took over the television channels to ensure that normality was properly communicated to the public on the afternoon of August 19. From now on, the Emergency Committee, and only the Emergency Committee, spoke. But who were these people? Kryuchkov did not like to show himself to the public, so he was hardly seen in the photos. But the KGB chief let his fellow putschists talk. Six of them went to the press at the Novosti news agency near the Park Kultury metro station. With trembling hands, the spokesman for the Emergency Committee, Gennady Yanayev, explained that Gorbachev was unfortunately too ill to fulfill his duties. Without sleep and marked by alcohol, Yanayev looked as if he himself had just come out of intensive care. His comrades-in-arms displayed no more vitality than he did. They were all dressed in gray suits. One of them had a runny nose, and another was coughing. A foreign reporter asked if the committee had met with General Pinochet, the leader of the 1973 Chilean coup. Laughter. The press conference turned into a disaster for the coup plotters.

Meanwhile, resistance was growing. More and more people gathered in front of the White House. Muscovites called each other, a local radio station even called for people to go to the seat of government. With each passing hour, Boris Yeltsin became more and more of an acclaimed tribune of the people, and by barricading himself in the White House was thwarting the coup plot. Soon, more than 100,000 people stood outside the White House, and they were carrying the Russian tricolor instead of the Soviet flag. The USSR was almost a thing of the past. As snipers waited in position on the rooftops, Yeltsin stepped out from behind bulletproof glass onto the balcony and addressed the crowd. Moscow celebrities joined him and warned of the danger of a »new dictatorship,« among them Yelena Bonner, the wife of Nobel Prize winner Andrei Sakharov, poet Yevgeny Yevtushenko, and Gorbachev's former foreign minister Eduard Shevardnadze. Mstislav Rostropovich, the cellist, played against the coup with his hair blowing in the wind. Their resistance found public support. Many felt they were on the right side of history at the White House.

For Vladimir Kryuchkov, bad memories were awakened. During the 1956 uprising against Soviet power in Hungary, Kryuchkov worked as a young press attaché in the Soviet embassy in Budapest, where his boss (the ambassador) was none other than Yuri Andropov. The Moscow leadership crushed the Hungarian uprising with tanks then. In Prague in 1968, the counterrevolution against Soviet power was prevented by similar means. Weren't these the real models for putting down a rebellion?

Kryuchkov consulted with Defense Minister Yazov. There were enough troops in the city to storm the White House. Tanks were everywhere, on Red Square, on Gorky Street, on Pushkin Square. The Taman Division and the Airborne Division from Tula had taken positions in front of the White House. The orders for »Operation Thunder« were given by Kryuchkov and Yazov: Early in the morning of August 21 at 3 a.m., paratroopers and police would surround the White House and disperse the crowd. The KGB's Group Alpha and an army unit then would storm the White House and shoot their way in, blast open locked doors with grenade launchers, and arrest Yeltsin. So much for that plan.

This was the reality: no one in the Emergency Committee wanted to take responsibility for »Operation Thunder.« Yasov's deputy Yevgeny Shaposhnikov rejected the attack. Some of the commanders did not carry out the defense minister's orders. They revolted against the idea of Russians shooting at Russians in the middle of Moscow. Nevertheless, there were casualties. Three protesters died at the entrance to the tunnel in the Arbat district while attempting to stand as a human barrier in the way of the tracked vehicles. The resistance had its martyrs, and the crowd in front of the White House grew bigger with every hour. More and more soldiers and civil servants refused to serve. At the end of the night, Defense Minister Dmitri Yasov took stock of the consequences. At 8 a.m. on August 21, he ordered a complete withdrawal from Moscow. Yeltsin had prevailed.

That was the preliminary military decision. The political decision was still pending. Vladimir Kryuchkov was busy on the phone. First, he called the presidents of the most important Union republics. Ukraine and Kazakhstan refused any support. Desperation grew, and Yanayev dove into a drunken stupor. In general, the Emergency Committee drank a lot. As a Russian historian remarked years later: »As typical Soviet people, they were familiar with the usual cultural exercises and drink often and with pleasure. Anyone who doesn't drink is suspect.« Yanayev's nickname was »Gena the Glass.« Kryuchkov, who liked to keep control, drank wisely, but when he did, it was top-shelf whiskey from the class enemy's distilleries. Kryuchkov liked to sip such a drink while talking on the phone. He called Yeltsin to let him know that »the troops from Moscow will be withdrawn.« In his memoirs, the KGB chief later claimed that a storming of the White House had never been planned. Now he had a big problem: He needed to neutralize Yeltsin in another way and save himself. Only how?

Kryuchkov then remembered the long-standing rivalry between Gorbachev and Yeltsin. Since Yeltsin was now his enemy, Gorbachev suddenly seemed like a possible supporter. And he made a decision that surprised many when, with Yazov and two comrades-in-arms, Kryuchkov flew to meet Gorbachev in Crimea at noon on August 21. Yanayev, who was indisposed, remained in Moscow. To his indignation, Kryuchkov learned on the plane that Yeltsin had ordered his arrest and was also sending his people to Gorbachev. When he arrived in Crimea, Kryuchkov had to wait while Gorbachev talked at length with Yeltsin's emissaries. On the TV in the anteroom, he saw how the demonstrators were already standing in front of the KGB building. He saw people waving Russian flags. He saw the other demonstrations in Russian cities. The putschists were openly condemned on the evening program. Things were going badly. What is worse, Gorbachev didn't even receive him in the end. An employee told him that the president would fly to Moscow and talk to him on the return flight. Then Kryuchkov knew: »The cause is lost.«

The failed coup accelerated what the coup plotters so loudly lamented: the disintegration. In Moscow, Yeltsin had all activities of the Communist Party banned and publicly forced CP leader Gorbachev to sign off on the ban. An important bond that held the USSR together was broken. After the coup, most republics declared their independence from the Soviet Union. And because the sequence is so impressive when viewed as a whole, I list it here:

Estonia declared independence from the Soviet Union while the coup was still in progress on August 20, 1991;

Ukraine followed on August 24,
Belarus on August 27,
Moldova on August 27,
Azerbaijan on August 30,

Uzbekistan on August 31,
Kyrgyzstan on August 31,
Tajikistan on September 9,
Turkmenistan on September 23, and
Kazakhstan on December 16.

Lithuania, Latvia, and Georgia had already declared their independence from the Soviet Union in the spring of 1991. Russia itself also broke away from the Soviet Union: Moscow said goodbye to Moscow. The Soviet Union was not shattered from the outside, as Putin and his followers claim today; it disintegrated from within. The Russian nation-state emerged from the ruins of the empire. When Kryuchkov and Gorbachev sat on the same plane and landed in Moscow on August 21, they were both practically disempowered. In the weeks that followed, Gorbachev lost the country he ruled, and Kryuchkov forfeited his freedom.

But Kryuchkov was in prison only for a short time; he was released in 1993. In Moscow, the democrats around Yeltsin triumphed for a few years, but not democracy itself. When Vladimir Putin took over from Boris Yeltsin in 1999, Putin's regret over the collapse of the Soviet Union as a »geopolitical catastrophe« became state doctrine. Newspaper reports even claimed that Putin, the intelligence man, had taken personal advice from Kryuchkov. The ex-KGB chief spent his last years in peace and freedom. Kryuchkov died in 2007, the same year as his opponent, Yeltsin. The secret service honored Kryuchkov with a large ceremony, whereas Yeltsin was ostracized and preferably forgotten.

In Russia, there was discussion about where Vladimir Putin was at the time of the coup and whose side he was on, especially since he has explicitly regretted the end of the Soviet Union several times over the past years. Unfortunately, there are no independently verifiable sources. Putin himself said in a May 2018 interview with television host Ksenia Sobchak that he resigned from the KGB on August 20,

1991, the second day of the coup. He was torn, he said. »On the one hand, I worked for Anatoly Sobchak, the mayor of St Petersburg, who was on the side of Yeltsin and the others,« he said. Anatoly Sobchak was an ally of the then-president—and the father of the moderator. Putin continued, »on the other hand, the security services were on the side of those who implemented the coup attempt.« He could not »be here or there,« said Putin. That is why, he said, he had called his ultimate superior, Kryuchkov, on August 20 and asked to be dismissed from the service. Putin repeated a similar narrative in an interview with American director Oliver Stone, who made a four-part film out of it. Putin, however, also amused Russian audiences by recalling that in 1991, in addition to his work for Sobchak in St Petersburg and reconnaissance work for the KGB, he still worked as a cab driver to earn money.

In these interviews, Putin distanced himself from the coup, but he always avoided a clear and unequivocal condemnation of the putschists and their worldview. No wonder, since the secret service, which he rejoined a short time later to eventually become its head, was the most important guardian of a worldview according to which the end of the Soviet Union empire was not a liberation but a disaster. Putin sees it the same way. He knows, however, that an official state tribute to the putschists, who were considered drunkards, would be unpopular even in today's Russia. Instead, he simply represses the memory of the inglorious August days of 1991. But he does honor the spiritual fathers of the Soviet uprising against Russia's opening. For example, Putin ordered that Andropov, the longtime head of the KGB, be given a highly visible stele and a commemorative plaque. In 2014, he also personally awarded a medal to Yazov, the defense minister in command during the coup. And he awarded the commander of the tank that deliberately ran over three demonstrators in the Arbat tunnel in 1991, Sergei Surovikin, with the highest honors. Putin made him commander-in-chief for the Ukraine campaign in October 2022. The small stele commemorating those killed in 1991 in Arbat disappeared behind a newly established car park in the fall of 2022. In addition, Putin forced the newspaper *Novaya Gazeta* to cease publication in Russia. It had already been an important liberal voice in the 1990s. Mikhail Gorbachev was involved with it and *Novaya Gazeta*'s editor-in-chief won the 2021 Nobel Peace Prize, but that didn't stop Putin's bureaucrats from cracking down on the paper. Perhaps it even was spurring them on.

The coup plotters had lost a battle in 1991. In the confusing years of reforms under Boris Yeltsin, their comrades-in-arms went into a kind of bureaucratic hibernation, from which Putin was later to awaken them. They and the associated security services never gave up the long war to restore the Soviet Union that was fought first in Russia and then against its neighbors. They left behind a legacy that Putin revived and has cultivated in all its consequences ever since. In August 2022, with an angry look back to 1991, the deputy chair of the Security Council and interim president Dmitry Medvedev threatened the Baltic states: they had not earned freedom, but Moscow had failed to prevent them from leaving the Union. Vladimir Putin set out to take revenge for the failed uprising against Gorbachev and Yeltsin and for the disintegration of the Soviet empire. He has revived and radicalized the spirit of the putschists.

# Exercises in Democracy

## The hopes of the 1990s

»Yeltsin's nineties ... how do we remember them? They were a happy time ... a crazy decade ... terrifying years ... the age of fantastical democracy ... the fatal nineties ... hands down, a golden age ... the age of self-denunciation ... mean and hard times ... a bright dawn ... aggressive ... turbulent ... That was my time ... It wasn't for me!! «

This is how the Belarusian Nobel laureate in literature Svetlana Alexievich sums up the 1990s in her book »*Secondhand Time*« (English edition, 2016; Random House, New York). People in Moscow will always talk about this decade at some point. It is the starting point of today's life, the big bang of modern Russia, and the model of an alternative concept of society that is rejected by the current rulers. It is on the condemnation of this era that Vladimir Putin bases his legitimacy. It is the epoch over which Russians scatter and divide into worshippers of freedom or the state, into pro-Westerners or nationalists, into liberals or authoritarians. The former are a small minority in today's Russia. This is a tragedy, for them and for their country. For the 1990s were an opportunity for Russia that does not often present itself in history. Russians were building a new model: a free society. They began to disarm their state and develop a cooperative understanding of Russia's role in the world. Today, that very alternative is being stifled. Its supporters are marginalized or persecuted. But a look back at the 1990s, the decade of missed opportunity, makes it clear why: because the Russian elite and Vladimir Putin would not be in power in this model.

»When they constantly badmouth Gorbachev and Yeltsin on television today,« says doctor Assya Kudryavtseva about the last Soviet Communist Party general secretary and Russia's first president, »I always think: Why, actually? For me, the era of Yeltsin was a really good time. I was happy and free; there were no limits for me. And that was the most important thing for me!«

I visited Assya in an area of new construction in southwest Moscow. She received me in a spacious apartment from the 1970s with rather low ceilings and double-wing windows with insulating glass. In the living room, there was rather plain, modern furniture and a window that looked out onto a courtyard with trees. Now 55, she was a doctor at a Moscow hospital. Her children, two daughters and a son, had moved out not long ago. She would not speak of her husband. The dispute over the 1990s also tore apart her family and circle of friends, but more on that later. Assya is known among her friends and colleagues for thinking more of Gorbachev and Yeltsin than of Russia's current president. That's how I got to know her—through her friends.

»So, what was so good about Yeltsin?« I asked her as she poured me a black tea and set out small bowls of honey, jam, and nuts.

»I liked him,« she said. »A strong guy who had charisma, convincing clarity, and was very courageous.« Russia needed someone like that at the time to eliminate the Soviet legacy, the dictatorship of the Communist Party. Unfortunately, he did not succeed completely. But that is not what he is accused of today. Today, he would be held responsible for the so-called chaos and the economic crisis.

The late 1980s and the 1990s were bitter years for millions of Russians. All the accumulated deficits of the Soviet Union collapsed in this decade: the bankruptcy of the planned economy, the blatant corruption, the inefficiency of the administration, a depleted infrastructure, an eviscerated industry. Russia and its post-Soviet republics slid into a permanent crisis. In the early 1990s, everything seemed dramatic. At that time, I saw professors and teachers selling their books in cardboard boxes on the street and engineers working as cab drivers. Even Putin claimed to have supplemented his salary by driving in 1991. An historically low oil price of ten dollars a barrel in some cases exacerbated the crisis in Russian state budgets and led to a financial crash in 1998. Assya and her family did not have it easy either. »I was earning next to nothing as a resident at the time,« she recalled. »In 1992, we were essentially living on noodles.« And everyone talked about the vouchers that the government distributed among the people. These were share certificates in the state factories that were privatized in this way. »The particularly smart ones bought the vouchers from the people for little money and created private industrial empires.« Yes, there was all that.

But that was only one side, Assya said. The other side was the freedom that was given to everyone after 70 years of Soviet rule. The state stopped bullying people.

»I was finally not controlled, in anything!« exclaimed Assya, still excited. »I could suddenly travel wherever I wanted, learn whatever I wanted, work wherever I wanted, even live wherever I wanted.« That had not been possible in the Soviet Union, she said. And one should not forget: Under Yeltsin, in July 1991, everyone was practically given an apartment as a gift, namely the apartment they had previously rented from the state. »A tremendous starting asset into free life.«

Assya was in her mid-20s in the early 1990s, full of energy and zest for life. The Yeltsin era, she recalls, was a »time of uninterrupted rebuilding.« In the Soviet Union, they were proud of women crane operators, but under Yeltsin, women suddenly were even driving cars themselves. They renovated the apartment, threw out the old Soviet cabinet walls, and built in something modern. »We painted the walls and houses red at first, then yellow, blue and purple.« Just no more Soviet brown and gray.

»Everything bloomed!«

Assya was not in the minority at that time. It was the feeling of a whole generation. A majority at that time no longer reveled in Russian greatness, in the inevitable downfall of the Western liberal system, and races with the US for lands, seas, and outer space. Russians were interested in their country and their personal freedom. They were free from the totalitarian domination, oppression, and persecution of the Soviet period. Fear had disappeared. Other people felt the same way. Assya had no problem at all with the fact that in the early 1990s the Lithuanians, Latvians, and Estonians found it was time to leave. »Finally, after half a century, the Baltic republics could find themselves and develop themselves. This was not a catastrophe after all, but a great happiness for all of us.« After the Baltic states came the Ukrainians, the Georgians, the Central Asian states, and the other republics hungry for freedom. Boris Yeltsin, she said, had ensured that all this could pass off peacefully.

»That was to his credit.«

Today, this is a minority opinion in Russia. Like their leader, most Russian citizens today believe that it was a mistake to let the non-Russian republics leave in peace in the 1990s. In 2005, Putin himself spoke of the dissolution of the Soviet Union as »the greatest geopolitical catastrophe of the 20th century.« And he and many Russians pin it on a specific date: December 8, 1991, one of the most controversial days in modern Russian history. For Russian liberals, this is the founding date of modern Russia. For the government and ruling elite of Putin's Russia, however, the day represents the betrayal of the Soviet Union. At that time, the Russian and Ukrainian leaders met with the head of state of Belarus at the Viskuli hunting lodge in the Białowieża (Belavezha) Forest to make an agreement formally dissolve the USSR. The former First Deputy Chairman of the Supreme Soviet, Yuri Voronin, spoke of a »coup d'état« and a Belavezha »conspiracy.« Books are available in Moscow with such titles as *Who Betrayed Whom?* and *How They Killed the Soviet Union*. The three presidents are accused in many variations of having disrupted an empire as a drunken collective in a state of intoxication. The official and pro-government accounts describe December 8, 1991, as the unlucky day on which the Soviet empire fell.

There is plenty of resentment and even more political calculation in these assessments. The judgment about December 8 has much more to do with justifying today's rule in Russia than with the historical facts. It is about judging Russia's attempts at democracy in the 1990s, the period of freedom of expression, the opening of the archives, the beginning of political competition. From the government's point of view, this pluralistic period in Russian history must appear as gloomy as possible such that the authoritarian present shines all the brighter. Accordingly, the day Russia freed itself from the grip of the moribund Soviet state must have been a bad day.

But the meeting in Viskuli went very differently from how many Russian officials would like to remember today. I spoke with key players and contemporary witnesses who are still alive or were alive at the time of the interview. I consider the harsh judgments to be politically colored and see the consequences of December 8, 1991, much more positively than today's elites want to admit. This date is central to the assessment of the 1990s. Let's look back: What was it all about?

The primeval forest of Białowieża on the western Soviet border was a special experience for those privileged few who were invited. The Ukrainian delegation hunted wild boar immediately upon arrival. The one-story white villa with light brown columns was a favorite hunting lodge of the nomenklatura in Soviet times. It was in this bucolic idyll that Russian President Boris Yeltsin and newly elected Ukrainian President Leonid Kravchuk met on the evening of December 7, 1991. They were the main characters, for if Russia and Ukraine agreed, the Belarusians had to go along. Stanislau Shushkevich, the chairman of the Supreme Soviet of Belarus, was also sitting at the table. The deputies of the two presidents, Yeltsin's confidant Gennady

Burbulis and Kravchuk's deputy Witold Fokin, were present. The latter two told me about every detail of that night. Yeltsin raised his glass and tried to convince Kravchuk of a new union treaty of Soviet republics. This was the agreement envisioned by Soviet President Mikhail Gorbachev to replace the old Soviet Constitution and, Yeltsin also hoped, save the Soviet Union as a loose confederation. Kravchuk also raised his glass and said flatly, »No.«

Yeltsin and his deputy, Gennady Burbulis, realized then that this could be a difficult, perhaps confrontational, meeting with unmistakable consequences. »Ukraine was swimming away, and we wanted to prevent that at all costs,« Burbulis recalled to me in his Moscow office. Yeltsin felt the pressure; he did not want to be seen as losing Ukraine after more than 300 years of union with Russia. All the representatives around the polished wooden table in the state dacha knew that Ukraine's strong negotiating position in Viskuli was based on the recent referendum in this young state between the Carpathians and Crimea.

Yeltsin, however, did not want to believe that the Russian-speaking regions in the east were also in favor of independence. »What, did the Donbas vote for it too?« he asked. The issue then was the same Russian-speaking region to which Putin sent his soldiers in 2014 and 2022.

»Yes,« Kravchuk answered confidently. »In no region is approval below 50 percent.«

On December 1, 1991, Ukrainians overwhelmingly affirmed their independence and elected their new president, Kravchuk. Ukraine was not only one of the last, but also the most important of the Soviet republics to take this step. The Baltic republics on the Baltic Sea were the first to declare independence, followed by the Caucasian republics in the south. In Russia, this was called the »parade of sovereignty declarations«; withdrawals that tore down the mighty edifice of the Soviet Union piece by piece. The strongest symbol, however, was provided by those who claimed to want to preserve the old Soviet Union: the putschists of the failed coup, as we saw in the previous chapter. The Communist Party of the Soviet Union had been in a long, almost unstoppable process of erosion since 1988. First in Armenia, then in the Baltic republics, national movements asserted themselves against the party and the Soviet organs. The dissolution of the party structures broke a crucial link that had held the Soviet Union together since the 1920s. With the coup against Gorbachev in August 1991, the CPSU was no longer a power factor in the Russian republic of the RSFSR.

Hence why it is an intolerable distortion of historical facts when December 8, 1991, is described as the cause of the downfall today. When Yeltsin and Kravchuk left for Viskuli, the Soviet Union had practically ceased to exist. No one had declared it dead—for fear of what might happen then. Everyone acted as if the state corpse would live on. After all, the USSR was, next to the US, the largest nuclear power on Earth. The nuclear weapons were distributed among several republics, including Ukraine.

Yeltsin declared that if Kravchuk did not want a new Union treaty, then neither did he. Then, finally, Kravchuk brightened.

»If the majority here wants an agreement, then we should not part without it,« he said.

Yeltsin suggested that the legal experts who had come along should not draft a document on the continuation of the Soviet Union but a new treaty of the three independent states. The word »*sodrushestvo*« (commonwealth) made the rounds. Kravchuk chimed in.

Boris Yeltsin had sent his young, excellent lawyer Sergey Shakhray and economist Yegor Gaidar into the nightly wrestling match. Gaidar is no longer alive; I was able to speak with Shakhray in his office at Moscow State University.

They met at Gaidar's dacha in the forest, he recalled. But the Ukrainians did not come. No wonder. Then-35-year-old Shakhray was aware that »the Soviet Union was already at an end with the departures of the individual republics.« Something new had to be created that would prevent a bloody breakup. Gaidar and Shakhray knew that the Ukrainians rigorously rejected the word »union.« Together with the Belarusians, they drafted a text. Gaidar wrote everything down by hand because no typists were traveling with them. Russia, Belarus, and Ukraine—the three republics that had created the Soviet Union in 1922—wanted to found a »Commonwealth of Independent States.« At the same time, as the originator of this idea, Shakhray, put it, »they issued a death certificate to the Soviet Union after its demise.« The agreement's preamble reads: »The Soviet Union as a subject of international law and geopolitical reality has ceased to exist.« By six o'clock on the morning of December 8, the text was in place and delivered to the three presidents a little later with Soviet champagne for breakfast.

On the morning of December 8, 1991, the three heads of the Slavic republics assembled in the billiard room of the Viskuli dacha. The new states mutually recognized their territorial integrity and borders. Their Commonwealth of Independent States was open to the accession of other republics. It chose to be based in Minsk, the capital of Belarus, rather than Moscow, the headquarters of the Soviet empire. It should have a joint military council, and, the crucial point for world peace, nuclear weapons were to be placed under joint control for the time being. Thus, Yeltsin ensured that the Soviet Union would not disintegrate as Yugoslavia had in 1990, with a dispute over nuclear arsenals threatening the entire world. Unlike his successor, Putin, Yeltsin wanted to contain the nuclear danger, not conjure it up.

By noon, all points were agreed upon in Viskuli. The final version was reproduced on an old facsimile machine. Yeltsin raised his glass to each of the fourteen articles. Then, the tables were brought from Viskuli's billiard room to the reception hall, along with three flags and some branches from the primeval Białowieża forest as decoration. At 2:00 p.m., the three heads took their seats in the large entrance hall at mirror-finished white tables and signed the documents. Everyone was relieved. Shushkevich suggested that they go hunting together. Now even Kravchuk was no longer hesitant: »Sure, I'll go with you!« The Belavezha Accords declaration was ratified by the parliaments of Belarus, Russia, and Ukraine on December 8. At a follow-up meeting in Almaty on December 21, 1991, representatives of 11 of the remaining 12 Soviet republics met and signed the Constitutive Act of the Commonwealth of Independent States. On the morning of December 25, 1991, Gorbachev resigned and handed over power, including the nuclear suitcase, to Boris Yeltsin. Thus, the bloody, possibly apocalyptic disintegration of a nuclear-armed superpower had been averted. This was not the »greatest geopolitical catastrophe of the 20th century,« as Putin said, but an historical stroke of luck. The events in Yugoslavia demonstrated how a country could sink into war. Putin's invasions of Ukraine in 2014 and 2022 showed that things could have turned out very differently in 1991.

Assya felt the end of the Soviet Union as a liberation. She enjoyed the opening of her country to the fullest. The doctor and her husband read a lot, they watched controversial programs on TV, and they let new impressions wash over them every day. Assya learned English, »not as a dead language as in the Soviet Union, but with a chance to use the language for a change.« Because under Yeltsin, she could suddenly travel!

»A whole new world opened up to us!« In the fourth year after the breakup of the Soviet Union, she had pulled enough money together to fly abroad. »We went to Austria to ski and spent the holiday intoxicated by the experience. We had never dreamed of doing that.« Two years later, it was off to the Czech Republic. Then France, Germany, Italy. Again and again, she went skiing; it was her obsession during those years. Then came the business trips to Europe, the medical conferences, the exchanges with Europeans.

Her neighbors couldn't understand her »obsessive traveling« and often shook their heads as she waited outside the house again with her suitcase for the cab to the airport, Assya recalled. »We Russians like to isolate ourselves, to be different from everyone else.« People like to speak only Russian. They are suspicious of the outside world. They barricade themselves in apartments with many locks, with a complicated code on the front door and a club behind it. »Fear of the outside world is inherited from generation to generation.«

Assya loved change. She was curious about the future and reveled in the opportunities that the 1990s offered her. But she knew there were many Russians who suffered from the multiplicity and choice. »Most people in Russia are interested in keeping things the way they are.« They wouldn't protest restrictions on freedom, they wouldn't protest police arbitrariness; they just wanted absolute security and enough to eat. »That's enough.« On that basis, the current regime would rule. People were not interested in the future; they were not bothered by the borders that were difficult to penetrate. They lived in the Russian here and now, no matter how sad it was.

Assya speaks from experience gained in her own family. Her eldest daughter, Anastassiya, was born in 1987 and spent a lot of time with her grandmother in the 1990s. »For my mother, those confusing years were harder than for me.« She shared many of her critical impressions with Anastassiya, she said. The daughter studied design, but mainly so she would be able to earn money. For her, security was most important: »Finding a suitable husband, having children, furnishing an apartment nicely, watching TV together in the evenings.« Anastasiya has different ideas about life than her parents. In the 1990s, she was still a child, but her memories are shaped by her grandmother's stories and TV: not a good time, she says. Today, Anastasiya works for an interior design company and has little interest in the world beyond her everyday life. She takes care of her husband, cooks for him and smiles when he comes home.«She also lives in the here and now, wants everything to stay the way it is.«

Her second daughter is quite different, more like Assya herself, she says. Darya was born in 1996, in the middle of the 1990s. She didn't experience the economic hardships, but she also didn't sit in her grandmother's lap quite as often. »Darya lives into the future, she lives for the future. She understands how isolated our country is, that we are turning away from the world, so she wanted to get out early.« Darya went to study in the US when she was just 18. She took economics at a College in Los Angeles, California. »That was her choice.« Of course, Assya would have supported Darya as much as possible, with advice and with money. Now, she lives in America and worries a lot about her family in Russia, Assya said. »We can't help her anymore; she's outgrown us. She wants to help us, but it's not clear yet how she can.«

Assya's third child, a boy named Ilya, was born in 2002. He graduated from high school and wanted to study. The poisoned atmosphere has a strong effect on him, »the obsession with Ukraine, the Crimean hysteria, the constant talk of war.« But he felt instinctively that of the two ways of his sisters, he would rather follow Darya. He learned English and gained his entry ticket to the world. Assya wanted to get him out of it all, but she did not know how. She was still in it herself. »With each passing year since the annexation of Crimea, it became clearer to me that our country was losing its future.« The memory of the Yeltsin years faded with each year under Putin.

Today, the Yeltsin era is relegated to a museum that is worth a look beyond Moscow. In the Urals region hometown of the first president of the Russian Federation, Yekaterinburg, a city of 1.5 million, stands a white, modern building whose architectural sophistication is eye-catching. The »Yeltsin Center« opened in 2015 and serves as a museum, a conference hall, a place of study, and a meeting center. In 2018, while I was on the grand flight of steps in front of the building, I looked up and found that the dynamic architecture was a perfect fit for Boris Yeltsin, who in his better years had an inexhaustible energy. Inside, I quickly found myself in front of some relics, and the exhibition began: Yeltsin's school kit, Yeltsin's workbook, Yeltsin's suit, Yeltsin's scarf, Yeltsin's atomic suitcase. His state car, an armored ZIL 41 052, was right there in the vestibule. In a display case a few meters away, I saw an orange sweater that his former Deputy Prime Minister Boris Nemtsov had given Yeltsin as a birthday present not long before his death. Next to me, four men in their mid-20s stood in front of the display case and almost devoutly read Nemtsov's congratulatory card: »Dear Boris Nikolaevich, I hope this sweater will warm you. Its orange color is an indication of what is so bitterly lacking in Russia today. Every day I love and appreciate you more.« The four young men in black T-shirts and black pants were from Chelyabinsk in the southern Urals. »Thank you,« they said, still standing for a long time in front of the sweater, which bore the color of Ukraine's 2004 revolution. There are more than a few Yeltsin fans in that country, but they have gone undercover to make a pilgrimage here.

I was greeted by Dina Sorokina, who had been director of the Yeltsin Center since 2016 and was replaced in 2021, in an office on the upper floors. From her room, she had a sweeping view of Yekaterinburg. The Yeltsin Center wants to keep alive the memory of the president and Russia's alternative path, she told me. Many Russians do not understand how the economic difficulties of the 1990s were a consequence of the »processes of the 1970s and 1980s,« i.e., that they originated in the Soviet Union. This is suppressed today. Just like the fact that »the Soviet Union could not be maintained as it existed.« Its end was not an arbitrary decision by individual politicians, but an historical development of disintegration.

The exhibition has two goals, Sorokina said. It aims to make the events of the 1990s tangible for everyone, so that they can connect the history of all Russians with their own personal history. »After all, the youth can hardly imagine that time,« she said, amused. »They laugh about the comical 1990s, about all the experiments of that time, when we tried everything in the political, cultural, economic and social spheres.« With films, exhibitions, and discussions, she wants to bring this »time of great experiments« back to the present. And not just to admire.

She knew that the 1990s were controversial because of more than poverty. There was also much to criticize about Yeltsin's political decisions, even from liberals. He was in a permanent fight for survival. In a political conflict with communist and reactionary forces in parliament, he had the White House, then the seat of parliament, shot up in 1993. He pushed through a constitution that was supposed to be democratic but left many authoritarian loopholes, which Putin later exploited. In 1995, Yeltsin sent the army into a confrontation with the restive republic of Chechnya in their battered country. And for the 1996 elections, Yeltsin allied himself with the oligarchs, who ruthlessly exploited the alliance for their business purposes. Many of the experiments in the 1990s went awry. The »Yeltsin Center is supposed to be a space for these debates: What was right? What was wrong?« said Dina Sorokina.

It was also Yeltsin, by the way, who made Putin prime minister and his designated successor in August 1999. Putin assured Yeltsin at the time that he and his family would not be persecuted. Perhaps this also explains why the center was able to open in 2015 at all. And why it even received support from the federal budget. »But that's only a small part of it,« said Dina Sorokina. Most of its income comes from sponsors, foundations, and companies. In addition, the center is allowed to sublease offices in the large building, which also brings in money. How long it survives ultimately depends on Putin, who does not like much of what can be seen here.

A cartoon film in a hall through which all visitors were guided was very moving. It presented an outline of Russian past as a history of democracy. Is that possible? Yes, indeed. I saw an animated tale of civic freedom, participation, initiative, distance from the state, civic spirit, and readiness to revolt when the ruler snapped. It focused on the fulcrums and turning points of Russian history; for example, the People's Assembly in the free republic of Novgorod in the late Middle Ages, where law was laid down in writing and military leaders and archbishops were elected. And the reformer and tsarist advisor Mikhail Speransky in the early 19th century, who recommended the separation of powers and wrote a constitution. And the Decembrists, who rebelled against the reactionary Tsar Nicholas I in 1825 and demanded a constitution and the liberation of the peasants. And the tsar and reformer Alexander II, who finally abolished peasant serfdom in 1861. And the legendary 1990s. Russia has a spectacular history of freedom, and here it was impressively demonstrated. The Yeltsin Center refuted the old prejudice that the country can only be ruled with a heavy hand.

It told a convincing counter-narrative to the major exhibitions sanctioned by Putin. These described Russia as a success story of tough, decisive leaders from Ivan the Terrible to Joseph Stalin who had made Russia united, great, and feared. In the 20th century, Russia had three chances to break away from this preordained track. The 1905 Revolution, which was followed by a brief period of parliamentarization that was soon stifled. The February Revolution of 1917, which led to the overthrow of the czar but was hijacked by Bolsheviks led by Vladimir Lenin in the October 1917 coup. And the end of the Soviet Union in December 1991, which was followed by eight eventful years of democratic, free-market experiments under Boris Yeltsin. All three experiments were accompanied by a severe economic crisis, the cause of which was not the fault of the democratic actors. The reasons were primarily tsarist mismanagement and the lost war against Japan in 1905, the continued war against Germany in 1917, and the legacy of decades of Soviet mismanagement, including an historically low oil price in the 1990s.

The upswings always benefited the autocrats.

But all these historical facts are forgotten in Russia today. The Yeltsin Center has long been a thorn in the side of the guardians of Putinism. And that is why it came under increasing pressure in 2022. Representatives of the regime and the elite spoke about what Putin would not because of his deal with the Yeltsin family. Putin's journalistic pit bull, television host Vladimir Solovyov, accused the Yeltsin Center of promoting homosexuality. The center, he said, had some time ago given a prize to a high school that had become the talk of 2022 with a dance containing homosexual innuendo. This is, apparently, the »style of the spirit of freedom« that the Yeltsin Center wants to promote, Solovyov caustically scathed. A little later, conservative film director Nikita Mikhalkov, who is loyal to Putin, spoke out and demanded (not for the first time, by the way, but the tenth) the Yeltsin Center be declared a »foreign agent,« which would prohibit any outside contact and funding of the Center. Patriotic-minded musicians, singers, and actors immediately joined in. Mikhalkov called for a »patriotic view of history« and demanded the demolition and ruin of »destructive influences on children's national identity.«

This elite is concerned with totalitarian control over the history and self-image of Russians. Built into this control is a fixed image of the 1990s that Putin himself has given. It has three components: decay, chaos and crime, and remote control by the Americans. The Russian ruler never misses an opportunity to paint his predecessor's time in office in the blackest colors. »In fact, a civil war was going on at the time,« Putin said in December 2021, adding that the country was on the verge of falling apart. But then, he said, he tightened the reins and unified the country—and drove out the US agents who were working in Moscow as advisors. In essence, that is his narrative: He is the firm hand that brought the Americanized, ungovernable, and chaotic country back together.

Anyone who knows history and lived in Russia in the 1990s, like me, knows that this is a lie. There was no civil war. In fact, it was Boris Yeltsin who held Russia together in the 1990s after the breakup of the Soviet Union. After the death certificate for the Soviet Union he signed in the Białowieża Forest, Yeltsin's nightmare was to have to issue another for the Russian Federation. This explained, among other things, his willingness to conduct the Chechen war in 1995 with all its harshness and to give Putin a free hand in the second Chechen war in 1999. Serious mistakes made crimes possible. But Yeltsin's real integration achievement took place at the negotiating table. He relied on persuasion and reconciliation and occasional grants to the regions. He concluded the first federation treaty in 1994 with the Volga Republic of Tatarstan, which demarcated the competences of the center and the periphery under the umbrella of the Russian Federation. Tatarstan got the best deal of all because it was the first republic, but its example was followed by all other regions and republics. This proved to be resilient even in the 1998 financial crisis. Boris Yeltsin had long since unified the Russian Federation when Putin took office. Putin's steps beyond that were not toward the supposedly necessary unification of Russia, but the establishment of an authoritarian system. The regime of today began with the second Chechen war and the destruction of federalism.

To justify this today, the big picture of the 1990s must appear as dark as possible. Putin's propagandists add black paint daily. Margarita Simonyan, the editor-in-chief of three state media outlets, noted that back then, as a state employee, you didn't get a salary, but were paid »in kind, like syringes or morels [...] That has stopped.« Billionaire Boris Titov, who entered the presidential race in 2018 with a sham candidacy to legitimize the election, credited Putin with bringing »stability after the chaos of the 1990s.« Patriarch Kirill thanked Putin from God for straightening out this »aberration of our history.« With these formulas, they all support the tyranny after the years of groping and experimenting with democratization. And would that it were only representatives of the Russian elite. No, in Germany, too, the Putin narrative was diligently propagated. Gerhard Schröder was the most platitudinous, and no wonder. The 1990s were »marked by plundering, corruption, and chaos,« the ex-chancellor and natural gas oligarch remarked at a discussion in Berlin's Adlon back in 2007. It had »no statehood« anymore. It was Putin who led the country onto a path of stability and reliability.

Many politicians, as well as many German business representatives, spoke like Schröder at conferences on Russia up until the pandemic years. At the same time, it was the fixed narrative of the Left Party: Yeltsin stood for US prescriptions, chaos, and impoverishment; Putin stood for stability and prosperity. The Germans who talked like this rendered outstanding services to the Russian regime. Schröder and numerous other Germans received posts, medals, and not-insignificant money in Moscow.

Dina Sorokina resigned as director of the Yeltsin Center in 2021. When I wrote to her in the summer of 2022, she was living indefinitely in New York to pursue »her own projects.« A new leadership was trying to survive in Yekaterinburg. After the invasion of Ukraine in February, the center declared that the war was an »unthinkable disaster for both countries and peoples« and called for an immediate cessation of hostilities. This was not well received. In June, the Center tried to correct the impression of being unpatriotic. Speakers loyal to the regime were invited. A »hero of Russia« lectured to students about the »operation« in Ukraine. A little later, two Russian military correspondents spoke about their trips to the Donetsk People's Republic and their experiences at the front. They warned against »fake news from Ukraine and the West« on the news channels and professed their »love« for »Russian Donetsk« and Donbas.

For Assya Kudryavtseva, the war against Ukraine brought a long development to a close. The rulers, as she saw it, were directing all the country's concentration and strength outward, toward savage conquests of Crimea and the Donbas.

»But nothing is happening internally,« she fretted. There is no development, for example, in her field of medicine. A lot had happened with the opening up since the 1990s, but at some point, development stagnated. Now, with the turn away from the West, the sciences, medicine, and educational institutions are being cut off from all exchange, and the opening of the 1990s is being reversed. Now the youth are being educated patriotically, she said. »They are taking away the future of my country and my family,« she said.

When I last heard from Assya before writing these sentences, she was preparing for a big trip. She wanted to join Darya in America. Ilya had already left Russia. Only Anastassiya, her eldest daughter, wanted to stay. When they talked about Russia's path, Anastassiya usually withdrew because she disagreed with her family's opinion.

»I see it all a little differently than you do,« Anastassiya said. End of discussion.

Assya would follow Darya to America. Ilya was studying in the Netherlands. »We're leaving,« said Assya, »before the country closes itself off so much that we can't leave at all.«

# Rogue Republic

## The Chechen model

I did not recognize the city. For the first time since the war in 2000, I was back in Grozny—and caught in a burst of happiness in Kadyrov Square downtown. Young men danced on clacking leather shoes, back and forth, on one leg and on their hands. Young women in long skirts swirled around them. I saw pitch-black sunglasses and white lace capes, dizzyingly high heels, and headscarves. A band played Caucasian pop music. Amplifiers carried the bass across the huge asphalt square in front of the big mosque. It was a folk festival in Grozny, the capital of Chechnya, where people were celebrating, as they do every year, the end of the »anti-terrorist operation,« a euphemism for Russia's brutal war in Chechnya, unleashed by Vladimir Putin in 1999.

But what I saw on that visit seventeen years later was not an anti-Putin demonstration—quite the contrary. A colorfully dressed procession of older women waved Russian and Czech flags. Several of them bravely held up large posters with photos of politicians: Vladimir Putin and Ramzan Kadyrov, the head of the Chechen Republic. Around them stood uniformed men dressed entirely in black with long beards, the feared »Kadyrovites« security guard. In Grozny, no one celebrates without authorization.

Suddenly, screams erupted from the crowd. A black Mercedes SUV raced into the square and stopped in front of the dancing people. A second SUV filled with security guards followed close behind. A Chechen hissed at me with raised eyebrows, »the deputy prime minister!« Indeed, Islam Kadyrov, red bearded, in sunglasses and a black T-shirt, the brother of the ruler of Chechnya, was sitting in the driver's seat.

People recognized the man at the wheel and backed away. He slowed down the Mercedes and drove slowly through the middle of the crowd. The music stopped. The people stared. Then the man stepped on the gas again, did a victory lap around the giant square, and roared away. »Celebrate!« the police officers shouted. But now the mood was subdued and deflated. People quietly packed up their things. The celebration was over.

Chechnya is both a maneuvering ground and a laboratory for Russia. It is a country where the powerful test the extremes, the limits of war, destruction, and bureaucratic despotism as well as the limits of tyranny and the people's tolerance. Putin came to power with the Chechen war in 1999. It was his first war, and it made him popular enough in Russia to win the presidential election in 2000. In subjugating Chechnya, Putin gained control of Russia at the same time. But in so doing, he awakened demons that haunted the entire country. Putin's campaign in Chechnya accustomed people to war and violence, and the Caucasus republic itself became a model for Russia's future under Putin. I would hardly have been able to understand the marketplace scene if I had not traveled around this Russian republic, probably the most unfortunate of them all, in 1999. To show what an important role Chechnya plays in Russia, I will briefly look back to the beginning of Putin's rule.

In 1999, Putin wanted to prove that he could deal with the small insubordinate Caucasus state. His predecessor, Boris Yeltsin, had launched a bloody campaign there in 1995. Like with Ukraine in 2022, there was no comprehensible reason for a major war in 1999. A Chechen warlord, Shamil Basayev, had occupied several villages in Russian Dagestan in August 1999. A targeted action by Russian special forces would have certainly solved the problem. There was no reason to break the peace treaty with Chechnya signed by President Boris Yeltsin in 1997. But Putin decided otherwise.

Like the invasion of Ukraine in 2022, Putin invented a justification for the war in Chechnya. To do so, he used a mysterious series of attacks in September 1999, when unknown persons blew up apartment buildings in Moscow, Volgodonsk, and Buynaksk. In the provincial city of Ryazan, residents of a house foiled one attack. Russian intelligence had placed explosive-capable material in the basement of an apartment building and, when residents discovered the strange bags, the whole thing was explained away as an »exercise«—for what remains unclear. So, who was behind the attacks in Moscow, Volgodonsk, and Buynaksk?

I asked Vladimir Putin that explicitly during a *Zeit* interview in November 1999. I was able to visit his White House office in Moscow. »Chechnya,« he told me with his fist clenched on the table, »Chechnya has become a world center of international organized crime and terror.« Putin spoke of kidnapping and arms deals, attacks, and bandit raids. The marketplace of Grozny, where the Russian army inflicted a massacre with over 100 civilian deaths in October 1999, was just a »weapons marketplace« to him.

Such early excuses are reminiscent of later propaganda formulas used by the Russians when they fired missiles at civilian targets in Ukraine in the spring of 2022. Putin claimed he was fighting the United States in Ukraine. In the fall of 1999, Putin justified the Chechen war thus: »This is an aggression of international terrorism against Russia.« He would not talk to moderate Chechen President Aslan Maskhadov. All efforts at political mediation were sabotaged by the intelligence services. Putin promised that »the bandits will be destroyed,« the same promise he made about the purported »Nazis« in Ukraine today. The FSB, a successor organization to the KGB, brought Maskhadov, who had long since been ousted from the presidency, to Chechnya in a special operation in 2005 after making Putin an offer of a cease-fire.

Russian forces surged ahead in bloody, internecine fighting in Chechnya in 1999. In retrospect, the Russian campaign in Chechnya and the war of aggression against Ukraine in 2022 have many similarities: poor planning, poor coordination of troops, high casualties, destruction of residential areas, and the increasing brutality of the war. For example, in early December 1999, 250 Russian soldiers died in one day alone in a battle near the capital, Grozny. In March 2000, 84 airborne troops from Pskov were killed when they were caught in an ambush. Today, in front of their barracks in Pskov, there is a monument as tall as a house commemorating this defeat. Due to a lack of coordination, a lot went wrong at that time.

At the end of March 2000, 43 elite soldiers of the Ministry of Interior died to friendly fire from regular Russian troops. Most of the fallen were buried in a tomb of silence, as was also the case in Ukraine in 2022. In November 1999, army spokesman General Valery Manilov had provided detailed information about the casualties suffered by Chechen fighters, and those figures revealed how little oversight he himself had. Then he claimed that the rebels numbered about 8,000, but in January 2000 he announced that the armed forces had killed 10,000 (!) of them. In July 2000, he put the number of rebels at 25,000.

The Russians were obviously dealing with an elusive enemy. Therefore, as in Ukraine in 2022, air warfare and artillery quickly gained importance. The only difference was that the Chechens had far fewer antiaircraft weapons to counter the bombardment than the Ukrainians did more than two decades later. Russian planes dropped their explosive charges over Chechen towns and villages largely unchallenged. Military specialists in Moscow accused the armed forces of using internationally outlawed cluster munitions and vacuum bombs. The diabolically intense pressure wave kills even people in bomb shelters.

I saw the result of this warfare for myself on a trip to Grozny in mid-February 2000. It was not easy to get there; the Russians did not like to see foreign journalists in the city. At a truck stop not far from the border with Ingushetia, I was able to convince a Russian army driver to give me a ride in his truck. He drove soldiers's clothes and laundry to Grozny. Our deal: I let him use my satellite phone to call his girlfriend and his mother in Siberia. In return, he improved my knowledge of the Russian vulgar language »Mat« and took me to Grozny.

The sight was bloodcurdling. The center of the city, which I later revisited, was the dead center of Chechnya in February 2000. Life was no longer conceivable on Minutka Square, around which Russian troops and Chechen rebels had fought for weeks. Instead, there was rubble, debris, metal parts, smashed vehicles, broken glass, and bullet casings. The alleged precision strikes of Russian bombs had devastated the houses and left meter-deep craters. Trees were shredded, and streetlamps had bent from the heat of the fire. Grozny's Lenin Street was a boulevard of ruins, the buildings standing along a tank track like a line of skeletons. In the center, no wall stood straight, no window was in its frame, no house was habitable. A few cellars had become the last place of retreat. On a mezzanine-floor, I saw scattered white flags and, again and again, the scrawled inscription, »People live here!«

I was able to talk to a woman who crawled out of a basement into daylight and was blinking into the winter sun. She said that »the soldiers come every other day and check our papers« before telling them they should leave.

»There is nothing left for us here« they would say, »but where should we go?«

Grozny's center was wiped out. Between the ruins of the houses, the Russian soldiers had posted checkpoints. I was detained at a checkpoint because I did not have special permission from the army to be there. After questioning me, the soldiers let me go on the condition that I leave the city and Chechnya as soon as possible. But I still had one appointment—in the filtration camp. I remember this visit today when I read the reports of Ukrainian soldiers returning from Russian captivity. They, too, were in »filtration camps.«

The camp was in Chernokozovo, a village not far from Grozny. It was actually a remand prison, the largest in Russian-controlled Chechnya. On the road to the prison stood parents, sisters, and friends of the detainees: »Ask for Akhmed!« »Look after Ruslan!« they called out to me. The road ended where barbed wire and fences began. The barrier opened only to authorized visitors. Major General Mikhail Nazarkin, the head of the remand prison, received me for a tour with a smile. Before me lay an old factory site: rusty tracks, cranes, a bombed-out hall.

»In the Soviet Union, this was an educational and labor colony for thugs, drunkards, rioters, and work-shy people,« the major explained. »Later, the Chechens maintained a penal camp here,« Nazarkin said. He pointed to a wall riddled with bullet holes. »That's where the Sharia court had the convicts executed.«

I saw young men painting the large gate to the prison courtyard green and carefully adjusting the barbed wire. From the courtyard, a corridor lined with bars led to the cells. »We are currently holding 113 people who fought in unlawful military units,« Nazarkin said. According to Russian legal thought, the opponent in war is not only imprisoned, but also prosecuted. He is a »terrorist.« This applied not only to men, but also to women who helped the combat troops. A guard soldier opened an iron-barred wooden door for me, then tore open a lattice shutter. Damp cold hit me from the dark cell. A hint of light fell through a filthy window no larger than a sheet of letter paper. Four prisoners startled from the cots. They were in their mid-30s. The emaciated men quickly turned away to the window and lowered their heads. On the floor, I saw cockroaches, many of them.

»What's the matter, don't they feed you well?« shouted Nazarkin into the cell. No answer. »Everyone gets bedding, medical aid, and food here,« Nazarkin said. »Everyone is happy, as you can see.« With a crash, he slammed the cell door shut. The women's wing was no less bleak than the men's. In one cell, right next to the entrance, a hole had been cut into the concrete, from which feces overflowed.

»Did you have a nice time in the bathhouse?« boomed Nazarkin into the cell. A timid yes came back. Why were the women here?

»Soldiers took me off a bus in a suburb of Grozny,« says Amina, a 38-year-old with deeply rimmed eyes, with whom I was allowed to speak briefly under supervision. »They took my ID and claimed I was a criminal.« Yet she had never fought, she said.

»My only guilt is being a Chechen.« She had been in Chernokozovo for a month and eight days.

Nazarkin intervened, and the door slammed shut. He waved it off. »No one stays here more than a week, then we either release them or send them on to another prison. That's for the investigators to decide.« Did lawyers have access to prisoners? He smiled at me mockingly, »Good luck finding a lawyer in Chechnya.«

Of course, I saw no instruments of torture and heard no screams during the tour, which lasted a good hour. But people who had gathered outside the prison claimed to have heard screams during the nights. »The Russians keep secret who is in the filtration camp,« agitated a 50-year-old woman who had traveled from a neighboring town to look for her missing son. »Relatives and friends just disappear. The soldiers use any pretext to arrest them.«

After returning from Chechnya, I met a former prisoner from Chernokozovo in the neighboring republic of Ingushetia. He did not want to tell me his name for fear of prosecution. He had been arrested by a Russian patrol in January 2000. »They wanted any confessions, any information about fighters who are still in the field,« he told me. For that, the law enforcers apparently were willing to use any means. »They tied me up and hit my arms and legs with a hammer because I didn't say anything useful,« he recounted. »Twice they ordered me to stand with my hands up all day until I collapsed.« When dawn broke, fear would spread among the prisoners. »Then the guards would get drunk and beat them senseless. They didn't want confessions anymore, they wanted money and watches.« He escaped in early February because a friend learned through a released detainee that he was in Chernokozovo. The friend bribed an officer—and he was able to leave half an hour later.

The prisoner's statements were similar to interviews I later read in Human Rights Watch reports on Chernokozovo. According to these reports, guards ran the detainees through gauntlets, beat them with rubber truncheons and iron hammers, robbed them of gold rings, leather jackets, and money, sprayed tear gas into the cells, and raped women and men. And these reports again corresponded to those from 1995 and 1996, when the Russian army had already overrun Chechnya. Today, we read the continuation of these stories in the reports of Ukrainians who escaped Russian captivity.

Chechnya is the laboratory for a type of warfare that compensates for a lack of efficiency and penetrating power with cruelty and revenge. Russian troops used and continue to use disproportionate force to demoralize and disarm the enemy to achieve victory. The wiping out of Grozny was the model for the destruction of Aleppo in 2016 and the obliteration of Mariupol in 2022. The cruelty of Chernokozovo and other Chechen crime scenes followed a logic that continued in Bucha, Ukraine in 2022. Despite military reforms and announcements of change, Putin's wars since Chechnya have followed the same formula.

Unlike the war, the development of Chechnya in the Federation was an absolutely exceptional path. And you can see that when you walk through the city. There were 17 years between my visits to Grozny, and there was a good reason why I did not recognize the city at all. During the years of my absence, it had turned into a Chechen copy of Dubai and Istanbul. The city rulers decided to completely clear the ruins of the center. Where I spoke with the woman from the basement in 2000, skyscrapers now tower into the sky, with glittering glass façades and gilded roofs. At night, the towers begin to glow and display banners with Qur'anic suras. In front of »Grozny City,« as the high-rise park is called, stands a huge mosque, a reproduction of Sultanahmet, the Blue Mosque in the old center of Istanbul, built by the Turks. A Qur'anic school nearby looks more East Asian with its golden pagoda roofs. The Chechen government district was built in a former park. From my hotel window on the 22nd floor, I could look at the buildings of power: white palaces with tall columns, pilasters, and green domes framed by triumphal arches, porticoes, obelisks, and freshly planted flowerbeds. The so-called parliament reminded me not of the gray box of the Duma in Moscow, but of the Capitol in Washington. That seems to be the minimum standard of the Chechens today. The only thing I dimly recognized from 2000 was Lenin Prospekt. There stood classicist houses from the middle of the 20th century, built under Stalin, destroyed under Putin, and now rebuilt as an »historical center« again. Today the street is called Putin Prospekt.

This also shows that the current rulers of Chechnya do not hold Putin accountable for the terrible war. Ramzan Kadyrov, the ruler of the republic, gets along well with the Russian president, who promoted him to colonel general of the Russian National Guard in 2022. Kadyrov is the son of former Chechen mufti Akhmat Kadyrov. Akhmat was elected head of the republic by Putin in 2003, then died barely a year later—not uncharacteristically for the country—in an assassination attempt. Today, his son, Ramzan Kadyrov, is the absolute ruler of the Caucasus republic. His subjects call him Padishah, what the Ottoman subjects called their sultan until 1918. He succeeded in forcing some of the Russian troops and overseers out of the country. He took over the repression himself with his bodyguard and security service. With Putin, he and his country have no constitution, no treaty, no model of federation, but a pact of the powerful. It is a personalized, quasi-feudal vassal model outside the institutions. Putin has given him

Chechnya as a fiefdom, and Kadyrov can do as he pleases so long as he remains loyal to Putin. Extensive independence in exchange for absolute personal loyalty. Putin acts as if he were also the all-powerful president of Chechnya, while Kadyrov acts as if Chechnya belonged to the Russian Federation like any other region. Putin pays for this with a lot of money, which Kadyrov uses to build his glittering palaces. Eighty percent of the Chechen budget came from Moscow in 2016. Russia has been subsidizing the republic, which was destroyed in 2000 and where the economy lies idle except for the construction industry and oil production and most people are unemployed. But Putin and Kadyrov have much more in common.

On Putin Prospekt, there is a corner house that bears a wall painting depicting Putin and Kadyrov in an oval frame. Kadyrov is a copy of Putin. Both talk about family values and a conservative worldview, but they interpret traditional family ties very freely. Both combine an obsession with power, mistrust of everyone, and macho nationalism. Both oppress homosexuals: one presumably has them tortured, whereas the Russian president harasses them with laws. Both love martial arts, Judo and Karate. Both like to pose for pictures with tigers, horses, and weapons. Both are populist leaders who rally the common people behind them with invective-laden speeches and abundant subsidies. And, of course, both like to go to church services and pray for the cameras, so the people can see: The leader fears none but God.

I was able to hear about what it means to be led by a ruler like Ramzan Kadyrov from Oyub Titiev in Grozny in 2017. He represented the respected Memorial Human Rights Center, which was »liquidated« by Putin's appointed judges in 2022. I met Titiev at his office, which still existed then but was threatened with closure. A predecessor, Nataliya Estemirova, had been murdered in Grozny in 2009. Titiev saw Putin and Kadyrov as having a symbiotic relationship, the one depending on the other. »Kadyrov is Putin's son, he is entirely his creature,« the human rights activist said. Many of the things that are being considered in Russia are being tried out here. Examples? »There are security forces everywhere, there are constant raids on the market in Grozny,« he recounted. People must show their papers and open their cell phones to the uniformed officers. They then look through the chats and search histories for anything suspicious. This method was not used systematically in Moscow until much later. Titiev reported that people would be arrested at the slightest hint of suspicion. This is why people flinch when they see the security forces. I immediately remembered the scene in Kadyrov Square. But it could be worse.

The first problem is kidnappings. People would simply disappear on the way to the grocery store, on a bus ride to neighboring towns, on the way home from friends. »Suddenly they are gone, don't answer calls, the phone is turned off,« Titiev recounted. Every month, he said, about a dozen people disappear or are kidnapped in the capital alone. Often, gangs were behind it, but without the connivance of the security forces, they would hardly be able to terrorize. Not infrequently, he said, they were kidnappings for hire.

The fear of this moved into every house.

Some people took revenge on the police for the violence. As a result, he said, there have been occasional serious shootouts between armed Chechens and security forces. When I visited Titiev, a heavy battle had taken place not long ago. Fourteen dead and 36 wounded. Ten of the dead came from Kadyrov's units, and they took the most brutal vengeance possible. They tracked down the relatives of their opponents and drove to their houses. They poured gasoline around the houses and set everything on fire. »Others have to watch their houses being flattened with bulldozers and Kamaz trucks.« This is how the regime takes revenge for resistance.

Another form of repression is expulsion from the republic, away from home, farm, and family. The expulsions are traumatic for many Chechens. This is reminiscent of the deportations of Chechens in 1944 under Stalin during the Second World War. At that time, about half a million people were expelled to Central Asia; only after Stalin's death were they allowed to return. Kadyrov had a monument to the deportees partially destroyed and relocated. There is no reference to the 1944 deportations in the Grozny State National Museum, and a conference on the expulsions earned the organizer a four-year sentence in prison. The memory is unwanted, and the method is still practiced today.

But can it work? How long will people allow themselves to be bullied and oppressed by a brutal regime? »This may take some time,« Titiev said. Kadyrov is not only oppressive, but also magnanimous in how he distributes social benefits from the Russian treasury and takes care of the spiritual well-being of Chechens. His trump card is Islam. His father, Akhmat, was the mufti of Chechnya, a legacy he is using to his advantage. Islam is the means. Since 2015, Ramzan Kadyrov has been staging gigantic marches in the city. In 2015, he called together half a million people to protest the Muhammad cartoons in the French magazine *Charlie Hebdo*. With Putin's blessing, Kadyrov latched onto a worldwide movement in the Islamic world of mostly authoritarian rulers who fanned people's anger over perceived insults to Islam. Of course, with anti-Western overtones— in this case against France. Kadyrov is one of Putin's bridges to that world. »Kadyrov builds mosques and madrasas, he pays people for the Hajj, the pilgrimage to Mecca,« Titiev said. I should definitely see the large mosque in the city center, he advised. When I said goodbye to Oyub Titiev, I didn't know it would be our last meeting, or at least our last meeting for a long time. A year later, he was arrested and sentenced to prison. Because nothing else was found against him, he was sentenced for alleged drug offenses, a popular way to keep human rights activists out of circulation.

I had an appointment with the mufti. I walked toward the Akhmat Kadyrov Mosque, the copy of Istanbul's massive Blue Mosque.

The Islamic University is right next to it, between them a park with Japanese cherries, laburnum, hibiscus, and far too many wrought-iron lights. The university was no less richly decorated than the mosque with arches on the outside and marble walls and floors inside. I had to wait a very long time, and I spent it looking at numerous pictures of Putin and Kadyrov, on celluloid and in oil, framed in gold with accent lights mounted over them. While I was daydreaming like this, suddenly the mufti stood in front of me. »Come, please!« said Salah Mezhiev. We went into his office, which was laden with new, heavy wooden furniture. He abruptly began a punitive speech against terrorism. The Chechen terrorists, al-Qaeda, the Islamic State, were all emissaries of Satan. They had nothing to do with Islam, I had to know that. I could hardly catch my breath to ask him a question before he continued talking. Chechnya was victorious over terrorism »because Akhmat Kadyrov and his son Ramzan paved the way for it.« For this, he was grateful. Kadyrov enjoys Putin's full confidence. »This trust is the basis of our unity and stability in the Caucasus.« Vladimir Putin is the most important Christian friend of Muslims, he said. »He does not allow insults and caricatures.«

I learned two things from this sentence. Official Chechen Islam is part of the anti-Western program in Russia, and the constant emphasis on the cartoon issue reminded me of the very similar campaigns in Syria and Iran. Through Chechen Islam, Russia was supposed to become compatible with the Middle East: Putin's soft power. As in many countries in the region, there was a well-controlled state Islam in Grozny. Religious institutions serve and are sustained by the state and only the state. The concept has no stranger to Russia since Peter I established the Holy Synod in 1721, effectively subjugating the Orthodox Church. Other religions have been controlled in Russia accordingly ever since. Incidentally, Turkey takes a similar approach with its religious office, Diyanet, which reports to the Turkish president. In return, everything is paid for. Imams are selected, trained, controlled, and paid by the state. This is also how it is done in Chechnya. »The mosques are financed by the Akhmat Kadyrov regional fund; here no Chechen has to pay for his worship,« the mufti said. Ramzan Kadyrov himself has also donated to mosques, he said. With good reason.

Islam is the second major source of control, alongside repression by the security forces. The mufti and imams watch over the war-torn country, as do Kadyrov's armed guards. And, of course, sermons are handed down from above, otherwise any imam could claim anything. Since radical preachers had infiltrated from the Arab world, especially from the Gulf, in the 1990s, the mufti is keeping a particularly close eye on things.

After my meeting with the mufti, I listened to one of the human rights activists in a side street off Putin Prospekt explain how Ramzan Kadyrov uses Islam for his rule. »Religion is something that helps everyone survive in war,« Heda Saratova explained. »People put up with the blows and the pressure better if they believe they can rely on Allah.« The government knows this too, she said, and that's why it's reinforcing the trend. »Religion gives the government legitimacy that it can't get through violence alone.« Kadyrov would burnish his popularity through vulgar Islamic measures. There are swimming pools, he said, where men and women must lie separately by the water—or can use the facilities only on women's or men's days. Alcohol is hardly found anymore; it is sold under the counter in stores. Islamization, which Putin has always warned against, is Kadyrov's means of rule, at least on the surface. Women, in particular, are the target of this religious oppression.

Girls are required to wear a headscarf in schools from the first grade, Heda Saratowa said. In all government offices, the head covering is mandatory. Women are expected to wear long skirts, even school-age girls. When they come home from school, they hear on television about how women should behave: patiently and obediently.

The woman should pray, then the man will go to paradise. She should sit at home, while the man goes outside.

»But that doesn't work!« cried Heda Saratova. Because men don't earn enough, so many women must go to work, too. The president had given her a flower and congratulated her on Women's Day on March 8. She had a surprising answer ready:

»I'm not a woman!«

»Why?«

»I am the third gender, woman and man at the same time.«

»I don't understand.«

»I pray, shop, clean, have kids—and on top of that, I go out and work to make money. And all just to hear some idiot on TV on Fridays telling me how to behave morally.«

How did the president react? »He kept silent,« Heda Saratova said. All values in Chechnya are twisted to make it as comfortable as possible for the man, she said. A woman is practically without rights. In case of divorce, the man gets the house, the money, and the children. The courts in Chechnya follow a religious logic or that's what they called it »if women even have the courage to go to court for their rights,« Heda Saratova said.

The discouragement is systematic. Ramzan Kadyrov, father of 12 children and husband of two wives, flaunts family values. Religion is at the service of the rulers in Grozny and in Moscow. Kadyrov praises Putin as a leader, but much of what Kadyrov tries out in Grozny is later applied throughout Russia: police terror, cell-phone searches, and displacement and expulsion of citizens from the country. Chechnya is a test ground and model for Russia.

Kadyrov's best service to the Russian president, however, is to provide firepower—both internally and externally. Chechen contract killers have murdered scores of Putin critics in Russia, including journalist Anna Politkovskaya and politician Boris Nemtsov. Who enabled or even ordered the murders in the Russian security services was never clarified. Most importantly, no shadow was allowed to fall on Putin.

Even more important is Kadyrov's service in Putin's numerous wars. Chechen mercenaries are said to have fought in Syria and Libya. Kadyrov's fighters played a central role in Putin's war of aggression against Ukraine. There, they tried to break the Ukrainian resistance with several battalions and the worst brutality. According to various sources, they were also present at the crimes in Bucha. Kadyrov has openly boasted about his fighters in Ukraine. He knows that many men in Chechnya can find no other job than in its mercenary armies. The commander of the combat unit »Akhmat,« Apti Alaudinov, said on Russian television in July 2022 that he had opened a »holy war« with his men against LGBTQ and the »antichrist« in Ukraine. Such formulas are reminiscent of Muslim fighters on behalf of European colonial powers in World War I. Putin is waging the Ukraine war in the colonial style of European powers 100 years ago. Especially in the first phase of the war, he had the dirty work done by non-Russian citizens of the Russian Federation.

But if the Russian president thinks that he has Chechnya so under control, he is mistaken. Despite the bloody war of 1999 and the years-long anti-terrorist operation, despite Kadyrov's loyalty, despite the loyal fighters in the Russian army, Chechnya is not Russified, but a separate state within the state of Russia. The tendency is the other way around. Russia has been Chechenized under Putin.

# Nationalists by choice

## Putin's good friends in the world

Ever since Putin said this sentence, I can't get it out of my head: »If someone wants to destroy Russia, we have the right to respond. That would be a disaster for humanity and the world. But as a citizen of Russia and as a Russian president, I ask: Why do we need a world where there is no Russia?«

A statement like a cannon shot. Putin not only claims that Russia is more important than all other nations and that Russians are worth more than all other people, but also proclaims Russia as the beginning and the end, the main component of human civilization in general. He says that a world without Russia would lose all meaning and right to exist—and threatens its destruction. The man speaks like a sect leader, which would be unbearable, but not dangerous to the world. But he is the president of the Russian Federation with the nuclear suitcase in his hand.

The quotation is excerpted from a television interview shortly before his re-election as president on March 18, 2018. Putin's statement is based on the two most important foundations of nationalist ideology: the exaltation of one's own nation and the assumption of the lesser or non-existent value of all other nations. And thus, Putin fits perfectly into our time.

Nationalism is back. An ideology that destroyed Europe twice in the 20th century and is responsible for the deaths of more than 100 million people dominates international relations today. After the devastations and genocides of the last century, this ideology should have been discredited for all times. But it is more powerful than ever. Today, its supporters claim that these crimes cannot happen again. Nationalists make a seemingly convincing offer to people who feel threatened by pandemics, immigration, trade competition, and economic decline. They praise retreat into the comfortable shell of the nation-state as a protective space. In this way, they suggest that there is a »good nationalism,« a »soft nationalism.« Protection and security are the illusions that authoritarian right-wingers use to capture votes. But there is no such thing as soft nationalism. Putin is living proof. His career demonstrates the radicalization of a nationalist who has normalized war.

I have been observing the man since the late 1990s, sometimes at close range, so I also know that he was not always like this. To be sure, Putin launched his long reign with a war, but he warned against nationalism in the early years of his reign and did not promote himself with nativist slogans. On trips to Tatarstan and Siberia, he praised diversity and non-Russian cultures. The Putin of today is a nationalist by choice. He is a man who has taken on nationalism as a mantle, and this also makes him a phenomenon of our time. There are nationalists by choice like him in Turkey and Hungary too. They exist in China, in Serbia, and in America. But he is the idol of them all.

Rulers like Putin, Turkish President Recep Tayyip Erdoğan, or Hungarian Prime Minister Viktor Orbán are quick-change artists. They slip into many roles and cling to power, but in a flexible way. In crises, they take on all sorts of guises. At first, they were economic liberals, distributors of wealth; for career reasons, they eventually became nationalists. Unlike the classical nationalists of the 20th century, they did not draft their agenda when they were young and before they began their political careers. They are nationalists by choice because the new nationalism of the 21st century is opportunistic in nature.

When I first met Vladimir Putin more than twenty years ago, he looked older than he does today: his cheeks looked hollow, his complexion was pale, and his shoulders slumped forward. He had received us, two editors from *Die Zeit* and our publishing director, for an interview. It was a freezing cold November day when we sank into leather chairs with lion paws at a smoothly polished, fine wood table. Putin's office was still in the White House then, the seat of government with an eventful history. In 1991, Putin's predecessor, Boris Yeltsin, had defied the coup of the KGB conspirators here; in 1993, nationalist and communist deputies entrenched themselves here—and Yeltsin order troops to fire on the parliament. We had come here for a somewhat peaceful discussion, while Putin was waging a brutal war in Chechnya. I had expected a tough, unapproachable man. But Putin surprised me then, for the first time.

I met a rather shy man, not loud, not muscular. He was not yet used to riding bare-chested on horses or thundering over the arctic circle in a fighter jet as would be in the 2000s. He also lacked the broad-legged macho posturing that he used to intimidate the West in the 2010s. He was very controlled, almost a tad clumsy in his movements. His Russian sounded bureaucratic. His German was that of a model student who did not want to make a mistake. Putin had not yet completely knocked the dust from his laborious rise out of the poor backyards of Leningrad and the bullock ride through the secret service all the way to the Kremlin off his suit. He talked carefully and surprised us: no nasty remarks about NATO, which had bombed Belgrade in the Kosovo war of 1999 and had just expanded to include Poland. No nasty words about the US, which was directing all this. »Working together« with America and with Germany on a transactional basis was what he wanted. The common enemy was terrorism, and he saw his role as fighting this very terrorism in Chechnya. He appealed for understanding. He wanted nothing to do with Russian nationalists. Putin remained true to this line during his first two terms in office. He also refrained from criticizing NATO's eastward expansion in 2004—in stark contrast to his later years.

When I think back to the meeting in late 1999, I am struck by how much of a construct the Russian autocrat of today is. A man who has been made into the tough guy by spin doctors, propagandists, tailors, orthopedists, plastic surgeons, and taiga hunters, who defies NATO, has opposition figures persecuted, and stages himself as his country's »greatest nationalist.«

But in the years before his change, he had rallied Russians behind him using other means. He led them out of the confusing, crisis-ridden, but free post-Soviet era. He gave Russians the outward impression of a stable state. He was helped by a petrodollar boost from steadily rising oil prices. For the first time in decades, Russians felt something like a modest economic miracle. Putin put the money primarily into buildings and infrastructure, so people saw that something was changing. Meanwhile, he targeted competitors and oligarchs who did not submit to him. Prosperity for the masses in exchange for giving up any say—that was the deal Putin offered Russians during his non-nationalist years. It did not last.

Putin embraced nationalism in 2012. There are two legends in the West, neither of which stands up to scrutiny. The first myth is that Putin took a nationalist line as early as 2007, when he delivered a harsh critique of America at the Munich Security Conference. In fact, Putin dropped the plan to ally with the West against terrorism at that time because he was increasingly critical of the United States. He was already seeking to distance himself from the West and their military interventions in the neighborhood. But nationalism was not yet a defining feature of his policy. For many years, Putin supporters persistently spread the second myth on German talk shows: Putin's turnaround was only a response to the lack of respect and the actions of the West. This is not only a mistake, but also disrespectful. Russia is too big a country and too independent an international player for its leadership to make fundamental policy direction decisions dependent on foreign countries. As is so often the case in large states, the reason for the change lay much more in Russia itself, in this case in a threatening crisis for Putin that erupted at the end of 2011.

Russians had grown accustomed to the small prosperity and, to Putin's surprise, demanded more: a say. In the winter of 2011 and spring of 2012, people protested against his return from the post of prime minister to the presidential chair and a brazenly rigged election. In Moscow, demonstrators gathered in Bolotnaya Square, comprised of lawyers, programmers, and managers, the winners of the past decade. They were no longer willing to be fobbed off with the old social contract of »consumption instead of participation.« In the Russian provinces, those who had not profited from the petroleum blessings of the early Putin years took to the streets.

Putin's popularity plummeted dramatically. His occasional appearances in military uniform and judo suit no longer had an effect, his speeches fell flat, and Putin suddenly seemed old. It was a shock. In polls conducted in January 2012, only 42-percent of respondents wanted to vote for him as president, and the trend was rapidly downward. He won the March election anyway, thanks to the coordinated TV media and a concerted effort by all security and counting personnel. After that, approval dropped again. Putin became nervous. Looking around the world, he saw protests. In Tunisia, Egypt, Bahrain, Syria, Yemen, and Libya, people went to the barricades. Before that, the uprisings in Georgia, Ukraine and Kyrgyzstan had already unnerved him. He suspected the American government and, of course, the CIA to be behind these »color revolutions,« as he called them. Was it all directed against him personally? The Bolotnaya protests showed Putin that it was time to act. He needed a whole new narrative, and the impetus came not from the West, but from the protesters in Russia.

In search of his new narrative, Putin committed himself to nationalism in a programmatic newspaper article in 2012 that appeared in *Nezavisimaya Gazeta*. In the text, he describes Russia as a unique space of many peoples, a special civilization that Russians must hold in one state. »The core and connective tissue of this civilization is the Russian people, Russian culture,« he wrote. Putin understood the Russian Federation as a countermodel to Western »multi-cultural experiments«; he saw it as a vessel in which many peoples lived together under a guiding ethnic-Russian culture. He propagated nothing other than a Eurasian Russocentrism, which many nationalists, like right-wing extremist philosopher Aleksandr Dugin, had been preaching for years.

Putin was to juggle many variants of Russian nationalism assiduously over the coming years. In particular, he promoted the »Russian world« in Russia's neighboring countries, an idea based on a narrow ethnic-nationalist worldview. On visits to non-Russian republics, he liked to invoke Russia as an empire of many peoples under Russian leadership. And with regard to Ukraine, he fell back on writer Aleksandr Solzhenitsyn, who saw Russia, Belarus, and Ukraine as part of a trinitarian Slavic entity. As a new nationalist, Putin plays with nationalisms, pursuing a »nationalism by choice.« In 2012, he described himself as »the greatest nationalist in Russia.«

This, as he was soon to realize, was the right tone for broader sections of the population. Putin, who was personally more devoted to the multi-ethnic state in the Russian–Soviet imperial tradition than to a narrowly defined Russian nationalism, increasingly spoke about Russians as an ethnic group and the threats against them. In the war against Ukraine two years later, he gave broad space to ethnic nationalists. After the annexation of Crimea, he was more popular than ever, but he recaptured, disempowered, and muzzled the ideologues of ethnic nationalism who overshot in the war. When I listened to him in a smaller circle at a conference in St Petersburg in 2015, he warned against overdoing it with radical nationalism. Putin has simply nationalized the new nationalism. In the war against Ukraine, he let the nationalists off the leash to immediately stifle burgeoning discontent in the country over the mobilization and defeats of the army. To this day, he allows himself to be carried in power by a wave of nationalism fed by military adventures and fierce competition with the West.

Other authoritarian politicians have had similar revival experiences. I saw the current Turkish president in person thrice, in 2002, then in 2010, and finally in 2019. The first time, I met him in a no-frills conference room. Back then, he still wore a gold tie pin with his shiny red tie. He was friendly, dissolved two sugar cubes in a steaming glass of tea, stirred it in a relaxed manner, and was the complete opposite of today's Erdoğan, who is constantly irritable and always in his interlocutor's face. Back then, he spoke in pro-Western, neoliberal terms, promoted »Anglo-Saxon secularism,« and warned against nationalism. Indeed, after winning the election, he reformed his country and started EU accession negotiations in 2004. In the early noughties, nothing pointed to nationalism and the campaigns in Syria and Iraq from 2015. When I met Erdoğan for an interview on a sprawling purple banana-shaped divan at AKP headquarters in Ankara in 2010, he delivered a monologue: He was deeply disappointed by the EU and its de facto rejection of Turkey's application for membership, but he was still talking about democratization. After several wars, I met him again in 2019, in the great hall of the TRT broadcasting company in Istanbul. The once athletic, tall man stooped like an aging general, ranting about past battles, brutal crusaders, and glorious sultans.

Erdoğan had become a nationalist hardly out of conviction, but to maintain power. This is quite different from the dictators of the 20th century, many of whom lived their nationalism from a young age. Erdoğan, in contrast, is a nationalist by choice who was first an ardent anti-nationalist and now uses ideology as a tool. He is flexible. His transformation into a warlord began in 2015, when he fell out with the Kurdish party that was supposed to help him win a new presidential constitution. After the rift, he lost an election. Therefore, Erdoğan entered into a coalition with the National Action Party, an alliance of pan-Turkists, ethno-nationalists, and fascists. Erdoğan's deal with the MHP provided him with the majority for a constitutional amendment to introduce an authoritarian presidential system in exchange for his change of course to the right. The MHP was allowed to occupy key positions in the state, the judiciary, and the army with its well-trained, ideological cadres. Nationalism has been Erdoğan's essential tool to transform Turkey into a one-man state since 2016. In the pandemic, he turned into an all-around interventionist. He provoked a war-in-sight crisis with Greece. He sent mercenaries and Bayraktar drones to Libya and to Nagorno-Karabakh against Armenia. Only in the case of the Russian invasion of Ukraine did the Turkish ruler want to mediate, while arms factories owned by his family supplied Ukraine with weapons. In recent years, there has been no war in Turkey's neighboring countries in which Erdoğan has not somehow intervened.

The 21st century has brought a colorful array of new nationalists who discovered this ideology as a tool of power in the course of their careers. Greek politician Antonis Samaras, the inventor of the conflict between Greece and northern Macedonia, warrants mention. As foreign minister, the scion of a Greek elite family started a dispute over the name of the new post-Yugoslavian state that was created in 1992. When the demonstrations against »Skopje« in northern Greece refused to end, Samaras split from the conservative Néa Dimokratía and founded the populist party, Political Spring. In this way, he wanted to seize power in Athens. But he failed and eventually returned to the Néa Dimokratía fold. In 2012, Samaras became prime minister with ND, and without any nationalist program at all. He was just a nationalist by choice who had temporarily used the ideology. Consider also Boris Johnson, who led Great Britain out of the EU as a nationalist-turned-opportunist but years later harshly condemned nationalism. Remaining flexible is how one stays in power. Other examples include Xi Jinping, who has turned China into a nationalist fortress, and Donald Trump, who dreamed of exactly that in America. We shall speak of him later.

The pioneer of this new brand of nationalism came from Hungary in the 1990s. In his youth, Viktor Orbán held a George Soros Foundation fellowship and was a favorite of liberals. Thanks to an American patron with Hungarian roots, the young man from a poor background was able to study in England. As a junior member of parliament for the Fidesz party, Orbán fought for a liberal Hungary, sporting a beard and long hair and wearing jeans and no tie. As parliamentary party leader, Viktor Orbán made a reputation for himself as a sharp-tongued and quick-witted liberal. In February 1992, he stood before the Fidesz party congress and declared: »Folkish-nationalist thought and populist politics are in sharp contrast to liberalism.« Anyone who hears the man today can hardly believe the words.

At barely 30, Orbán was elected vice president of Liberal International and hosted liberal political party leaders from around the world at a conference in Budapest in 1993. Fidesz's popularity ratings skyrocketed, and the party became known as the »Liberal Party.« Orbán was expected to play an important role in the next government, but the divisions and discord among the liberals, previously known only from the communist splinter groups, intervened. Orban fell out with his party colleagues, and many resignations followed. In the 1994 elections, the plucked Fidesz party only took 7-percent instead of the expected victory. It was a catastrophic defeat, and Orbán's political dream was in tatters.

At the nadir of his career, Viktor Orbán felt he was getting nowhere as a nice, young, liberal star in Hungary. It was a similar experience to Vladimir Putin's after the Bolotnaya riots in 2012 and to Recep Tayyip Erdoğan's after the election defeat of 2015. Facing the possible end of his career, Viktor Orbán decided to make a sharp turn to the right into the new nationalism.

His biographer Paul Lendvai could detect »no deeper ideo- logical soul-searching« and »a clear-sighted calculation of what it would take to win power.« In the months that followed, Orbán began to talk about Hungary, the homeland, national interests, family, citizenship, and decency. He saw room for political expansion only to the right. Orbán suddenly wore a suit and tie, his hair was short, and his shoes were polished. He raged against the EU, but he gladly took money from Brussels to distribute among Hungarians in his name. He won the following elections, with only one slip. Today, Orbán has a firm grip on Hungary, and there is no end to his rule.

The breakthrough of the nationalists by choice on a global scale, however, required an election in the economically and militarily strongest country in the world. The most important nationalist by choice entered the world-stage in 2016: Donald Trump. Once a supporter of liberal immigration laws and abortion rights, as president he built walls on the border with Mexico and courted the Christian right. He had not previously pursued a right-wing political agenda, and at most he had isolationist impulses. As early as the 1980s, he indulged in the banal and sophomoric economic conviction that the whole world was screwing America over.

Trump donated money to Democrats and canvassed Republicans to somehow become a politician. In 2016, in his 70th year, there was opportunity to stir up his muddled resentments into a nationalist agenda with the help of his advisers, which he stated in simple words. Trump changed himself and the world.

His term in office became a nationalist nightmare: tariff barriers, trade wars, sanctions against Iran, Russia, and the EU, walls against migrants, caution against foreigners and Islam! Trump twisted US patriotism, which unites all US citizens of whatever origin in pride for their country, into a white American nationalism that divides the country along ethnic and racial criteria.

Trump thus became the figurehead of a new Nationalist International. Putin, Erdoğan, Orbán, and Trump formed a male cartel that supported each other, even if their countries sometimes compete geostrategically. When they met or spoke on the phone, the aides were sent out of the room. Trump allowed Erdoğan's chief adviser, who spoke good English, to translate from Turkish into English during face-to-face meetings. Trump smugly blustered and confided state secrets to the Russian president and made fun of the Europeans. During Trump's tenure, Putin filled the gaps that the US left in the Middle East, Africa, and South Asia. This is also why the US had such a hard time convincing the countries of the Global South to impose sanctions against Russia after the invasion of Ukraine.

The second stopgap was Erdoğan. The Turkish ruler would never have been able to wage his wars if Trump had not specifically withdrawn his military. Trump blocked the sanctions imposed by US Congress on Turkey over its purchase of Russian defensive missiles. He protected shady gold traders and bankers associated with the Turkish president against prosecution in the United States. Erdoğan railed a lot about the West, about the EU and its alleged Islamophobia, but he never did so about Trump, who is actually Islamophobic. Putin, in turn, tolerated Erdoğan's expansion in the Middle East. Erdoğan retaliated by undermining NATO with the deployment of Russian S-400 missiles. What else remained secret in NATO when the Turks sat at the table, no one really knew. Putin had made his sympathies clear in the 2016 and 2020 US election campaigns, still refusing to congratulate Joe Biden many weeks after the November 2020 election. This intergovernmental nationalism does not end with Trump's departure from the White House.

Nationalists by choice like Putin, Erdoğan, and Orbán are now waiting. They have three good reasons for doing so.

First, they have set up their game to last. They see themselves in a long war of attrition that they intend to win, so they save up. Take Russia, for example: Putin put money aside during the Covid-19 crisis. Putin gave himself up to the huge debt that Western states were incurring from 2020 onward, which will restrict how they can address the coming energy crises. In the first Corona wave in the spring of

2020, Putin did give workers weeks off, but he did so without even considering corresponding replacement payments to businesses. After the shock of the first Covid year, he refrained from further drastic measures and accepted the many Covid deaths. Putin saved for the long haul, the war. His biographers Fiona Hill and Cliff Gaddy have described him as a »survivalist« who has always built networks, armories, and sovereign wealth funds. If you look at Hungary's eager military buildup or Turkey's rise as an expansive military power on the cheap, you can see here, too, that Putin's is setting a precedent among the survivalists.

Since the occupation of Crimea, the West has been saying that Putin is running out of money and can no longer afford his expansion in Ukraine, Syria, and elsewhere. It was also assumed that after the invasion of Ukraine, the Western sanctions would quickly cause the Russian economy to collapse. This hope did not come true in 2022. This was due to Putin's austerity warfare. Putin has been conducting his campaigns with much lower stakes than, say, the United States under President George W. Bush for a long time. Low-budget war with proxy armies, cheap mercenaries, military advisors, and air power had proved efficient in Syria and Africa. In the war against Ukraine, of course, much was different because Russian soldiers were deployed. But Putin was able to produce his war machine in Russian factories at ruble prices that he could pay from the budget bloated by oil sales. From abroad, he bought cheap Iranian drones with which he terrorized Ukrainian cities. The costly reconstruction and humanitarian aid measures that NATO struggled with in Afghanistan are not planned for in wars of annihilation. In the long run, however, it was clear that the mixture of war of attrition, mobilization, sanctions, and dwindling sales of raw material would also cost Putin a lot.

Second, the new nationalists are learning from the West. They not only entrench themselves in their nationalist fortresses but also help each other. Autocratic solidarity was already Putin's means of extending his influence in the Middle East. When the Syrians threatened to overthrow their bloodthirsty dictator Bashar al-Assad, Putin intervened to save his friend. If Egypt's ruler felt criticized by the Americans, Putin offered arms and loans. If the Belarusians stood up against their oppressor Alexander Lukashenko, Putin demonstratively backed him. And during the unrest in Kazakhstan in January 2022, Putin sent airborne troops to stabilize Kassym-Jomart Tokayev's rule. With China, Russia practiced joint defense against an American attack in September 2022. As Putin turned off gas deliveries to many European countries, the nationalists by choice Viktor Orbán in Hungary and Aleksandar Vučić in Serbia were supplied continuously. In return, he expected their solidarity.

Putin could indeed rely on his nationalist friends. The Serbs essentially sold their gas industry to Gazprom. Viktor Orbán took over the role of Putin's hasty ambassador to the EU. Orbán visited Putin in Moscow several times after Putin's invasion of Ukraine. He dodged the EU's unanimous oil sanctions against Russia and negotiated for himself to continue importing Russian oil. In Brussels, he deliberately blocked aid packages for Ukraine and legislative projects to set international standards and give the EU global influence, e.g., the global minimum tax for companies. Orbán also prevented EU sanctions against the Russian Patriarch Kirill, who blessed and supported the war of aggression against Ukraine. He stopped critical EU statements about human rights violations in China with his veto. Whenever Orbán could, he paralyzed the EU.

Nationalists by choice also weaken the West's sanctions against Russia. Turkey and other states imported Western goods, which they continued to export to Russia even though the manufacturers explicitly no longer wanted to supply the Russian market. Russia welcomed and allowed such parallel imports, and China purposefully purchased Russian oil that the US and Europe had embargoed. Russian gas that no longer goes to the EU will be partly delivered to China in the future, even if the pipelines still have many years of construction ahead. India's national populist President Narendra Modi bought not only Russian weapons but also Russian oil on a large scale. In return, Putin supplied the fossil fuel at fire sale prices. This is likely to have consequences for the environment. While the EU forces its companies to meet tough climate protection requirements, nationalists in Russia, India, and China will deliberately and collectively disregard international targets to gain advantages on the world market. The nationalist alliance relies on fossil fuels to overthrow the liberal world order.

The third and last reason for the nationalists by choice to wait lies in the world power they actually want to defeat. For Putin and his consorts, America is not lost for all time. They are betting that a President like Joe Biden will only be an episode. A democratic politician may have won the 2020 election, but the nationalist by choice Donald Trump managed to receive 73 million votes, the largest number ever collected by a Republican candidate in a US election. Trump is gone for now, but Trumpism remains. There are millions of Americans today who prefer a divisive, even racist, American nationalism to the classic one-sided US patriotism. This US nationalism is only half-beaten; the narrative lives on. Trump's ardent supporters tell each other stories of voter fraud and vote theft. They seek to redraw electoral districts and bring electoral institutions under their control. Many don't want to move the country forward; they just want to see Biden fail. No compromise, no handwringing, no bipartisan cooperation in the world crises of our time. Trump has used strategic appointments to refashion the highest courts in the land to their liking. The result was on display in the Supreme Court's reactionary and divisive decision on abortion. Despite losing the election, Republicans have retained their position of power in many institutions and courts. The next nationalist by choice could run in the 2024 US election—and would not have a bad chance. Putin and the Nationalist International would be delighted to welcome him into their ranks.

# Information War

## How the Russians are incited

Like fighter jets on a runway, viewers flew into this program on channel Rossiya-1: the talk show *Evening with Vladimir Solovyov*, one of Putin's best-known propagandists. The camera swooped into the studio and zoomed in on two people, talk show host Solovyov and Margarita Simonyan, editor-in-chief of both the Rossiya Segodnya and RT propaganda factories. They stepped up to deprive their viewers of sleep. It reassured no one that Simonyan laughed the whole time while talking about Russia's war against Ukraine:

Simonyan: »So either we lose this in Ukraine or World War III starts.«

Solovyov (in the background): »Possible.«

Simonyan: »I think yes, a world war is more realistic. I know us and our leader, Putin. The unthinkable, that everything will end with a nuclear strike, seems to me more and more likely.«

Once again, she laughed out loud.

Simonyan: »To my horror, on the one hand, but, on the other hand, I realized that this is how things are.«

Solovyov: »Well, we're going to paradise, and they're going to hell.«

This exchange aired at the end of April 2022, two months after Russia's invasion of Ukraine began. This is how it continued. In early June, Solovyov roared at the West in his broadcast:

»Give it a try! I hope we survive this. If everything goes on like this, only a few mutants will live on at Lake Baikal. The rest will die in a massive nuclear strike. Everything goes in this direction, no matter what both sides want. And then nothing will remain, bang!«

The end of the world was regularly longed for on Russian television. The message to viewers was that the apocalypse was near, so it did not really matter how many more sanctions were imposed on Russia, what war Vladimir Putin might start, or how bad Russia's reputation was in the world. Anyone who consumes such programs every evening runs the risk of personality deformation. If I want to spend a nice evening in Moscow, I leave the TV off. But for my work, I often have to watch these programs.

Because Vladimir Solovyov and Margarita Simonyan are not just anyone. He is Russia's best-known and most notorious talk show host, a metallurgical engineer by training with a doctorate from the Institute of World Economy and International Relations in Moscow. Taught in the US, Solovyov became a businessman, then a radio host and television rabble-rouser. Simonyan is the editor-in-chief of the propaganda institutions Rossiya Segodnya and RT, promoted by Vladimir Putin. Even though Solovyov talks much more, Simonyan is the more powerful person. She became famous at 24 when she reported on a hostage disaster in the Caucasus; she became influential at 25, when she rose to become editor-in-chief of Russia Today, a media factory founded in 2005 and the forerunner of RT. Margarita Simonyan significantly helped direct the fall of Russian journalism into an apocalyptic propaganda machine. These state broadcasters are among Vladimir Putin's willing helpers in turning Russia into a repressive intelligence state and Ukraine into a ruined landscape, while most Russians are left cheering on the couch.

Years ago, some smirked at Margarita Simonyan, the country's youngest editor-in-chief, and attributed her appointment to close relationships with top bureaucrats. But Simonyan is to be taken very seriously. As a reporter, she did good work. She is well-read and has a good feel for language. It is difficult for foreign correspondents to see this for themselves in an interview. For years, Simonyan has only given Western journalists written interviews, if at all. Therefore, I had to ask colleagues and former companions who know her well and want to remain unidentified for their safety about her. The following insights come from them.

Margarita Simonyan often invited her coworkers to her workroom for meetings in which too many of them fought over the floor in temperatures that were too high. She herself talked at length, interrupted only by incoming telephone calls that often tore the conversation apart. At the station, Simonyan appeared very self-confident, which impressed her co-workers. When others were talking, she liked to look at the large screens showing the news of major networks in other countries. She was not afraid of confrontation. In discussions peppered with Russian swear words, it was hardly possible to convince her of any point of view other than her own. Phrases like »maybe« or »we don't know exactly« are unknown to her. Compromises were not made. She resolutely insisted on her point of view. Above all, she always gave her employees the impression that it was not the boss who owed them anything, but the whole world owed her.

Perhaps this had something to do with her background. Simonyan liked to say that she came from a poor background in southern Russia. Her father was a craftsman who repaired refrigerators. She once described him to coworkers as a »bandit« who was barely present and then suddenly showed up with a pile of money from an unknown source. Her mother came from an Armenian family whose ancestors were deported from Crimea in 1944 on Stalin's orders along with other Armenians, Crimean Tatars, Greeks, and Bulgarians. Her mother temporarily ran a restaurant in the seaside resort of Adler on Russia's Black Sea coast. Simonyan broke out of these circumstances and fought her way up in a flash: She studied journalism in Krasnodar in southern Russia, was an exchange student in New Hampshire in the US, worked as a reporter for the Rossiya television channel, and then became editor-in-chief of RT and Rossiya Segodnya in Moscow. She is now responsible for many news programs that follow completely different values, different standards, and different production methods than Western and German news formats.

These programs have almost nothing in common with the ponderous Evening News in Europe; they are more like over-the-top Netflix series with lots of guns and lots of blood. Let's take a quick look at a documentary.

It is a pitch-black night. Headlights flash. A helicopter lands with a roar. Black boots impress their treads into the damp sand. Soldiers hold Kalashnikovs at the ready. Armored limousines drive up. Several people run quickly through the dark of night and jump into the limos and into the helicopter. More limousines drive up. Russian special operations troops take a politician and his family to safety. They drive off with screeching tires as heavily armed men are securing the road against a deadly threat. The enemies are Ukrainians who want to kill this politician. At least that's what Vladimir Putin claims in the documentary *Return to Crimea* when he talks about how he pre-empted »the bloodthirsty Ukrainian nationalists« to protect »the elected president of Ukraine.« Putin was referring to Viktor Yanukovych, Ukraine's corrupt ruler and Putin's friend, who ran into trouble in the Maidan Revolution in 2014 and then quietly fled the country. The less-than-glorious exit was his political end. Russian television ennobled the Russian ruler, depicting a wiry, lightning-fast Putin, who first saved Yanukovych from the nationalists, then saved Crimea, and finished off by achieving world peace.

This is what Russian propaganda looks like today. Not like a Soviet-era black-and-white poster that depicts little girls presenting flowers to dictator Stalin. Not like a cast-iron Lenin with a bronze cap in front of the local city council. Not like the nasty old Pravda with quick-dissolving printer's ink and blurred photos of Leonid Brezhnev's kolkhozes. Russian propaganda today is cool, young, and ultra-modern.

The news broadcasts of RT and other Russian channels no longer have anything to do with Soviet propaganda broadcasts. They are often faster, hipper, louder, and more modern than Western news broadcasts. »Never uncool again,« noted Putin's one-time chief strategist and political technologist Vladislav Surkov. Russian propaganda works with tablets, smartphones, Telegram, and TikTok.

These are the new weapons in hybrid warfare. In the 20th century, the Soviets were heavily armed. It was important which army had more soldiers and missiles. Today, in the 21st century, it is at least as important whose narrative wins, which story prevails. In 2013, Russian Chief of General Staff Valery Gerasimov gave a speech that he later published in the *Military and Industrial Courier*. Because of its strong theses on the war, the text was called a new »military doctrine,« although not a doctrine in the strictest sense. This essay had it all. It argued that wars and conflicts of the present would have an »ambush-like character.« This is exactly what Ukraine has experienced twice in the past eight years. It argued that in the future, Russia would also have to use »nonmilitary means«: diplomatic, economic and, of course, media.

In Russia, nobody talked about »propaganda.« They thought they were in a »hybrid war« with the West. In other words, journalists loyal to the state were waging an »information war.« Putin himself set the tone for this. Of course, only in a distorted reflection of presumed Western strategies, so as not to be caught in the act. In a 2017 greeting, for example, he said that in »Europe in recent years, authoritative media have turned into a weapon for manipulating public opinion. [. . .] Information wars have become a daily occurrence, reality,« he said. This choice of words was very Russian and had little to do with actual circumstances in the West. At the same time, however, it suggested to Russian journalists what they should do now: respond to the attack with precisely these means. And the public relations department of the presidential administration was happy to help.

Russian state propaganda today is essentially based on three principles. First, cynicism: the world is bad, and the West is at least as corrupt and immoral as we are. Second, schadenfreude: in fact, everything is even worse in the West than it is here—because we have Putin! Third, apocalyptic: The West wants to destroy us and attack us, but we will defend ourselves until the nuclear strike!

In Moscow, I often drove past the propaganda factory on Zubovskiy Boulevard just before the Krymskiy Bridge. It was not far from my apartment. A gray block of concrete, Soviet brutalism stretches for half a kilometer: the headquarters of the information warriors, the headquarters of Rossiya Segodnya (»Russia Today«) and formerly RT. It is not easy to get in. The director general, Dmitry Kiselyov, has been banned from entering the EU because of his inflammatory broadcasts. He does not give interviews. Simonyan is also subject to Western sanctions and does not give interviews. Ordinary editors cannot be met in the editorial building, only in Moscow's cafes. When I got accredited for Victory Day on May 9, 2022, I was supposed to meet at Zubovskiy Boulevard and was hoping for entry. It was a freezing day with a sharp north wind, but the journalists were told to queue on the street and in the courtyard to board buses to Red Square. At the entrances to the building, strict controls barred visitors from entering. Passports, PCR tests, and accreditations were carefully checked for access to only the courtyard. It was like entering an army barracks. This was probably an intended association in times of information warfare.

I did gain access to the editorial office on another occasion, before it had moved to a more modern building. I got to know an employee with an office on one of the upper floors on Zubovskiy Boulevard. For his protection, I will not mention his name. I appreciated deeply that he had an access card issued to me with which I got through all the controls in no time. As forbidding and defiant as the building looked from the outside, it was transparent on the inside. The doors were made of glass. A huge newsroom opened up in front of me. Plants were growing between white desks, and news was running on a digital ticker under the ceiling, just like at CNN headquarters in Atlanta. The walls were painted white. No one had to touch the glass doors; they opened when you held your accreditation up to a card reader.

There was a gym on the seventh floor. »You have to take a break from Ukraine, too,« joked someone who was about to go on the machines. Those who were hungry took their seats in chic cafes and restaurants. At lunchtime in the trattoria, people chose between risotto ai funghi and the tuna carpaccio. There was nothing to suggest the solyanka soup, dry bread, and over-fat pelmeni dumplings that I ate here in the 1990s, when the Foreign Ministry still had a press and information office in the same building.

General Director Dmitry Kiselyov and Chief Editor Simonyan have shaped this factory for more than a decade now. Former employees describe Simonyan's management style as »moody and chaotic.« Important emails, requests, and vacation requests from subordinates tended to go unanswered; text messages from higher up interrupted any conversation she was having. If someone approached her about a forgotten request, she would open her eyes wide and look her co-worker in the face: »Never heard of it!« It was part of her style to be able to represent even obvious untruths quite casually. She had a talent for believing deeply in something that was in her interest in a matter of seconds. Both on and off the air, she defended absurdities and madness with the natural charisma of someone who was firmly convinced of them.

How she got away with this method so well was also due to how she had stacked her institutions with confidants and relatives. Three criteria were important in the selection process, say her former employees. First, were they from the intelligence service; or second, did they belong to her age group; or third, did they come from Krasnodar in southern Russia, as she did. Several of her classmates were hired in the newsroom as correspondents and producers with enviable starting salaries. These friends then received preferential treatment and were sent on coveted reporting trips throughout Russia, with accommodations in luxury hotels, or even on foreign trips with the president. »Simonyan's generosity,« reports a former companion, »did not stop at her family members.« Her more low-key sister, Alissa, was allowed to sit in her anteroom and later work as a producer. Simonyan's husband is said to have been paid for a feature film from the state treasury in 2018, for which Margarita Simonyan wrote the script and in which Alissa also participated. This is what researchers from the team of the murdered opposition leader Aleksei Navalny found out. Even in the early days of RT, documentaries were a way for Simonyan to spread charity far beyond the channel, say former employees. She herself had reserved the decision on commissioning such video products. She was interested in who the author was and who the production company was, even before the topic and content. The relationship between the producer and Simonyan often decided the purchase. Such arrangements never disturbed anyone in the government, or at least nothing to suggest that it did was reported to me.

Vladimir Putin had Rossiya Segodnya, the headquarters of the Information War, reestablished in December 2013. Today, Rossiya Segodnya and RT are hugely bloated. According to its own figures, Rossiya Segodnya had 3350 employees in 2022, while RT had more than 2500 employees when the pandemic broke out. State media in Russia are financed from the budget, with no upper limit. For 2022, the equivalent of almost 1.5 billion euros in direct payments was planned, of which almost one third was for RT alone. But Rossiya Segodnya and such other state media as VGTRK, TASS, and Perviy Kanal (Channel One) were also lavishly endowed with money. All the more so in times of war. The independent online platform *fontanka.ru* and *The Moscow Times* calculated from Finance Ministry figures that payments to state media tripled from January to March 2022 alone. Most of it went to television. In percentage terms, the media received a much larger budget increase than the military. This demonstrates that the propaganda machine was at least as important to Putin in the war, both internally and externally, as the military machine.

With so much money, Rossiya Segodnya can come across as an ultramodern news factory. »Russia Today« uses television, radio, news agencies, the Internet, social media, polls, and satellite programs. It includes RIA Novosti and Sputnik News, a station with radio and Internet presence with videos in 30 languages. Sputnik operates in 34 countries just as RT broadcasts around the globe with its foreign channels.

According to the management's programming mandate, their stations carry the »Russian point of view« to the world. But what is the Russian point of view? That is what English TV reporter Peter Pomerantsev, who worked in television in Moscow, asked RT's managing editor.

»There is always a Russian point of view,« the managing editor answered. And then he explained it by analogy to a banana. »For one, it is something to eat. For another, it is a weapon. To the racist, it is a tool to annoy Black people.« Anything is possible, he said. There is simply no objectively clear view of what a banana is, the chief said. And just as the banana is crooked, these broadcasters bend the truth. That is the essence of the »Russian point of view.«

The first time the Western public really got to know this point of view was in 2014. When flight MH17 crashed in a Ukrainian field in the summer of 2014, there was only one cause, but many assumptions. The real cause, a Russian Buk missile fired from Russian-controlled territory, has since been confirmed in several elaborate international investigations. Russian state channels, however, focused exclusively on the conjecture. When the shock of the first moment had passed, General Director Dmitry Kiselyov discussed the course of action with the Kremlin. Then, like Katyusha rocket launchers, Sputnik and RT kept firing out new variants of how it might have been every second: The Ukrainians were behind it; an airplane had crossed MH17's path; a Ukrainian missile hit the plane; maybe NATO was involved; maybe aliens? Anything is possible! Only the one very obvious fact, that a Russian Buk missile took the plane out of the sky, was lost in the story cocktail. That was the »Russian point of view« fresh from the factory.

Margarita Simonyan once explained this cynical point of view to *Der Spiegel*: »There is no objectivity, only many approximations to the truth.« There are current examples from the war against Ukraine: The Russian attacks on civilians at the Kramatorsk train station were allegedly perpetrated by the Ukrainians themselves. The rocket attack on the shopping center in Kremenchuk was only aimed at an ammunition depot. The attack on Vinnytsia airport was an attack on military objects. And of course, the city of Mariupol was destroyed exclusively by Ukrainian fascists. The Russian position is to spread lies.

»Telling the untold«: that was Sputnik's motto. Wild conjectures, false reports, and conspiracy theories were processed into news. The station worked on multiple truths: It reported invented news, for example, that US soldiers were fighting in Ukraine, waited for Western media to take over the false report, and then did not correct it. Something will stick. This coverage is designed to create the cynical impression that everyone is a villain and a criminal. Contradictions? Never mind. Ukraine is full of nationalists—but according to Russian interpretation, it is not a nation. Russia was liberating Ukraine, but the fierce resistance of Ukrainians who did not want to be liberated by Russia was a surprise. Russia stands against the fascists, but Russia is firmly on the side of Marine Le Pen, the AfD, and Matteo Salvini. Anything is possible.

Since the 2014 annexations of Crimea, Russian information war cyber-soldiers have worked on this principle in several Western languages. In 2015, some Russian media, including *Novaya Gazeta*, identified an office building on Savushkina Street in the Primorsky district of St Petersburg as a troll factory. The three-story white box in which young people worked online for the Kremlin was located on a suburban street with residential buildings from the Stalin era. I saw them myself during a visit to St Petersburg around that time. Trees lined the street, and there was a restaurant on the other side. After the Russian independent media exposed them, the building was locked and appeared uninhabited. A neighbor said the company had moved.

*Novaya Gazeta* spoke to an employee who had worked in the building for a long time. Lyudmila Savchuk recounted how she wrote daily from 9 a.m. to 9 p.m. on online forums, on social media, and in comment sections of Internet newspapers. What she had to write in English was dictated by the bosses.

In the West, people had hoped for years that the Internet would weaken authoritarian systems and open a window to the world for oppressed citizens. What a mistake! Moscow broadcasters hired cohorts of Western journalists in the 2000s to gain broadcasting space and viewer time in the Western public sphere. Peter Pomerantsev was just one of many. Authoritarian systems learned from the West and turned Western technology against its inventors to confuse, incite, and disrupt their publics.

RT used millions of euros to build a German station in the Adlershof district of Berlin. So far, this investment has only paid off to a limited extent. The declared goal of being able to broadcast on German cable networks like ARD and ZDF was denied by the German state media authorities, who cited clear state funding, which is prohibited in Germany. Russia's ban and ejection of Deutsche Welle in early 2022 did not help RT either. The EU banned Russian propagandists like RT and Sputnik from broadcasting and posting their content in the Union. But even after that, RT continued to spread itself undaunted on the web to reach its German audience.

Support came from the German side. Russian propagandists have reached an eight-figure audience in Germany since 2014 with the collegial help of ARD and ZDF. For years, such Russian propagandists as Ivan Rodionov and left-wing politicians like Sahra Wagenknecht, retired German army generals, and journalists were able to present the »Russian point of view« undisturbed, especially on the talk shows of the public broadcasters. Their statements were aimed at ill-informed German viewers who hoped that the war, the gas crisis, and Putin's aggression would go away if the West would only stop supporting Ukraine. In doing so, they inserted important elements of the Russian narrative into the German discussion. Some examples: »No one is served by heavy weapons«; »Crimea has actually always been Russian«; »Ukraine is corrupt and not a real state«; »Russia had to act this way because NATO expanded«; »The 2014 Maidan Revolution was financed by the Americans.«

It is particularly convincing for some Germans when former German politicians present arguments that are strikingly similar to the Russian narrative. Former-Chancellor Gerhard Schröder or former-Mayor of Hamburg Klaus von Dohnanyi are prominent examples in the SPD. In the FDP parties; Wolfgang Kubicki stood out even after the invasion of Ukraine with his support for Nord Stream 2. From within the CDU party, one heard Russian points of view from discarded backbenchers like Willy Wimmer or recently deceased Karin Strenz. But the Greens also have sympathizers of the Russian view among their alumni. In the summer of 2015, Ludger Volmer, ex-minister of state at the German Foreign Ministry, called the Maidan uprising a »coup« on Deutschlandfunk radio and accused the West of »double standards and hypocrisy« in Ukraine. Such claims justified Putin's war and delegitimized Western criticism of Russian actions. The result was a general uncertainty, in which all possible truths and versions apply.

General Director of Rossiya Segodnya, Dmitry Kiselyov, is a master of this discipline. Together with Simonyan and Solovyov, he forms a media triumvirate that likes to spread its propaganda in nuclear terms. The 66-year-old Kiselyov is known for detonating nuclear bombs over Western countries in presentations and in animated videos. In 2014, after the annexation of Crimea and Western sanctions, he said Russia was the only country that could »turn the US into radioactive ash,« while a mushroom cloud rose over Washington D.C. in the background of the image. After the invasion of Ukraine, he declared in May 2022 that a Russian Sarmat intercontinental ballistic missile would be enough to wipe out the »sinkable« British Isles. In an accompanying animation, a missile launched near St Petersburg and hit central England. »Then there will be no more England. Everything is already calculated,« he concluded. Kiselyov, like Simonyan and Solovyov, nurtured the Russian belief in fate and that the world was nearing its end anyway.

Kiselyov had Germany in his sights. He loved historical depictions from World War II in his »News of the Week« program, which stretched for hours over Sunday evenings. In many reports about Ukraine, German SS troops appeared in black-and-white pictures to prove that Ukrainian soldiers were fascists. Even the Pope had to suffer comparison to Nazis. In March 2022, Kiselyov praised Pope Francis's criticism of NATO for »barking at Russia's gates.« But when Francis received the wives of soldiers from the Ukrainian Interior Ministry's Azov regiment the following week, Kiselyov showed the Pope in an incriminating series of pictures with such Nazi criminals as Martin Bormann and Josef Mengele. In May 2022, Kiselyov anchored a segment on the German government's Ukraine policy with quotes from Hitler's Minister for the Occupied Eastern Territories, Alfred Rosenberg, about the colonization of Ukraine by Greater Germany.

Today's Germany was also presented in detail on Russian television. Every correspondent for the Russian broadcasters that was in a German city was busy filming empty supermarket shelves, crowded airports, and stalled trains. They often showed immigrants from Africa and Asia in city centers and claimed that they now ruled Germany's streets. In the summer of 2022, in anticipation of what they hoped would be a winter natural-gas crisis, correspondents showed German homes growing cold and German industrial plants rotting because Russia stopped sending gas. »That's what they get from their sanctions,« was the most frequently heard comment. In the West, the message was that fear, chaos, and decay reign.

The propaganda machine also regularly issued apocalyptic threats against Germany. When the Germans supplied heavy weapons to Ukraine in June 2022, Vladimir Solovyov had experts report on his talk show that the Bundeswehr was completely exhausted and had been reduced to a single rifle company. Berlin was practically defenseless. Then Solovyov stood up in front of the camera and said, »Listen up, Scholz!« In 1991, Mikhail Gorbachev made »a fatal mistake when he allowed reunification,« and so did Joseph Stalin in 1945 when he »allowed Germany to continue to exist.« Russia can correct these mistakes, he said, because it has missiles that reach Germany.

These are not just empty speeches. Russian politics are hammered out in Russian television: narratives are played out, reactions are tested, new realities are experimented with. They prepared in exactly this way for years for the war in Ukraine.

Russia's propaganda factories succeeded in making Germany one of the most popular countries in Russia for decades. Countless films about World War II, the denunciation of Merkel as a »puppet of the US« and Scholz as a »troublesome moth,« and the reports about a »fascist,« degenerate Germany destroyed by refugees were enough to turn that around. According to surveys by the Levada Institute, in 2013, barely 3 percent of Russians saw Germany as an enemy country. In July 2022, this figure had risen to 37-percent. Only 3 percent of Russians still considered Germany a friend.

This is how hatred among nations is stirred up.

No one should be under any illusions about how this reporting came about. Margarita Simonyan, Vladimir Solovyov, and Dmitry Kiselyov were powerful, but they were still under orders. What they said and how they said it was ordered from the highest level. A central role was played by the First Deputy Head of Putin's presidential administration, Alexei Gromov. He helped Putin bring Russian television stations to heel during Putin's first term. At that time, he headed the Kremlin pool of journalists, among other responsibilities. According to research by the investigative portal Proekt, he called together the directors and editors-in-chief of the major broadcasters every week and laid down the law. The journalists from Proekt explained why very similar or partly identical comments and wording could be heard on current topics on various state broadcasters within a very short period of time. Often, they were also Putin quotes, which Gromov then urgently recommended for further use. A former employee of Rossiya Segodnya reported that Alexei Gromov would instruct the leaders directly. Margarita Simonyan would cancel all meetings when he called. »Yes, Alexei Alexievich,« she would then chirp into the phone, adding a broad smile and sending the staff out of the room with a wave. Those conversations gave birth to Russian propaganda.

The pollster Lev Gudkov of the independent Levada Center in Moscow once said very aptly: »Propaganda does not create and does not introduce new ideas or rationales.« It only reproduces and exposes the »layers of mass consciousness of a totalitarian political culture.« This is not copied from anywhere abroad but a revival of the traditions of the Soviet era.

According to Levada's surveys, between 63 and 67 percent of the Russian population watched state television in the first half of 2022, and a full 50-percent considered state television to be the most credible source of information. Social networks, where the state broadcasters are also active, were a distant second. The propagandists are Putin's pillar and most important helper in the war against Ukraine and the West. Without them, his rule might have ended long ago because he might not have survived the recurring crises of his popularity in 2011, 2012, 2018, and 2021. The invasion of Ukraine and Putin's numerous misjudgments, especially in the early days of the war, are also a consequence of the state's misreporting. Putin, who is said to have difficulty with smartphones and the Internet, prefers to watch television. The ruler obviously fell for the propaganda he himself ordered.

# The Putin Archipelago

## Russia's system of penal camps

»First of all: night. Why is it that all the main work of breaking down human souls went on at night? Why, from their very earliest years, did the Organs select the night? Because at night, the prisoner torn from sleep... is more vulnerable.«

These lines were written by Russian author Aleksandr Solzhenitsyn in his *Gulag Archipelago* (English edition, 1973; Harper & Row, New York), which revealed the horrors of the Soviet camp system in 1973, but they would still accurately describe the situation of Aleksei Navalny, who was woken up every hour on his cot in the Russian prison camp »because of increased risk of escape.« In January 2021, the opposition politician was caught in the mills of this equally violent system. There are many ways into the Putin archipelago. By describing Navalny's case, who died in a prison and torture camp, I would like to shed light on the perfidious judicial regime that is likely to send many more Russian politicians, journalists, and scientists to the archipelago as prisoners.

Aleksei Navalny was by far the most prominent political prisoner in Russian penal camps. He was a man who was poisoned with Novichok by Russian intelligence and narrowly escaped death, who garnered millions of clicks for his exposé films about the corruption of the state leadership. He personally challenged Vladimir Putin.

This man seemed so dangerous to the Russian ruler in 2021 that he did not even mention his name. Navalny survived the poison gas attack by Russian secret services. His return from Germany to Russia and his prompt arrest at the airport in January 2021 plunged the country into demonstrations and street fighting. From Yakutsk to Kaliningrad, at minus 51 degrees and at zero degrees, across eleven time zones, the indignant and the supporters of Navalny gathered across Russia. Many men, fewer women, young people, students, young professionals, many of them for the first time, attended a demonstration. Well over 100,000 people demanded the release of Aleksei Navalny. They demonstrated against police violence, arbitrariness, and repression, despite the authorities forbidding it. Tens of thousands of people were arrested, according to the independent organization OVD-Info, including associates of Aleksei Navalny. Many got caught up in the maze of charges, show trials, and prison sentences, but most of all their idol himself. Navalny was initially convicted for merely failing to appear in court, then the criminal justice system kept fabricating new indictments to deprive him of his freedom. It is hard to imagine that Putin and his services had nothing to do with these highly politicized accusations.

The arrest was preceded by a bitter duel between Navalny and Putin: the president against the political activist, the intelligence man against the lawyer, the commander-in-chief against the political underdog. Their weapons could not have been more different. Putin had security services and propaganda factories, the state apparatus, and the penal system. Navalny had his supporters, social media, energy, and courage. Navalny lost; we all know that. What made this 2021 duel so dramatic was that Putin and Navalny shared two tactics: First, they both wanted to show no fear. Second, they sought to destroy each other as public figures. When Putin came under pressure in the process, he sent Navalny to a punishment camp. Let us take a quick look back.

Aleksei Navalny hit Putin in his most sensitive spot in early 2021. Navalny's associates uploaded a film to YouTube shortly after he landed in Moscow on January 17. »The Palace« had over 100 million views, and a whopping majority of Russians clicked on the documentary. They saw detailed research and a virtual journey into the realm of new corruption, old networks, hubris, and wellness-paradise resorts. Putin, as the presumed builder, was the focus of the film, which illuminated the gigantic palace on the Black Sea. At the same time, it showed how thoroughly and persistently Navalny's team worked. Dangerously persistent for Putin.

Members of Navalny's research team told me at the time that they had obtained the plans and pictures of the palace from a man who was directly involved in the construction. They had checked these documents »at least 35 times.« They went to Dresden and to the Black Sea. To mislead the secret service while taking aerial photographs, one employee traveled to southern Russia with the cell phones of two colleagues and three train tickets. The two colleagues, however, got off the train earlier, bought a rubber dinghy, and approached the heavily guarded palace from the sea. Three of their drones crashed because of the jammers before the fourth took the pictures of the 7000-hectare area. »This research,« Navalny's collaborator told me, »was the response to Alexei's poisoning.«

The goal of the operation was public exposure. What Navalny presented in such a palatable and ironic way were attacks on the illusion of Putin's virtues and strengths, which state television had been cultivating for years. Example one: Putin, the defender of traditional conservative family values. Navalny led the viewer into the palace's strip club, bathed in red light, complete with a dancing pole on a stage. Example two: Putin, the abstainer. Navalny showed in detail the winery, the bars, and the »cocktail hall« of the palace. Example three: Putin, the Russian outdoorsman who goes ice swimming when it gets frosty. Navalny unveiled the palace's decadent spa and gold toilet brushes worth $700, just under half of the average Russian annual pension. Navalny called Putin a »grandpa in the bunker« who is afraid of viruses and the truth.

This film was more than a revelation. It aimed to destroy public image. Navalny had taken Putin's virtues of earlier years and turned them to his advantage. Back in the noughties, Putin was the tough-as-nails cleanup man in the fight against the oligarchs and the corruption and theft of the 1990s. Back in the noughties, Navalny was still a nationalist, going on Russian marches and ranting about Caucasians. By the time of the film, Putin had turned into a nationalist who spent a lot of money on wars, on nuclear missiles, and on himself and his comrades-in-arms. In contrast, Navalny had taken on the role of the fearless clean-up man, exposing corruption under an increasingly fearful Putin. Navalny played the counter-Putin, strong and courageous. Again and again, he said he was not afraid. He liked to show himself with his children. He kissed his Julia in front of all the cameras shortly before his arrest, whereas Putin's wives and children were kept a big secret.

This was the biggest direct political threat to Putin since he came to power. It hit Putin at a time when his popularity, boosted by the Crimean annexation and Donbas adventures, was collapsing. A pension reform with noticeable benefit cuts starting in 2018 and mismanagement of the Coronavirus pandemic had caused him to lose the trust of Russians and his popularity to shrink. In the past, Putin had resorted to media manipulation, endless court cases, and expulsion from politics to deal with rivals. Now it was time for vengeance. He was aiming to destroy Navalny as a public actor and private person.

First attempt: Navalny as an agent of the West. State television accused him of vacationing in the Black Forest, sheltered by the German secret service, instead of facing the courts in Russia. He had been living in German luxury and was taken back to Russia in a sealed wagon, as it were. This was an allusion to Vladimir Lenin, who was smuggled into Russia by the Germans in a sealed train in 1917. Second attempt: Navalny as a Nazi. Putin's most riotous talk show host, Vladimir Solovyov, claimed that Navalny was a »collaborator with Nazi views.« Third attempt: Navalny as a criminal. Here, Putin coldly exploited the power asymmetry between the two opponents. Whereas the isolated Navalny was in jail, Putin was in the Kremlin—steeled by the full force of the repressive bureaucracy. The Russian ruler has a powerful instrument at his disposal for cases like Navalny.

The Russians call it »the zone,« a country within a country, with a long tradition, its own rules, its own administration, its own supplies, and even its own language. This is the system of Russian penal camps, which extends over eleven time zones of Russia, but makes any division of time and any calendar superfluous. Contact with the outside world is undesirable; it is a closed empire. What does it look like from the inside? Take a journey through the Putin archipelago.

In several trials, Aleksei Navalny was sentenced to many years in the camps after returning from Germany. The first sentence was handed down in 2021 for failing to comply with a request to turn himself in to the authorities in Russia during his poisoning. Finally, in May 2022, he was sentenced to nine years in prison. These trials are tribunals with pre-determined outcomes. The accused is allowed only a pro forma defense, and the conviction is a foregone conclusion. Navalny served more than a year in the IK-3 penal camp in Vladimir, »under a strict regime« with a heightened level of surveillance and discipline. The camp is located about 100 kilometers east of Moscow and has existed since the 1950s. It has had an infirmary since 1964. Navalny broke off his initial hunger strike on the urgent advice of his doctors and friends. Navalny decided not to finish the job that the secret service had started with his poisoning. Powerless, he had to watch from the camp as his regional representative offices and his foundation for the fight against corruption were destroyed by the authorities. They were all banned as »extremist organizations.« In June 2022, Navalny was transferred to the IK-6 penal colony in Melekhovo. It is located near the city of Kovrov, just over 250 kilometers northeast of Moscow. Melekhovo is a camp with harsher conditions. At the end of 2023, he was transported to the IK-3 penal colony in the settlement of Kharp in the Yamalo–Nenets district above the Arctic Circle in north-central Siberia—at the end of the world. There, he died in February 2024 under mysterious circumstances. This is the result of the treatment which Putin had in mind when he gave the judges and prison officers their marching orders in 2021: revenge.

Navalny lived deep in the Zone, in one of the 666 penal camps run by »FSIN,« the Federal Penitentiary Service or »Federal Service for the Execution of Punishment.« In Russia, about half a million people were incarcerated in 2022, most of them in such penal and labor camps. Olga Romanova heads the Moscow organization »Russia Behind Bars,« which provides legal and humanitarian assistance to prisoners. Her husband spent several years in prison because a former business partner had him prosecuted. He got caught up in the mills of the system in crooked trials. The camp facilities often date back to Soviet times, Romanova told me in a detailed interview in 2021. Low-lying barracks contain workshops and small factories where prisoners work for very little money. Other barracks serve as housing. The prisoners do not live in cells, but in large dormitories with over 100 people. There is often only one toilet and one sink per barrack. For safety, only spoons are distributed in the canteen. Conditions of the dark Soviet past are a present reality in the Zone.

The former-FSIN deputy director dismissed all comparisons with the Soviet era in a 2019 interview. »That era is long gone,« Valery Maximenko claimed to the Interfax news agency. On the Internet, the FSIN pretends to be ultra-modern. Online, one could find the latest information about Corona vaccinations in the camps and a YouTube channel to follow camp ski competitions, cooking lessons, and children's choirs singing patriotic songs. Maximenko contradicted all reports by hiding the prisoner mistreatment behind this façade. If one of his employees beats a detainee, he said, this is not the legacy of the gulag but a personal problem of this colleague who cannot control himself. »We are resolutely fighting against this.«

The Gulag was the Stalinist system of penal camps, subordinated first to the secret service, then to the Ministry of the Interior. Its prisoners were punished for wrong thinking or wrong origin. They built canals and cities for socialism, and they were destroyed as »pests and enemies of the system.« In this archipelago, which Alexander Solzhenitsyn describes so stirringly, at least 18 million people were imprisoned between 1930 and 1953. In 1940, a year before the German invasion of the Soviet Union, no less than 10 percent of the Soviet population was locked away. The camps were located on the permafrost of Siberia, on islands near the Arctic, in the Far East on the Bering Sea; in other words, far from the world. Almost three million people died in the camps, and more came out crippled and broken. This system was slightly reformed only once and put under the control of the Ministry of Justice, and that was after Stalin's death. After the end of socialism and the Soviet Union in 1991, the penal system was not dissolved but renamed. Since 2004, it has been called FSIN.

»The Gulag was a dragon that ate people alive,« Olga Romanova told me in 2021. »Today, the dragon has grown old, wrinkled, no longer breathes fire, has less hunger. But it is the same dragon.« Dmitry Medvedev admitted in a speech in 2011, when he was still Russian president, that the Russian penal system was still »95-percent Soviet.«

What does that mean in reality? How are people broken today?

In 2008, at the age of 21, Ivan Belousov was framed for a bomb explosion and sent crisscrossing between prison camps all over Russia for six years. »этапировать« (etapirovat') has a meaning close to relocation and has been a preferred method of imprisonment since the time of the tsars. Aleksei Navalny had also been relocated several times in two years. A prominent predecessor, businessman Mikhail Khodorkovsky, who fell out of favor with Putin in the early 2000s, was sent to penal camps in Siberia, among other places. Belousov was first imprisoned south of Moscow, then in Siberia in the north, and later in southern Russia. »Travel is pure torture,« he told me in a 2021 conversation. »They squeezed fifteen men into a compartment for eight in an old wagon.« Other relocated people report being pedantically searched when getting on and off the train and having to strip completely. Sometimes they beat you in the process. In the confines of the wagons, people are robbed and get on each other's nerves. One smokes, one whistles, another airs out their socks. In general, you never forget the smells, Belousov recalled. The journey to Siberia lasted for weeks, and the locomotive just sped along. Or not. Often the train just sat for hours or days and nights. There were rules and humiliating regulations for everything. While the train was stationary, no one was allowed to use the toilet; the guards were meticulous about this. The prisoners would scream in agony, and those who were able would secret away pilfered bottles. »With their rules, they make an animal out of you. Don't think, just do,« Belousov said.

»It's bad when you get sick,« explained Belousov. Medical treatment is simply a continuation of the punishment by other means. There are virtually no medications, and, if some turns up, they vanish immediately. At most, the doctors give out analgesics. He once had pneumonia and a high fever. Despite this, he had to wash himself on the street in minus-20-degree temperatures. »Without the medication my relatives sent me, I wouldn't have survived,« he said.

Belousov left the country after serving his sentence. Today, he lives in freedom in Germany. But in Russia, the flow of convictions of opposition members and dissidents increased at an alarming rate in 2021. Before the invasion of Ukraine, people were still being sentenced for specific or imputed acts. After the invasion, all it took was a simple statement of opinion that judges found to be in violation of the harsh censorship laws. A »No to War« sign displayed several times or an opinion expressed about the Russian military in Ukraine could result in a long prison sentence.

In July 2022, a court sentenced Alexei Gorinov, a lawyer and city councilor for Moscow's Krasnoselsky district, to seven years in prison. The charge: he had violated Article 207, Section 3 of the Criminal Code. This is the war censorship law that has made any criticism of the war against Ukraine a punishable offence since March 2022. Gorinov had said publicly at a city council meeting that children were dying in Ukraine. He argued that Russia should end the war and withdraw all troops. He was convicted for »knowingly spreading false news.« False, as the judges understood it, consisted of what is perfectly true according to everything the world knows about Putin's war in Ukraine.

Alexei Gorinov was the first political prisoner to be sentenced to camp imprisonment on the basis of the censorship law. It became apparent that many would follow him during his trial in July 2022. A former associate of Mikhail Khodorkovsky was sentenced to four years at a penal colony in July 2022 for running an »undesirable organization.« The organization in question was the non-governmental organization »Open Russia.« Journalist Ivan Safronov was sentenced to 22 years in prison for »treason« in September 2022. The judicial authorities brought charges against opposition politician Ilya Yashin for violating Article 207, Section 3. He was immediately placed under arrest and sentenced to imprisonment for ten years. Police officer Vladimir Kara-Murza was arrested under the same pretexts. The judicial authorities punished every statement about the war that deviated from the official line. If an opposition politician said what everyone could see on the Internet, namely that the Russian military bombed residential areas, hospitals, and schools, it was interpreted as »misinformation« with the »motive of political hatred.« This, the prosecutors said, would »harm the interests of the Russian Federation.« Many politicians were investigated on flimsy premises.

Couldn't a lawyer have immediately refuted these accusations in court? Attorney Maria Eismont, who, among others, represented Ilya Yashin, said that »political hatred« is a relatively new and »difficult to interpret« criminal offense. There is nationalist, anti-religious, and racist hatred, but political hatred? It came into vogue as an accusation against political prisoners. As a lawyer, she can hardly stop the process and sentencing, she said in July 2022, but it is not uncommon for lawyers to be the »only link« the prisoners have with the outside world because authorities often refuse to allow relatives to visit. »As a lawyer, I can argue publicly against the illegality of detention and prosecution and about the violation of the Constitution and procedures,« she said. Lawyers like her can inform the public about the process. »It's important for society and history.« And that's exactly why some trials are held in closed sessions, she said. Then, the attorneys are deprived of the opportunity to speak publicly about the proceedings.

Those who end up in court have little chance of getting off without punishment. Judges almost always deliver a sentence, said Romanova. This is not only due to political requirements, nor is it necessarily due to corruption. »Judges are quite well paid and enjoy many benefits, such as free housing.« The criminal trial authorities are very interested in increasing their budgets by »performing well.« Justice, she said, is less important than handling as many cases as possible. Indeed, former Moscow police investigator Alexander Salamov said that many investigators are »obsessed with numbers« and that mass prosecutions are »the only way to get ahead or keep your job.« Thus, trials in Russia degenerate into a mere formality that is no longer about finding the truth but about completing the work of the prosecutor. And the prosecutor is instructed to put people in pre-trial detention centers and penal camps where the conditions are such that they can no longer pose a threat to the ruler and the system.

Grinding down a prisoner's resistance and making them lower their gaze to the ground: how does that work? According to investigators, businessman Vladimir Pereversin was supposed to incriminate his former boss Mikhail Khodorkovsky. He refused and ended up in a prison camp. There, he worked in cement production, among other things. He suffered greatly from the loss of privacy, he says. »I slept with up to 100 others in a barracks. The cots were full, the toilets were full, I shared a shower with five men—people, people, people everywhere.« The toilets had no doors, so you sat on a concrete beam with eight holes next to each other, and the guards would watch. Today, cameras are mounted at every corner. Arbitrary surveillance, a lack of distance, and humiliation: »The penal camp is an exaggerated copy of our society,« says Pereversin. Envy, hatred, lawlessness, arbitrariness, cruel pedantry—all are present in the camp.

The guards tortured the prisoners with petty rules. Not putting the kettle down properly? Smoking in the toilet? Top shirt button undone? Shoelace untied? »Off to the Karzer!« There, you sit in a cold, damp room, often in the company of vermin. At one point, Pereversin thought it would be a good idea to complain, and in writing. That was a mistake. The guards set his fellow inmates against him. It was his fault that they could not sleep during the day and were not allowed to eat anything in between meals.

This is an ominous situation. Beatings and torments are part of everyday life. Sometimes prisoners are raped by fellow inmates as punishment, and the guards film it. Afterwards, everyone finds out, and the raped person becomes a leper—or fair game.

Pereversin was threatened. Everyone was angry with him over the agitated guards. If things went on like this, he feared that his fellow prisoners would kill him. Pereversin had to get out of the barracks before the situation escalated, so he stole a blade from a machinery tool and slashed his stomach. He got to the prison hospital cracked but not broken.

Confinement in the prison camps can be life-threatening, says Olga Romanova of Russia Behind Bars. In the camps, an above-average proportion of inmates are infected with HIV, hepatitis, or tuberculosis. »Poor food, lack of hygiene, and little light make prisoners vulnerable to disease.« Tea with lots of sugar, porridge with water, watery soup, potatoes, bread, more tea with sugar—those who have to live on that for a long time get sick. According to the Council of Europe, Russia spent the least in Europe on prisoners in 2021, no more than 2.40 euros per capita per day; the European average was 68 euros. The FSIN spent one euro per prisoner per day on food. Medical care was abysmal, Romanova reports. »Military doctors work in the camps, following orders from their superiors rather than the Hippocratic Oath.« The goal, she says, is not treatment but punishment. Belousov and Pereversin experienced this firsthand.

In any case, human life is worth less in Russia than in Europe. In the penal camps, this attitude has become radicalized. The cynicism is great. Dying is considered part of life, especially when it affects others. In the Zone, the life of the individual has worth only as an object of torture, because the prisoner still feels the pain while alive.

In October 2021, the human rights organization Gulagu.net published a full series of recordings with concrete cases of torture in Russian penal colonies and prisons. A former prisoner who had been commissioned by the prison management to archive and organize the recordings from the surveillance cameras provided several videos from Saratov. The videos comprehensively document systematic torture in the Russian penal system.

One prison in Angarsk, Siberia, became particularly notorious in 2021. Former inmates there reported incidents of torture after a prisoner protest: »We were taken out of the cells at midnight. We had to lie naked on the concrete until 9 o'clock in the morning. No one was allowed to rise.« Those who had to go to the toilet could only relieve themselves in place and lay in their excrement, he said. »We were beaten and ridiculed,« reported the prisoner, who suffered several broken ribs that night.

The evidence of torture was so overwhelming that even Putin had to act. In November and December 2021, he dismissed the head and several officials of the FSIN. In January 2022, on the 300th anniversary of the founding of the Prosecutor General's Office, he called for »stronger monitoring of enforcement in law enforcement agencies.« In doing so, the agencies were to cooperate with »state structures and human rights organizations.«

Human rights activists feared that this was a cover-up. In fact, the organizations and associations that cared for prisoners, the tortured and the abused, had to leave Russia or close down. Olga Romanova has lived permanently in Berlin since 2017. Vladimir Osechkin, the head of Gulagu.net, has been living in France since 2015. He has been wanted by the prosecutor's office since 2021. The Russian Committee for the Prevention of Torture disbanded in June 2022 after 20 years of advocating for abused people, after authorities branded the organization a »foreign agent.«

These conditions explain why Aleksei Navalny went from a hero in the courtroom to a physically exhausted shell on his sickbed within a few weeks in 2021. On the web, FSIN describes Navalny's camp, where he was held until June 2022, as a penal camp for 1211 prisoners, including a hospital for 379 patients that specializes in multidrug-resistant tuberculosis. It describes a church and a prayer room for Muslims to pray and a place where people can work as bricklayers, carpenters, and locksmiths. Navalny's supporters reported something quite different. In the Melekhovo camp, they said, conditions were much harsher than in the first penal colony where he had served time. »A torture camp, not a hospital,« said Navalny's Chief-of-Staff Leonid Volkov, who left Russia in 2021 after the politician's arrest. Though such judgments are difficult to review, former prisoners told the Open Media platform that patients had been beaten in the hospital. There were »traces of violence« on their bodies. Tuberculosis patients were locked outdoors in winter. The camp in Melekhovo also has a reputation as a »torture camp.« In 2021, the independent Russian platform Mediazona published a harrowing letter by detainee Ivan Fomin. In it, the Uzbek-born prisoner described torture rituals, systematic rapes, and murders of fellow prisoners that he had witnessed or even participated in. Aleksei Navalny was experiencing the conditions in this prison camp in the summer of 2022.

At the time, the opposition politician was still at the beginning of his long journey through the Zone, with at least nine years ahead of him. Vladimir Pereversin, who lived in Berlin during our interview, was allowed out after seven years and two months. But the Zone did not let him go, even in Germany. He is scarred by this time. »Several times a month, I have nightmares that I'm back in,« Pereversin said. He dreams of getting up at 5:30, gymnastics, breakfast, roll call, and work.

»I tell the wardens in my dreams that I have already served my sentence.« But no one listens to him. And then he wakes up in a cold sweat.

# Elections Without Choice

## Descent into dictatorship

A few days after the Russian invasion of Ukraine, I stood in a long line at the foot of St Basil's Cathedral. Thousands of Muscovites had come, women and men, all carrying a rose. People waited patiently to get through the police barriers.

»Please open your bag. No posters, no leaflets, no weapons?« the officers barked. »No? Well, go!«

Slowly, I pushed my way through the crowd onto the bridge. There you could almost see over the wall of the nearby Kremlin, but that was not what people had come for. They were lining up to commemorate Boris Nemtsov, who had been assassinated on this spot seven years earlier. Roses lay next to photos of the politician. Roses were also laid out next to a *Novaya Gazeta* frontpage that read in large letters, »Russia. Bombed. Ukraine.« No one was talking about the war, but everyone was thinking about it. They knew Boris Nemtsov would have been vocally against it. That's why they were here.

The shooting of Boris Nemtsov on this bridge over the Moskva River and right next to the Kremlin in February 2015 was one of the severe shocks of the Putin era. There have been many political assassinations under this president, but this was of one of his predecessors as prime minister. Nemtsov had been appointed deputy prime minister in 1997 and was a passionate reformer of the 1990s. I knew him well and interviewed him several times. He was not offended like other Moscow politicians when I asked him tough questions. On the contrary, he enjoyed it and answered with a quick and sharp wit. He jokingly called then-President Boris Yeltsin »the czar« and told him to his face about his having »made many mistakes.« That's how Nemtsov was: fearless, spontaneous, clear, decisive. Until 2015, he was one of Putin's fiercest, most fearless critics. For this, he was shot, right at the Kremlin, in front of the lenses of dozens of cameras and the eyes of many police officers. The crime scene is one of the best-guarded places in Moscow. The perpetrator is said to have been a Chechen. Who let the man shoot in front of the Kremlin was never solved, as in many other political murders. Those behind it were suspected to be in the state apparatus. Hence why so many people came to this bridge right after the invasion of Ukraine to protest against violence, violence by the state, directed first inward and then outward.

Murder and war are the alternating faces of power.

This was already apparent at the beginning of Putin's term in office in the Chechen war and in the targeted killing of journalists. Every murder was followed by a misunderstanding that this was an isolated act, that the murder of one person would have no effect on others, and that the violent extinction of one indomitable voice would nevertheless allow all others to live and speak in peace. Murders accompanied the rule of Vladimir Putin and were often not solved. Only pawns were condemned because no judge dared to follow the tracks into the world of the Russian security services and the Chechen state mafia. Putin's »dictatorship of the law« punished dissidents, not violent criminals.

Nevertheless, Putin had to come a long way since his first steps to tame the oligarchs before he arrived at the suppression of any dissent and the rule of unlimited violence. In the West, these 22 years were accompanied by many illusions. First, Western politicians believed Putin's claim that he »only wanted to stabilize« the country. In Germany, Putin's speech to the Bundestag in September 2001, when he described the »guarantee of democratic rights« as the »main goal« of his domestic policy contributed to this. It was a deceptive maneuver. Later, the ostensibly soft-spoken interim president Dmitry

Medvedev grew into a figure of hope. Then, many reassured themselves that Russian civil society would not stand for it. They were hoping in vain. What Putin impressively shows the world is how anyone who starts bending the law, empowering the security apparatus, and trying out repression is on a slippery slope. The curtailment of freedoms, the intimidation of citizens, the fear of speaking openly, a corrupt judiciary, and a bent law are wounds to a country that can no longer be healed. You cannot bend the law »a little bit,« intimidate »a little bit,« or suppress »a little bit.« What touched only a few at the beginning of Putin's term in office now affects all Russians—and their neighbors. The decline began slowly, with a gradual backslide of the rule of law in the early 2000s, but it culminated in dictatorship. How did it come to this?

Putinism went through several phases: a hybrid phase in the early 2000s, an authoritarian phase from 2012, and the current phase of destruction of civil society from 2021. The first phase in particular was supported by a frightening level of approval not only in Russia but also in the West. In the process, Putin turned away from the almost-decade-long attempt to copy Western democracies. Former role models served only as decorative elements for the showcase to the West. The Putin system emerged at the beginning of the 2000s as a hybrid stabilitocracy in the West, in the gray area between democracy and dictatorship.

The first phase consisted primarily of eliminating the counterweights to central power in the presidential system. Putin's first stroke was against parliament. He reformed the recalcitrant Duma by growing a clone of the Soviet Communist Party (CPSU), without its ideology. The Party of Unity, later renamed United Russia, moved broadly into the Duma after a media campaign and a compliant vote count. Together with the free-riding system opposition, it formed a power bloc in parliament; henceforth the Duma exercised loyalty and probity. The occasional cries of the real opposition could no longer interfere with Putin's governing.

The second stroke was aimed at the governors and presidents of the republics, who ruled like little kings in the federal system of the 1990s. They formed a real counterpart to the center, which was an intolerable idea for Putin, the ex-intelligence chief. Putin took away their immunity and influence at the federal level. Russia's once powerful upper house, the Federation Council, degenerated into an organization of bureaucrats who could be called upon quickly. From then on, the regional princes were allowed to simulate influence in the »State Council,« which was devoid of influence. The many councils had only one purpose: to assist the president's power.

The third strike against the media was most important. Putin deprived private owners of the nationwide television channels of their property. What he called a »fight against the oligarchs« was, in fact, a state takeover of the influential television stations. The oligarchs were made an offer they could not refuse by a collective of judges, intelligence agents, and government officials: Give up their stations and flee abroad with some of their money.

Unlike Western systems, Putin's »dictatorship of the law« was dominated by politics. The prosecutor's office and the judiciary degenerated into the Kremlin's legal department. Putin's political technologists built a hollow façade of democracy in the still-unoccupied space between European values and Eurasian traditions. At that time, Vladimir Putin managed without camps and police terror. He worked in the penumbra of a hybrid system in which much was under control while a residual pluralism flourished. In Moscow, there were politically critical newspapers that served the needs of liberals and intellectuals with very small circulations. Journalists were allowed to criticize Putin as long as the masses reliably voted for Putin. Moscow celebrated itself as a city for freedom-hungry people, and power encouraged the party as long as it did not become political. Putin spoke out against the death penalty, but the murders by Russian soldiers of Chechen civilians went unpunished. The executive power professed »freedom« while the secret service knitted its surveillance net. Since one thing was true while its opposite was also true, everyone could see in Putin what they liked. He created a hybrid system that misled Westerners and Russians alike. By gradually growing oil and gas revenues, he and Dmitry Medvedev, while he served as president from 2008 to 2012, were able to give Russians a modest prosperity. That was the social contract: welfare in exchange for a refusal to have a say. And complaining was still possible, for now.

This deal lasted about ten years—until Putin's planned return to the presidency in 2012, when people revolted against a rigged Duma election in late 2011 and the bending of the constitution to enable Putin's desire to run for president for a third time. The demonstrators marched to the center of Moscow and almost to the Kremlin's walls. The protest marches ended at Bolotnaya Square on the other side of the Moskva River, and this name was used, both among the protestors and in the subsequent court cases against them, for this movement that lasted from November 2011 to May 2012. Putin's return to the Kremlin in 2012 marked the beginning of the second, authoritarian phase, in which the regime systematically cracked down on Russian pluralism and expanded the repression of individual oligarchs into indiscriminate mass repression.

The »foreign agent laws« were an important instrument for this phase as a decisive extension of the laws on non-governmental organizations. These laws require any association that is even remotely socially or politically active that receives money from non-Russian sources to label itself as a »foreign agent.« This branding was accompanied by close monitoring of these associations and harsh penalties for violations of a wide range of bureaucratic requirements.

»The direction was absolutely clear,« Maria Eismont described the process. »Putin wanted to stay in office, come what may.« Eismont was a journalist, an excellent reporter, and tireless researcher at the time. Small in stature, she is powerful in everything she says—and very persistent. I had met her at an award ceremony where she was being honored for her work. Her work is exactly what became difficult under Putin. The more she wrote about the shrinking political freedoms, the more she had to deal with the courts. »And that's why I decided to become a lawyer,« she proudly announced at a later meeting. After additional legal training, she found herself in court defending not herself but others. New changes in the law had to be studied constantly. The foreign agent laws were expanded. A law on »undesirable organizations« was passed. »There was always more to do.«

Eismont remembers a hybrid attitude toward life. Putin ruled at the top, while the great search for niches began at the bottom. The state systematically restricted everyone's personal and political freedoms, while it allowed the expansion of personal amenities. Restaurants, bistros, private clinics, summer cafes, amusement parks, animal welfare societies, and dance clubs sprouted up in Moscow and the country's major cities. People had jobs, and some had good-to-very-good salaries and went on vacation to Europe, Dubai, or Bali. »We became hostages in a highly comfortable world,« Eismont recalls. »You could have a good life beyond the political.«

But only if you kept your distance from politics. Russia changed profoundly during these years. Putin ordered the invasion of Ukraine in 2014, and he annexed Crimea and occupied part of Ukraine's Donbas. The nationalists cheered. The critics were terrified. The murder of Boris Nemtsov on the bridge near the Kremlin showed how heated the atmosphere was. Nemtsov had sharply criticized the invasion of Ukraine in 2014. Shortly after the murder, I met a close confidant of Nemtsov, the liberal politician Vladimir Ryzhkov, not far from the crime scene. He was angry about the portrayal of the assassination on state television. Putin's chief propagandist, Dmitry Kiselyov, claimed that Nemtsov was actually an insignificant, unpopular, and by no means key figure.

»He was not dangerous to anyone,« Kiselyov causticized about the dead man. The moderator sought to deny any Kremlin interest in his death. Vladimir Ryzhkov, however, was convinced that the government was partly to blame. Putin himself had started the hunt for the opposition, Ryzhkov told me, by speaking as president about Russia's »internal enemies.« In December 2014, a few weeks before the assassination, Putin had warned, »It's hard to understand where the opposition ends and the fifth column begins.« That statement, he said, has become a constant turn of phrase on television and in the Duma. There are whispers that anti-Russian forces are getting paid by America and conspiring against Putin with the money. Foreign agents. Ryzhkov considered the danger to oppositionists under Putin greater than in the late Soviet Union. At that time, under General Secretaries Leonid Brezhnev and Yuri Andropov, only the state and its organs exercised violence; it was controlled repression from above. Dissidents went to prison for their convictions, or they were expatriated. »Today, the opposition faces violence from above and below,« Ryzhkov said. And that can quickly turn deadly, he said, if a hired assassin is put on the trail. The outcry over Nemtsov's death was limited to liberal supporters of freedom in Russia. The other Russians were in a Crimean delirium.

Here we come to one of the central reasons that Putin was able to establish a new authoritarian regime less than 20 years after the collapse of the Soviet Union: the vast majority of Russians willingly supported him. It was precisely in times of particularly great restrictions on freedom that Putin's popularity rose to dizzying heights. According to the independent Levada Institute, it was at 86-percent at the time of Nemtsov's murder. The majority eagerly gave up their civil rights and free elections for pseudo-stability, minimal prosperity, and the Crimean festivities. Of course, the votes were manipulated in advance and additionally falsified directly at the ballot box.

Nevertheless, the polls confirmed that a majority supported the ruler. These people apparently did not see elections as a means to change the country with their vote. They looked back in anger on the confusing but free 1990s. They approved every constitutional amendment to perfect their own domination. And they cheered their oppressor.

As far as a relative majority of the population is concerned, Russia is a dictatorship of consent, or at least this was the case until the mobilization in September 2022. Putin's archetypal supporter can be found in Moscow, but he is not part of the majority there. He is the resentment-laden »sovok,« the *homo sovieticus* who survived the Soviet Union. He usually lives in a medium-sized town in the Russian provinces and works in the administration or a similarly bureaucratic business. He watches only state television, and a lot of it. From the sofa, the sovok watches the screen in a frenzy of revenge and satisfaction as the minority is stomped under police boots.

Putin's showdown with Aleksei Navalny in 2021 heralded the third phase of the descent into dictatorship: the destruction of Russian civil society. First, the secret service poisoned the opposition politician on a trip to Tomsk. After narrowly surviving thanks to German doctors at Berlin's Charité hospital, Navalny returned in January 2021. He was immediately arrested on a flimsy pretext. The protests against his detention were decided to be the last free demonstrations in Russia. A gigantic wave of arrests swept the country. Schoolchildren, university students, and other activists were arrested en masse and interrogated before they were put on trial. Within four months, well over 13,000 people were detained. Aleksei Navalny was sentenced to several years in a penal colony and died in February 2024.

All charges against him were fictitious. The goal of his imprisonment was to ensure that the popular Navalny no longer played a role in Russian political life. Putin took personal revenge on him for the challenge.

The results of repression all over Russia were already apparent in the Duma election in September 2021. In polls before the election, Putin's United Russia party was well below 30 percent. Only a few opposition candidates were allowed to run. When a liberal Yabloko party candidate in the city of Kazan announced in democratic fashion that his party would also like to govern at some point, the prosecutor's office intervened. The man was accused of »political extremism« and investigated on suspicion of foreign funding. Naturally, he was excluded from the elections along with more than a dozen candidates from the small liberal party. On election day, many liberal voters cast protest ballots for the Communist Party, a national-patriotic system party. In fact, Communist candidates won many constituencies. But during the night, the counting was stopped, election observers were denied access, and the votes were recounted. By the next day, United Russia had won more than two thirds of all seats. »You vote, we count,« a principle formerly attributed to Leader Josef Stalin.

Shortly after the election, the prosecutor's office, with a suggestion from Putin, brought charges against the renowned NGOs Memorial and Memorial International, which were awarded the Nobel Peace Prize in 2022. Maria Eismont sat on the bench with Memorial's other defense lawyers in front of the Moscow High Court. On the other side of the courtroom, the prosecution presented the indictment, a collection of false and unlawful allegations. Former journalist Eismont responded with a fiery statement, refuting every single point of the indictment. She looked upon motionless faces with small eyes and tight lips. After several days of trial, both Memorial societies were banned in Russia. Memorial, co-founded by Nobel Peace Prize laureate Andrei Sakharov, was »liquidated,« as it is called in official Russian. Putin was erasing Russia's memory and installing his own historical legends in the empty space. This was internal mobilization for the external war.

A few days after the invasion of Ukraine on February 24, a private camera crew stood in Red Square and asked Muscovites for their opinion. One woman said that she was against the war. Before she could give her reasons, police officers dragged her away in a squad car. After her, a second woman stood in front of the camera and very firmly expressed her unconditional support for the ruler, Vladimir Putin. She too was dragged away by the police.

The opinion did not matter at all. Since the outbreak of the war, it has become dangerous to speak out at all, without prompting, authorization, and as dictated by those in power. Public space in Russia has become toxic. Meanwhile, holding up an empty sign is an arrestable offence because it is interpreted as a forbidden expression of opinion. »Even for that, you can be sentenced to a heavy fine,« says Maria Eismont. »And in the case of a repeat offence, there is the threat of prison.«

With the invasion of Ukraine, the authorities set in motion their plans to destroy civil society. The last free media, Radio Echo Moscow, the television station Dozhd, and *Novaya Gazeta*, headed by Nobel Peace Prize laureate Dmitriy Muratov, were forced to cease their work. A new wave of arrests swept the country. People who protested the war with leaflets, without leaflets, with their voices, or with silence were arrested. In Russia, there has been no public voice except Putin's since 2022.

What should we call the Putin system of today? Is it fascism? There are not only frightening parallels but also differences. It lacks the extermination camps for »racial aliens,« the red-brown socialist rhetoric, and the fight against church institutions and terror by storm troopers in the streets. In their inherent radicalism, National Socialism and Italian fascism were also revolutionary movements; Putin shuns revolutions of any kind. One does not fully understand his system if It is pressed it into a familiar template of Western European models. It builds on Russian and Soviet traditions of violence and lawlessness that have never been overcome.

Putinism is a kind of USSR without socialism, a pseudo-clerical conservative moral rule, a venom-spraying police state that is internally repressive and externally aggressive. But even this is not, in itself, a new system. Putin, who is divorced and in a wild marriage with an athlete, has the image of the conservative family painted as the ideal of society. State propagandists strive for control over minds. They create a hermetic »Russian information space.« They create the ideal of the strong, conservative man who defends his wife and children, who cultivates his fields outside the city and fights for the fatherland. They mobilize the masses to isolate the country and to attack the neighbors. People are allowed to cheer war, annexation, and Putin. Across the country, people denounce each other. Society is atomized and has hardly any forms of organization beyond the vertical power of the state. The politician Andrei Kolesnikov speaks of »hybrid totalitarianism.«

Such assessments are dangerous under Putin today. Many are drawing the consequences. The intellectuals are leaving, the foreigners already were. The young people, the artists, the journalists, the IT technicians, and the free-thinking scientists are all leaving the country. Meanwhile, most Russians are getting what they have repeatedly voted for in elections and referendums: a Russian dictatorship with increasingly totalitarian features. This is Putin's new system.

The anti-war march for the murdered Boris Nemtsov on the bridge at the Kremlin ended in a trap. No sooner had the people put down their roses and bowed before the politician's picture than police officers pushed the men and women into a narrow space between the barriers. Secret service agents with press badges on their jackets filmed every face. Police officers checked IDs. Blue police vans were parked on the side of the barriers. The demonstrators were then

sorted: Some were picked out and locked into the vans. The others walked on, depressed, back down the bridge and took a deep breath.
　　So did I.

# Executor of History

## Putin's abuse of the past

It was the strangest declaration of war in world history. In a televised speech that was part angry outburst, part history lecture, Vladimir Putin justified his recognition of the Russian-ruled separatist republics in Ukraine's Donbas on the evening of February 21, 2022. This marked the beginning of his assault on Ukraine. Between wood paneling, potted plants, and corded telephones, the Russian president spent nearly an hour shouting about 20th-century history, which he said had disadvantaged Russia from beginning to end. Gasping for breath, he criticized his two predecessors for doing everything wrong. He condemned the West, which had taken over everything. He wanted to correct the hated world, which had gone in the wrong direction since the collapse of the Soviet empire. It was his historic moment of revenge. Putin was driven by history, befuddled, almost hypnotized. With the invasion of Ukraine, he drove it forward, in a completely different direction. In February 2022, he saw himself well in the league of Czar Peter I, the founder of the Russian Empire, and Josef Stalin, the victor over Hitler and conqueror of Europe as far as the Elbe. To their colossal legacy, he now wanted to add his work: the forcible return of Ukraine to Russian rule. And after that—we will see.

Vladimir Putin justified the raid with a long tale of Russia's suffering, betrayed by the West, threatened by genocide, and betrayed by Ukraine. This narrative accompanied the Russian invasion of Ukraine and pressure on the West backed by nuclear flailing. It shows that misused and misinterpreted history can provoke and justify wars even in the 21st century. Putin claimed a deeply moral right. He sought to legitimize the revision of the European order and Russia's uninterrupted westward expansion with his bizarre interpretation of history. He portrayed the West as in breach of treaty, disrupted Ukraine, divided European and German public opinion, and poisoned his own country with his narrative of grievance and betrayal.

Vladimir Putin was not a born ideologue when he took office in 1999; he became a new nationalist. Power was always in his foreground: its acquisition, its preservation, its expansion. The narrative of deception and disregard suffered by Russia is part of his strategy to expand power internally and externally. Internally, the reference to his country's history of suffering and grievances justifies his waging of wars. Externally, especially to countries in Asia and Africa, it justifies Russia's fight as against only the West and for its own good. Both narratives have had quite some success: see his approval ratings in Russia and the rejection of sanctions against Moscow in countries like India, South Africa, Nigeria, and Indonesia. But he also hoped to make an impression in the West, especially in vulnerable societies like Germany or Italy. To Putin, history is both intellectual intoxication and a means of power.

With an overdose of history, Putin radicalized himself and the Russian public. Wherever he appeared, he liked to rant about history. On June 9, 2022, he met young entrepreneurs and researchers at an exhibition site in Moscow and had little to say about their concerns for the future since the beginning of the war. He had all the more to say about Russia's great past. He spoke about Peter I and the Northern War that he had »fought for 21 years« with a great deal of patience. He spoke of territories that were Russian, but which Europe had maliciously regarded as Swedish.

»And yet Slavs had lived there!« he said indignantly. Russophobia and historical injustice were said to have existed even then. No one whispered such insights to him. Putin had replaced or dismissed most of his advisors and spin doctors from earlier years. Who could tell him anything after 22 years in power? Putin advised Putin. For his history essays, he read national patriotic literature, which he charged politically. For him, memory was a continuation of the war by other means. He started the war with a history lecture. He justified the invasion of Ukraine with three main assertions:

First, Ukraine is not a state but a variation of Russia, and, if anything, Ukraine is an invention of the Soviet Union.

Second, Russians and Russian-speakers in Eastern Ukraine would have suffered genocide and neo-Nazis were at work.

Third, the West cheated Russia in 1990 during the reunification of Germany and NATO betrayed all its promises.

These claims fell on fertile ground in the West, especially in Germany, where politicians, generals, and journalists eagerly repeated them on talk shows, in articles, and during interviews.

What is possibly true? What is a lie?

*First assertion: Ukraine is not a state.*
Putin's war against Ukraine is directed against the very existence of the independent country. It is a war against the existence of a Ukrainian language, a Ukrainian national consciousness, and a non-Russian Ukrainian culture. Putin repeatedly announces his conviction, including in his attack speech of Feb. 21, 2022. Ukraine »is not just a neighboring country for us,« Putin said, »it is an inseparable part of our history, culture, and spiritual space.« In an essay published by the Kremlin on its web site on July 12, 2021, Putin called the »wall between Russia and Ukraine a tragedy.« What he called a »wall« is Ukrainian independence. He considered Ukraine's borders to be nothing but the administrative divisions of Soviet times. Putin claimed 30 years after the end of the Soviet Union that Russians and Ukrainians were »one people.« The fraternal embrace was already seen in 2021 as an attempt to stifle Ukrainian independence. Putin wrote that Ukraine was »wholly and thoroughly a creature of the Soviet era« and created in large part at the expense of historic Russia such that »Russia was

effectively robbed.« He was alluding to the nationality policy of Soviet leader Vladimir Ilyich Lenin, who in the 1920s thwarted Great Russian centralism and granted Soviet republics self-government within limits for the cultivation of their language and culture. Along with brutal conquest, this was Lenin's means of containing the aspirations for independence of non-Russian peoples. Ukraine was not the only independent state at the end of the First World War and the break-up of the Russian Empire.

In Putin's twisted view, however, all periods of Ukrainian statehood had been a Western conspiracy, part of an »anti-Russia project.« Putin applied this grotesque claim to the early modern period and the First World War as well as to the most recent period since Ukraine's declaration of independence in 1991. He said that it was not Ukrainians but Poles, Lithuanians, Swedes, Germans and, of course, Americans who were behind Ukraine's independence and secession from Russia. Looking back before the 20th century, he spoke of Ukrainians only as »Malorussians« [Little Russians] and even as »Russians,« and defined Ukraine as »borderlands.« Ukrainian is, for him, a »dialect,« and Ukrainian culture is local folklore. Putin reproached modern Ukraine for its pro-Western course. It had never had a »tradition of statehood« and was today »mechanically copying foreign models« that would »alienate it from its history.«

It is perhaps superfluous to say that Putin revealed an almost pathological view of history here. It dripped with nationalism, sniveling blood-and-soil pathos, and delusions of persecution. Putin stirred up ethnic Russian, Russian imperial, and Slavophile nationalism into a furious turmoil. He repeatedly spoke of »a triune people of Velikorussians [Greater Russians], Malorussians, and Belorussians,« an ideological formula for the peoples of Russia, Ukraine, and Belarus that Archbishop Feofan Prokopovich introduced during the reign of Peter I. The writer and Soviet dissident Alexander Solzhenitsyn also picked it up later. Putin mixed Solzhenitsyn's East-Slavic cry of woe with new nationalism and personal vindictiveness to create a project of destruction unparalleled in the history of the 21st century.

Before and since Russia's attack on Ukraine, I was surprised to see the strong the circulation of Putin's revanchist thoughts in Western Europe. In letters to the editor, I read that Ukraine was a corrupt and failed state, that Crimea had always been Russian, that the West had split Ukraine off, and that the Americans had organized the Maidan Revolution to weaken Russia. Ideological Putinism is quite common among Western Europeans. Therefore, it cannot be reiterated often enough that Ukraine is a normal European nation-state. It has the same right to exist as France, Germany, or Poland, and its demise would be just as great a catastrophe.

Putin's convoluted claim that Ukrainians and Russians are »one« also refers to the predecessor state of today's Ukraine, Belarus, and Russia: the historical Rus of the 10th–13th centuries. This medieval state perished in the Mongol attacks. Since then, the southern and western territories of the former Rus developed independently and quite differently from the northern territories, where centuries later the Moscow Grand Duchy emerged. It is as strange a claim as it would be to argue today that the French and Germans not only must be united in the EU and by the euro, but also urgently needed to harmonize their culture, internal administration, and language because both peoples once emerged from Charlemagne's empire.

The territories of today's Ukraine fell into disarray in the early modern period. The region was part of the Polish–Lithuanian Union from the 16th to the 17th century. Only the famous oath of allegiance of the Zaporozhian Cossacks to the Moscow Tsar Alexei Mikhailovich in 1654 brought them closer to Moscow. The subsequent appropriation of Ukrainian territories by Moscow's rulers in the 17th century was not a »reunification,« as national–patriotic Russian historians claim. Ukrainians and Russians did not live in »nation-states« at that time but in a personalized relationship with one ruler; loyalty was to him alone. Crimea became Russian in 1783 and was part of Russia for only 171 years. Before that, the peninsula, which Putin transfigured into a »Russian Jerusalem,« had been part of the Ottoman Empire for much longer. Despite Russian rule, a Ukrainian national movement emerged in the 19th century that was no less vibrant than that of other Eastern European peoples. It was suppressed in Russia in the same way as the Polish national movement. The prohibition of Ukrainian literature, culture, education, and language in the 19th century was an attempt by nationalist Russian bureaucrats to prevent nation-state development in the western territories of the empire. An 1863 circular issued by the tsarist Minister of the Interior Pyotr Valuev stated: »A separate Malorussian language has never existed, does not exist now, and will never exist. The dialect used by the common people is the Russian language, only corrupted by Polish influences.« Similarities with today's assessments of Ukraine by Russian politicians are not accidental.

Despite mass oppression, Ukrainians established their first nation-state at the end of the First World War. In January 1918, the Central Rada in Kyiv declared the Ukrainian People's Republic a »free and sovereign state of the Ukrainian people.« This young nation-state had four governments by 1920. It did not, however, survive the turmoil of the Russian Civil War between White Monarchists and Communist Bolsheviks.

It was not only the Whites and the Reds who had no interest in an independent Ukraine within the desired borders, but also the newly formed Polish nation-state. Unlike the Poles, Estonians, Latvians, and Lithuanians, who also founded their modern nation-states after the First World War, the Ukrainians remained under Moscow's rule and became part of the Soviet Union. Only when this empire collapsed in 1991 did the dream of the Ukrainian national movement come true. Ukraine emerged as a nation-state not out of an anti-Russian reflex— Putin got that completely wrong—but out of an anti-Soviet reflex against the communist empire. Thus, Ukraine was no different from other Eastern European peoples who liberated themselves from totalitarian Soviet rule between 1989 and 1991. Anti-Russian sentiments in Ukraine grew only with Putin's incessant attacks on the country.

*Second allegation: a genocide against the Russians in the Donbas.*
One of the phrases repeated like a prayer in Russia is that a »genocide« is underway against the Russians and Russian-speakers in the Donbas. Putin spread the rumor in February 2022, but this was not the first time. In February 2015, shortly after the Minsk agreement, Putin accused the Kyiv government of not supplying enough natural gas, if any at all, to the areas under Russian control in the Donbas. »What do you call that?« Putin asked eight years ago. »This already smells like genocide.« In light of Russia's 2022 gas supply stoppages against Germany and other European states, it seems bizarre that Putin called the failure to deliver gas genocide, but it precisely demonstrates his arbitrary and meaningless use of the word. In February 2022, he claimed that Ukrainian forces had killed so many civilians over the past eight years that »millions of people« were affected by genocide.

During my visits to Donbas and Ukraine since 2014, I regularly met UN observers and OSCE representatives in the region, who monitored the conflict area and recorded all ceasefire violations. They never told me anything about a »genocide.« The United Nations noted in a 2021 report that from 2014 to January 31, 2021, a total of 3,391 civilians, both Ukrainian and Russian citizens, died in the Donbas. Of these deaths, 58 percent were killed by mines or unexploded ordnance. Many people were killed during careless demining or while trying to scrap or recycle the mines and ammunition. Nearly 90 percent of the civilians killed died in 2014 and 2015, and the number has dropped sharply since. The total number of civilians killed in the region was no more than 26 in 2020 and 25 in 2021. The declining numbers prove beyond doubt that Putin's genocide claim is a lie. The months and year immediately preceding the Russian incursion offered no reason for intervention. The alleged »genocide« was for internal Russian propaganda to justify an illegitimate war of aggression. The same is true of Putin's claim that the Russian army was fighting fascists and wanted to »denazify« the country. In his first war speech on February 26, 2022, he called on Ukrainians to overthrow the »drug addicts and neo-Nazis« in the Kyiv government. The Jewish origins of Ukraine's president, Volodymyr Zelensky, to whom the »denazification« was primarily directed, made Putin's words seem absurd from the start. There were no right-wing extremists in the Ukrainian government. The far-right Svoboda party failed to win even three percent of the vote in the 2019 parliamentary elections.

Russian propaganda then latched onto the »Azov Fighters,« who fought against Russian troops in the east. The Azov battalion had indeed been founded in 2014 as a fighting group that included many right-wing extremists. After the Azov battalion was incorporated into the National Guard under the umbrella of Ukraine's Ministry of the Interior in late 2014, however, many right-wing extremists left the Azov Regiment, as it has henceforth been called. Its political founding father, right-wing extremist Andriy Biletsky, also left in 2016. Azov fighters today adorn themselves with symbols that are common in Germany on city coats of arms and among right-wing extremists, e.g., the Wolfsangel, a heraldic charge that consists of a Z-shaped hook. Russian propagandists deduce from this that the regiment is an ideologically fascist force that has remained unchanged since 2014. Numerous interviews and investigations have refuted these claims. Ukraine does not need to be de-nazified, and certainly not by Russia, a regime that has fallen for a destructive radical nationalist ideology.

*Third claim: The NATO states had promised to not expand NATO in 1990.*
The Russian president justified his military deployment in Eastern Europe in 2022 with a »broken promise« from the West. Before the

reunification of Germany in 1990, the Americans and Europeans agreed with the Soviet Union to not expand NATO eastward. In return, Moscow agreed to reunification. But then NATO was expanded. The Russian president fueled this highly topical dispute about a negotiation process that took place more than three decades ago in almost every speech, including his history lecture and declaration of war on February 21, 2022. Was there such a promise?

Putin's indictment targeted statements by German and American politicians in 1990. In February 1990, for example, then–US Secretary of State James Baker declared that »NATO jurisdiction« will move »not one inch eastward« with reunification, a formula Putin cited again in his attack speech. Putin also invoked then–NATO Secretary General Manfred Wörner, who said in May 1990 that no NATO troops should be stationed »beyond the territory of the Federal Republic.« Putin interpreted these statements as a binding promise never to expand NATO. This is wrong.

In 1990, the great powers negotiated the so-called Two Plus Four Agreement, which made German reunification possible. It was signed in September 1990 by the US, the Soviet Union, France, Great Britain, and the two German states. »What will become of NATO membership for a reunified Germany?« was the decisive question in the negotiations. This was precisely what Baker and Wörner were referring to and exactly what the negotiations were about. Baker declared in February 1990 that »the jurisdiction« of NATO would not extend to the territory of the former GDR after reunification. For US President George H.W. Bush, this was all too vague. He instructed his Secretary of State that he did not want to bring up the future of NATO at all. Neither did Gorbachev. The West finally accommodated Moscow by limiting NATO's presence. When the Two Plus Four Agreement was concluded in September 1990, Gorbachev got what he had insisted on: no nuclear weapons and no foreign troops would be stationed on the territory of the former GDR. There was no »promise,« as Putin says, or written note to back it up.

In Germany, proponents of the promise thesis like to point out that German Foreign Minister Hans-Dietrich Genscher, in a speech in Tutzing on January 31, 1990, suggested that NATO should not expand »closer to the borders of the Soviet Union, whatever happens in the Warsaw Pact.« In this keynote speech, Genscher presented a vision for overcoming the Cold War bloc confrontation through the dismantling of military alliances. A bold idea, but by no means a concrete proposal that became a coordinated Western policy. Moreover, Genscher was only a foreign minister of one of the two German states negotiating with the Four Powers, who still set the tone at the time. Even Chancellor Helmut Kohl did not agree with such thoughts. The question of a general expansion of NATO eastward was not part of the Two Plus Four negotiations on Germany.

The contemporary witnesses clearly contradict Putin's thesis. Horst Teltschik, Helmut Kohl's foreign policy advisor at the time, took part in all the talks and has assured that »there was no discussion of an expansion of NATO beyond Germany« in 1990. Gorbachev himself has spoken out on the matter several times, most recently in 2014 and 2019, and with unequivocal clarity. He told *Rossiyskaya Gazeta* that Baker, Kohl, and Genscher had spoken to him only about the question of »the expansion of NATO military structures and the stationing of Allied troops on the territory of the former GDR.« The question of a possible NATO expansion »did not come up at all.« His translator at the time, who accompanied him during all talks, confirmed this in 2018 on the Echo of Moscow radio station. It would have been »an absurdity« to talk about it, Gorbachev reiterated in 2019. The eastern counterpart to NATO, the Warsaw Pact, still existed—and its eventual end was not foreseeable. The reaction of the Polish head of government at the time clearly illustrates the mood in 1990. Tadeusz Mazowiecki had such strong reservations about reunification that he wanted to keep Soviet troops in Poland at all costs. This changed abruptly the following year.

For Putin, the disintegration of the Soviet Union in 1991 is the »primordial catastrophe« that ushered in an historical aberration, namely »US dominance« via NATO's eastward expansion. This, too, is a distortion. In February 1991, Lithuanians voted in a referendum for independence from the USSR. The disintegration of the Soviet Union had begun, and the events came thick and fast: at the end of February 1991, the Warsaw Pact states decided to dissolve the alliance. This raised the concrete question of a possible NATO expansion for the first time. Western politicians reacted with extreme restraint. In March 1991, British Prime Minister John Major rejected any form of NATO expansion. The French expressed similar views, as did German diplomats. According to a British memo, the German Political Director of the Foreign Office, Jürgen Chrobog, told Western representatives in March 1991 that NATO could not »offer membership to Poland and the others,« especially since NATO had not wanted to »expand beyond the Elbe« in 1990. All these statements were issued in March 1991 and not in negotiations with Moscow, but in a Western discussion. The Paris Charter had already been signed, as had the Two Plus Four Agreement. There was no »promise« in exchange for Russian concessions but an announcement: The West did not want NATO to expand eastward when the Warsaw Pact collapsed.

But why did it happen anyway? The impetus came from outside, through pressure from Central Europeans and the troubled development of Eastern Europe. In several countries, e.g., Moldova, Georgia, Armenia, and Azerbaijan, conflicts broke out, soldiers fired, and separatists split off. The Russian army played a sometimes very sinister role in these events. At the same time, Russia's internal development, i.e., the shelling of the parliament in October 1993 and the outbreak of the Chechen war in 1994, raised anxieties in Central Europe. In the elections of the mid-1990s, parties that advocated a clear orientation toward the West won in Chechnya, Hungary, and Poland. They pushed into NATO, while the debate in the West continued. A number of retired US politicians warned against the expansion, whereas US President Bill Clinton changed tack and wanted to open NATO. The Germans also campaigned for it, but only if Russia remained closely involved. This is why NATO agreed with Russia in 1997 on a Founding Act that regulated the security relationship and ruled out the stationing of nuclear weapons in future NATO member states. Under the terms of this Founding Act, Moscow agreed to the subsequent expansions.

Putin did not even mention this crucial condition in his long indictment of the West. In his speech, he very indignantly listed the accession countries: in 1999, the Czech Republic, Hungary, and Poland joined NATO, then in 2004, Estonia, Latvia, Lithuania, Slovenia, Slovakia, Romania, and Bulgaria. Putin downplayed his own role in this process. The 2004 expansion, in particular, could really have been a problem for him because it included three former Soviet republics, along with the Baltic states and, at the time, Putin was Russian president and Gerhard Schröder was German Chancellor. Both protested loudly against the US war in Iraq in 2003, but, and Putin may have forgotten this, not against NATO's eastward expansion. The German chancellor pushed it forward, and Putin let it happen. At a joint press conference on April 2, 2004, three days after the Baltics joined, Putin stood smiling next to Schröder and praised the »positive development« of Russia's relations with NATO. He went on to say: »With regard to NATO enlargement, we have no concerns about the security of the Russian Federation.« When the NATO secretary-general came to Moscow six days later, Putin said that »every country has the right to choose its own form of security.« Not a word about broken promises or a threat to Russia.

Putin's words in 2022 were contrary to those he spoke during the actual expansion and, above all, refuted his own claim of a promise.

But why? There had been no eastward enlargement of NATO to include former Warsaw Pact states since 2004. Instead, it was two other occasions, both involving independent Ukraine, that made Putin so angry in 2022.

At the 2008 NATO summit in Bucharest, Americans and Germans argued over an offer of membership to Ukraine and Georgia. Ukraine already had a security guarantee, the Budapest Memorandum of 1994, under which Russia took over Ukraine's nuclear weapons in return for a guarantee of Ukraine's »territorial integrity.« The US under President George W. Bush still wanted to make Ukraine a NATO offer in 2008, but German Chancellor Angela Merkel and French President Nicolas Sarkozy were against it. The result was a compromise: Ukraine and Georgia were to become NATO members at some point, but they did not receive the prerequisite, a Membership Action Plan. It was an invitation with no value.

German Chancellor Olaf Scholz referred to this aborted invitation in the days before the start of the war in February 2022 when he said that Ukraine's accession had not been under discussion at all. But for Putin, the sheer possibility was enough. In his speeches in the first half of 2022, he painted completely hypothetical scenarios. Ukraine was planning to produce nuclear weapons. The US would attack Russian territory from Ukrainian airports. They could set up missiles in Ukraine that would reach Moscow in four-to-eight minutes or less. The US was putting »the knife to Russia's neck.« This is what they intend to do today, just as they have expanded NATO, Putin said.

It is astonishing that such obviously imaginary threats made at least some sense to many politicians and journalists in Germany. They willingly tried to understand Putin in order to appease him. Ten days before the invasion of Ukraine, the chairman of the SPF parliamentary group, Rolf Mützenich, also attributed Putin's security concerns to »major mistakes« by the US administration under George W. Bush: the »invasion of Iraq,« the »farewell to arms control,« the »rejection of the war on terror,« and »distortions here in Europe.« Mützenich said of Russia's complaints, »I don't share certain concerns, but I can certainly understand them.« What now?

Politician Klaus Ernst of the Left Party and veteran SPD leader Klaus von Dohnanyi took a similar view, agreeing with Putin's assertion that NATO had broken its »promise of non-expansion« toward Russia after 1990. Some German journalists echoed this and questioned NATO's sincerity on enlargement—except during those crucial weeks in the spring of 2022, when Putin tried to spread his concocted legitimization of the war of aggression in Germany. Thus, Putin was able to sow doubts about NATO far beyond the Telegram channels of German contrarians and right-wing extremists, undermine the resolve of the German government, and spread his narrative in Germany.

In fact, however, he was concerned with something quite different when he wrote his speeches. To understand this, it is worth looking back at an important exhibition that Putin personally praised and recommended to every Russian. I visited it in 2015 at the exhibition grounds of the Ostankino Tower in northern Moscow. It was called »My History,« and it was a monumental history production first shown in Moscow and then moved around the country. »My Story« told the story of Russia's statehood from its medieval predecessor states in the 10th century through the first tsarist empire to the present. I saw a massive sense-making project of state-controlled nationalism organized by Putin's confessor, Bishop Tikhon Shevkunov. Millions of Russians have seen the show to this day. People queued for hours to get in. Schools, barracks, and universities organized excursions. In this exhibition, the church propagated a new »Russian idea,« which avowed four principles to visitors: the Russian people unite behind a strong leader, Russia is fought by the West, the people heroically bear their role as victims until the inevitable war, and (the bottom line) why Stalin is still needed today. In addition to display boards, movie screens, papier-mâché statues, paintings, and robes, the exhibition showcased a variety of maps. Each featured a scale showing the square kilometers of the East Slavic principalities and later the Tsarist Empire, as a »territoriometer.« This unique measuring instrument, used only in Russia, indicates the fortune and misfortune of the patriot. The scale recorded continuous expansion from the 10th century—with swings up and down—until the Soviet Union in 1945. In between, there were painful shocks of shrinkage, with the disintegration of Eastern Slavic principalities in the 12th century, in the period of turmoil at the beginning of the 17th century, after the collapse of the Russian Empire in 1917/18, and in the implosion of the Soviet Union in 1991. The exhibition organizers touched on current traumas of Russian elites and ordinary people. Everyone who examines the territoriometer of the various maps cannot help but notice that Russia had grown again for the first time since 1945 with the conquest of Crimea in 2014, thanks to Putin and the unity of the people. The lesson of the exhibition is that Russia's happiness and mission lie in expansion.

For Putin, history is a succession of glorious victories under military leaders who united the people and ignominious defeats in times of fragmentation. History is the glorious enlargement or shameful reduction of Russian territory. History celebrates triumphs, and it passes over losses. The most important reason why Stalin is not condemned under Putin as the greatest mass murderer in Russian history is the victory over Nazi Germany in World War II. As a result, the Soviet Union expanded enormously after 1945. The criminal Hitler–Stalin Pact, by which the dictators divided Eastern Europe between themselves in 1939, was justified by Vladimir Putin. He called the pact, which was the basis of the Soviet invasion of Poland and the Baltic states, a »defensive measure.« Thus, according to Putin, the criminal partition of Poland was also »defensive.« Soviet troops, he said, had only advanced at that time when the Polish government had »lost control of the territory.«

That whoever loses control will be gobbled up by others is a core element of Putin's understanding of international relations. Let us look back at his appearance before young entrepreneurs in June 2022. The meeting took place at the same fairgrounds as the Orthodox Church's history exhibition a few years earlier. Putin said that each country must »guarantee its sovereignty« on its own. This was a jab at Europeans under the US nuclear umbrella. »Either a country is sovereign,« Putin opined, »or it is a colony.« To control its own territory, he said, a country needs »technological sovereignty,« which Russia has with its hypersonic weapons. In addition, he discussed the »consolidation of society,« without which everything would fall apart. At this meeting, Putin outlined the conditions for Russia's modern expansion: nuclear weapons and an authoritarian-dictatorial society that follows its leader anywhere.

From Putin's point of view, this is also how Peter I, who hangs on the wall in his offices and to whom he so readily refers, is best understood. Peter did not have nuclear weapons, of course, but he did have an army and a fleet with which he expanded Russian territory. Yet Peter »took nothing away. He only took back!« opined Putin. »Brought back and strengthened, that's how he did it.« And since, in his view, he and Peter I stand in the same pantheon of Russian history, Putin also drew the oblique comparison with his campaign against Ukraine: »To all appearances, it also falls to us today to take back and strengthen. And if we assume that these values are the basis of our existence, then we will go far in solving the tasks ahead.«

Putin has truly come a long way in making a reputation for himself as a great destroyer. He invokes history, but, in fact, he breaks with all the traditions of the world that we know. His Darwinian war of aggression and nationalist radicalization have nothing to do with the development of Ukraine, imagined genocides, or supposed NATO promises of 1990. They only show what a frightening pathological state of mind he and Russia as a whole have developed under his more than

22 years of leadership. Putin proves how history becomes a deadly weapon that is costing thousands and possibly hundreds of thousands of lives. Putin did not have a comprehensible reason or even a cause for this war. This, above all, is proven by his speeches and essays. History never provides a moral justification for war.

# Special Operation

## How to wipe out Ukraine

Ukraine and the war seemed far away when the night train from Moscow rolled into the station in Pskov right on schedule. At six minutes after eight o'clock, brakes squealed and doors swung open. The first passengers who stepped onto the platform were in light jackets or light-colored trench coats and had rolling suitcases. These were Russians on a sunny spring day in May 2022. Then people who were in winter coats and thick sweaters climbed off the train carrying lots of bags and suitcases. A lot of suitcases. A woman from Pskov greeted these people very kindly, counted them, and led them from the platform to waiting transports. Sleepy but grateful, the people followed her. They were refugees, bombed out and displaced people from Ukraine. Thus, the war came to Pskov, an old Russian city with a mighty fortress on the northwestern border with Estonia.

Hundreds of thousands of Ukrainians have traveled through Russia since 2022. Women and men, children and seniors, they passed through the country of their attackers. It was not easy to meet these people despite their numbers. I wanted to talk to them because, as a correspondent in Moscow, it had not been possible for me to continue visiting Ukraine since the outbreak of the war, a trip that I had made regularly until February 2022. Russian state television broadcasted how wonderfully the Ukrainian refugees were housed, but my requests to visit these reception camps went unanswered by the authorities. A request to the Orthodox Church, which housed refugees, was refused for »scheduling reasons.« Then I got to know a Russian woman who helped the refugees. She and her comrades-in-arms wanted to remain unidentified for their safety. There were entire networks that took care of Ukrainians seeking help along the escape routes to Russia's western borders with Estonia and Latvia. There were Telegram groups where people exchanged ideas. There were refugee shelters that Russians provided for Ukrainians. There was help in the country that invaded Ukraine that came mainly from the citizens.

Putin's campaign against Ukraine had driven nearly a third of the Ukrainian population from their homes by the end of August 2022. Ukrainian Foreign Minister Dmytro Kuleba said in July 2022 that 1.9 million Ukrainians had been relocated to Russia—against international law, against their will, and by force. Some were mishandled. Some simply disappeared. In Russia, however, the TASS news agency cited a source from the security services who, in May 2022, was talking about over 1.5 million Ukrainian »refugees« in Russia. The Ukrainians spoke of »deportees,« whereas the Russians said »refugees.« The distinctions were seamless. Most Ukrainians who have entered Russia since the outbreak of the war came as refugees, but they were forced to leave. Whether they were forcibly displaced, injured, or frightened, they had to leave their destroyed homes, give up their old lives, and head to Russia because it was the last resort. It was an escape into the clutches of the enemy, from their destroyed cities into a broken country.

The Ukrainians drove through a Russia that supposedly has not been »at war.« The March 2022 censorship law forbade the media and people from speaking about »war« in Ukraine or demonstrating »against the war.« Russia waged an internal war against all those who were against the war. The Russian government enforced the censorship law with the same radicalism as it enforced the war externally and the stabilization of the country internally. While the Russian army bombed and shelled Ukraine, the security authorities in Russia completed the repression. Inside and outside could no longer be separated. Aggression in Russia was followed by aggression against the outside world and vice versa. Putin's nationalism by choice poisoned society and radicalized the entire country. The outbreak of war was the culmination of the Russian elite's pent-up anger, imagined humiliations, and need for vengeance against the Western world. They wanted revenge for the lost Cold War and the past 30 years on the bleachers of European history.

But this second attack since 2014 would not have been possible without the personal factor: Vladimir Putin. He made the decision to attack. In the previous chapter, we saw how the war was begotten in the ruler's historical fantasies of the mind and his completely unrestrained claim to power, without cause and without provocation from the outside. Putin even underlined his personal responsibility by having his closest subordinates and aides in the Kremlin lined up and stammering pledges of loyalty before the attack. This humiliating ritual made it clear that he, Putin, and no one else had started this war. It was a »war of choice,« his choice. And it became a war of complicity because so many Russians supported him without resistance.

The campaign began with a double surprise. First, Putin surprised the Ukrainian and Russian people with his order to invade that few had expected in the preceding weeks. Then the Ukrainians surprised Putin with an unexpectedly strong military force. The planned rapid capture of the capital Kyiv failed. At the end of March, the Russian army left Kyiv's outskirts, e.g., Irpin and Bucha, and these places became the cruel symbol of this Russian war right at its outbreak. Conditions in other areas conquered by Russia cannot be assessed as long as the Ukrainians have not regained control, but in Bucha, things were clear: the incoming Ukrainian soldiers, as well as the journalists who arrived shortly after, saw civilians murdered in the streets, disfigured corpses, devastated houses, a plundered town. A Russian conqueror had scrawled on a wall, »Who allowed you to have a nice life?« Bucha, among other Ukrainian towns, has gone down in history as a place of savage war crimes and extreme brutality.

In July 2022, Ukrainian Foreign Minister Dmytro Kuleba said the Russian war was a »genocide against the Ukrainian people.« There was ample circumstantial evidence to suggest »that Russia was not only waging a war of aggression against Ukraine,« but also committing »another genocide against Ukrainians in the course of it.« There it was again: the accusation of genocide. This time from the opposite side. Those responsible in Kyiv now turned against the Russian ruler this same accusation he had made without justification against Ukraine. American historian Timothy Snyder added his analysis of fascism, which he took for granted in Russia, to the accusation. What kind of war was Russia waging against Ukraine?

In Pskov, I listened to the refugees. The city was such a good place for this because the Estonian border was only about an hour's drive away by car. In this Russian provincial town, many Ukrainians who wanted to continue their flight to the West gathered here. Oksana Merezhko and her boyfriend, Oleg Fedorchuk, stood on the platform in Pskov. The slender 23-year-old blonde woman only had a thin black sports jacket and was visibly shivering in the morning chill. A Russian on the platform gave her a hoodie. She briefly refused, then she cried with emotion and exhaustion and put it on. Very slowly, she described her experiences, dramatic stories from destroyed Mariupol. The war came to her in the first days, she said. »At the beginning of March, I was standing on my balcony when a shell hit.« A splinter entered her back, and she was bleeding. At first, she was relieved that it was a small wound, »but then my left leg was paralyzed, and I had to go to the hospital.« There, they were told that the splinter had hit the nerves near her spine. Her treatment ended abruptly when the bombs hit. She found it hard to believe, she said, but Russian units attacked the hospital directly. »My friend picked me up, and we hid.« They moved from basement to basement in embattled Mariupol while Ukrainian troops were still resisting. They remained in the cellars as the Mariupol City Theater was bombed. More than 1000 people had sought refuge there, and more than 300 were killed in the attack. Oksana and Oleg realized that the Russians would occupy the whole city but destroy it first.

»We just wanted to get out!« But where to? »Going west was impossible, so we went to Russia.« On May 17, Oksana's parents drove her and her boyfriend, Oleg, east on a country road to the Russian border. Her parents wanted to stay in Mariupol; they lived on the outskirts of the city, where the disruption was contained. Oksana and Oleg took the risk of heading to Russia.

At the same time, Pavel Krivonos was hiding in the cellars of his neighbor's house. I met Krivonos not far from the citadel of Pskov weeks later. He was very depressed. The first thing he did was apologize for his mismatched shoes; he had lost one while traveling through Russia. The 56-year-old no longer had a passport, so he could not cross the border into the West. We sat down in a corner of a café. While he was talking, he kept looking around to see if anyone was watching us. The Russian secret service did not appreciate it when refugees met with Western journalists. He showed me photos of his former home in Mariupol. Hollow windows, sooty walls, a ruin fourteen stories high.

It was his birthday when the shelling began on March 13.

The first bullet hit the 13th floor, another the first, where it killed the owner of the apartment building. Smoke drifted through the whole house, and panic broke out. Krivonos lived on the 5th floor and left the apartment in a hurry with his wife, Yuliya. They passed a dead neighbor his age. He broke out in a cold sweat. They spent the first night in the garden in sub-zero temperatures and got up before 6 a.m. when the shooting started again.

While this was happening, I was watching reports on Russian television about the fighting in Mariupol. The propagandists traveling with the Russian army were filming and unabashedly showing the burned-out apartment buildings, but they claimed that the »fascists,« i.e., the Ukrainians, were shelling the Ukrainian civilian population. I asked Pavel Krivonos about it. He told me that they had been able to see exactly from where their house was attacked. The shells came from the suburb of Staryi Krim, where the Russian artillery was located. So, it was a planned shelling of the civilian population, an eviction by means of long-range weapons.

Pavel and Yuliya did not see their apartment again over the next few weeks. They lived in different cellars in the village. »We had to share two liters of water a day in a small room with 12 people,« Pavel recalled. Everyone got sick, in the stomach, in the head, in the gut. When the shelling subsided, he and his wife went back to their home. Their apartment, which they had renovated the year before, had been robbed and destroyed in the meantime. They tinkered with their car, an old Nissan. The plan was to get out of there. When the Nissan was ready to go, Pavel and his wife packed the trunk and back seat. They drove off, heading west into free Ukraine, but they quickly got stuck in front of checkpoints. There was no way across the front line, so they turned around, heading east. They too wanted to get to Russia, the last exit before Mariupol's final downfall.

Pavel Krivonos and his wife, and Oksana Merezhko and her boyfriend went to the country whose leaders had declared their intention to destroy their homeland. There were many explanations given from the president to the propagandists. When Vladimir Putin insisted that Ukraine could only be »truly sovereign in close partnership with Russia,« everyone knew, of course, that Ukraine »in partnership« had no chance of survival from Putin's point of view. Putin's coded death threats were often translated into very direct Russian by Dmitry Medvedev, the vice chairman of the Russian Security Council and ex-president. Over the course of the war, Medvedev evolved from Angela Merkel's former »partner in modernization« into a diabolical herald of the apocalypse. »Who actually says Ukraine will still exist in two years?« he asked in June 2022.

The state media prepared the Russian people for a new government policy: the obliteration of Ukraine. A good five weeks after the start of the war, in early April 2022, the well-known scientist and political adviser Timofey Sergeyev published an article titled »What Russia Should Do with Ukraine.« Sergeyev comes from the »methodological« circle founded by Georgy Shchedrovitsky, who strongly influenced the curricula and programs at Moscow's Skolkovo Institute, where many top Russian managers and officials were educated. This school sees values, humanity, and emotions as disruptive elements for administrative efficiency. Above all, the power of ideas is important. Society can be controlled from above. Sergeyev pondered how Russia could carry out the »denazification of Ukraine« demanded by Putin. Only a »victor« with »full control« over the country's institutions could accomplish the task. Therefore, he argued, a »Ukraine to be denazified cannot be sovereign.« This process could take less than a generation, he said, because Ukraine had »nazified« itself since 1991. The name »Ukraine« could not be preserved; »denazification« would inevitably mean a »de-Ukrainization« and further a »de-Europeanization« of the territories of »Little Russia« and »New Russia.« Ukraine could not remain as a nation-state because »Ukrainianism is an artificial anti-Russian construction« that has no »civilizational value.« Sergeyev wrote this in earnest.

This erasure program appeared on RIA-Novosti and was widely circulated in Russia and beyond. Sergeyev certainly spoke with knowledge of the country. He had formerly served as an advisor to a Ukrainian oligarch and then to Ukraine's pro-Russian president, Viktor Yanukovych. His ideas found their way into the daily sounds of Russian news broadcasts. On the state-owned RT channel, one of editor-in-chief Margarita Simonyan's star anchors, Anton Krasovsky, launched into a punitive speech about Ukraine spiced with Russian invective: »This country must cease to exist. We will do everything so that Ukraine will cease to exist. I will personally come and burn your constitution on the Maidan.« Krasovsky was later put on leave after he suggested locking Ukrainian children in huts and setting them on fire in October 2022. Simonyan herself felt inspired by the burning wheat fields and the seizure of Ukrainian grain by Russian troops, and she conjured possible famines at the St Petersburg Economic Forum in June 2022. To every Russian and Ukrainian, of course, »famine distress« immediately brings to mind the Holodomor, that catastrophic famine in Ukraine and neighboring areas wantonly triggered by Josef Stalin that killed millions of people. »People do want to eat,« Simonyan told an audience looking forward to the evening's gala dinner. She then proceeded with »a joke«: »All our hopes now lie in famine.« What was the punch line? »This means that the famine will now begin. Then they [the West] will lift the sanctions and be friendly to us.«

Public appeals to wipe out Ukraine increased in Russia in 2022 with each month of war. Live on Radio Komsomolskaya Pravda in early August 2022, host Sergei Mardan called for potentially lethal punishment of Ukrainian teachers who would not teach what the occupiers wanted in the occupied territories. Chewing on his fingers, Mardan suggested that they should be expelled from their homes, their families arrested, and the »good old Gulag« for the lot of them. »They want the Gulag, so give them the Gulag to really enjoy it,« Mardan barked into an orange microphone. »A small local gulag under the scorching sun of the steppe for all the students who have not yet learned to love our wonderful fatherland.«

There were many fantasies of extermination in Russia. Mass murder was spreading in people's minds. None of the presenters or authors of these fantasies were reprimanded for their words. Nothing was taken back. The destruction of the Ukrainian nation, culture, and state was part of the daily propaganda diet in Russia. It was from these fantasies and their implementation that Ukrainians had to flee, people like Pavel and Julija Krivonos, Oksana Merezhko, and Oleg Fedorchuk. Their city, Mariupol, burned in the extermination frenzy. They crossed the border into Russia at Taganrog, a Russian port city on the Sea of Azov. Russian officials and police led them directly to the »filtration camp.« These centers are familiar to many Ukrainians and Russians from the Chechen war. In these camps, Russian officials question and inspect Ukrainian refugees. It is particularly important for them to »filter out« former soldiers and members of paramilitary units from the masses.

»The camp was crazy crowded. I was standing among thousands of people; we had to wait for many hours,« Oksana Merezhko told me. When it was her and her boyfriend's turn, »they asked us about friends and acquaintances, whether any of them were in the Ukrainian army, whether we knew people from the territorial defense or from the intelligence service.« Her boyfriend, Oleg, was particularly targeted by the officers. He had to undress completely, was x-rayed, and checked for tattoos. Russian officers look closely for tattoos with Nazi symbols on Ukrainian prisoners and refugees. The idea is to support their ruler's claim that they are fighting Nazis in Ukraine. Oleg had no tattoos and got through. Pavel Krivonos had a similar fate. He was stuck in the camp for more than a day, but in the end was waved through because he had no tattoos and could credibly assure that he had not fought in the Ukrainian armed forces. At the exit of the camp, Oksana Merezhko and Oleg Fedorchuk as well as Pavel and Julija were released to Russia. Proceed at your own risk.

It doesn't always go so smoothly, a Russian aid worker in Pskov told me. The interrogations of the refugees are very hard:

»Unpack everything you have!«

»Open your cell phone!«

»Why are you wearing a camouflage uniform in the photo?«

»Who is this contact: 'Stepan Security Service'?«

»Who did you meet with on January 14?«

Women traveling alone can be grilled for hours about where their husbands were. Men are subjected to humiliating strip searches. They are always on the lookout for soldiers.

The Russian helper and Ukrainian refugees told me in unison that the Russian authorities would make offers to the Ukrainians: »We have an apartment and a job for you—in Vladivostok! And 10,000 rubles (170 euros) of starting money! Please sign here!« Often the refugees do not understand that Vladivostok is far away on the Pacific coast and that 10,000 rubles is a pittance. Anyone who goes there can never leave because there is not enough for a return trip. There are also offers in European Russia, in less-attractive provincial cities beyond Moscow and St Petersburg. But one could also reject these offers and simply be released onto the street. Then the refugees are left to fend for themselves.

Not all refugees are granted this mild indifference. Ukraine claims hundreds of thousands of deportees. For example, Mikhail Boyko, who told his story to reporter Andrea Jeska, who was researching for *Zeit* in Kyiv. Boyko was deported from a village near Chernihiv. He had been persuaded to drive around in his car to look for Russian soldiers. Boyko spent a few days exploring the area, something many civilians did in Ukraine. He hid in a forest near the village to look for suspicious vehicles and uniformed men.

This went well for fourteen days, then, on March 7, he saw Russian army vehicles. He called his liaison, and he notified the Ministry of Defense. But what he had not expected was that his phone was being tracked by the Russian soldiers. On his way back, a Russian tank blocked his way. They took him to their camp, where he was interrogated every day for a week. They wanted him to reveal the position and numbers of Ukrainian troops. Because he had a tattoo, the soldiers thought he was a Nazi. They beat him, and they threw him into a hole in the ground for two days. »When they got me out again, they said they would kill me and throw my body on the street in the village as a warning of what happens to partisans.«

After many interrogations, he was taken to the Kursk area of Russia, which is not far from the Ukrainian border. He was sent to a penal institution. There, they took samples of his blood, hair, and nails, and they shaved his head clean. »The interrogations took place in room 5.4; I will never forget that number. There were people from the intelligence services and the military police.« He said he was always asked the same questions, and when he said he knew nothing, they abused him with fists and electric shocks. »There were 24 of us in the cell, and every day they took some away and brought in new ones.« The other men in the room were also deportees from Ukraine. He lost hope of ever getting out of there alive. He was not allowed to make phone calls; his relatives considered him lost. That's what he thought.

He returned to Ukraine by pure chance. The Russian soldier who drove Boyko's car into the forest and burned it posted a video of the fire on Telegram. Mikhail's wife came across the footage and clicked through hundreds of videos in search of her husband. Eventually, she discovered where he was trapped. On their end, the villagers had captured a Russian soldier and offered him to the Russians in exchange for Boyko. Such man-for-man, directly-organized prisoner exchanges are happening more frequently. It is only because Boyko was very lucky that he could talk about his case.

Many deportees can no longer say anything or do not want to because they are stuck somewhere in Russia. The numerous cases of deported children caused a particularly big stir in Ukraine in 2022. Putin had signed a decree on the naturalization of Ukrainians at the end of May 2022 to make children whose parents were killed by Russian attacks and children in foster homes Russians. Orphans had been deported to Russia and the occupied territories, he said. This was reported by several Ukrainian organizations and the Minister for Reintegration of the Occupied Territories, Iryna Vereshchuk. There, they were given up for adoption, although they still had relatives in free Ukraine. This form of »child theft« was already a widespread means in 2014 of robbing Ukraine of another piece of its future after the annexation of Crimea. After Russia's annexation of occupied territories in southern and eastern Ukraine, thousands more children »became« Russian. Russian authorities denied these allegations. In March 2023, the International Criminal Court in The Hague issued arrest warrants against Putin and his children's envoy Maria Lvova-Belova for the abduction of children.

Yet reports of human rights violations committed by Russian forces filled archives as early as the fall of 2022. International human rights organizations the OSCE and the United Nations regularly reported abductions of Ukrainian citizens to Russia after field research in Ukraine. They reported torture during interrogations and mass shootings of civilians in more than 30 localities near Kyiv, Kharkiv, Chernihiv, and Sumy. They reported mass killings of prisoners, rape, looting of houses and apartments, theft of civilian property, and the murder of children and old people. They reported targeted shelling of train stations, shopping malls, civilian airports, hospitals, kindergartens, and schools by the Russian armed forces. The OSCE's Office for Democratic Institutions and Human Rights wrote in a report on July 20, 2022, that the »conduct of hostilities by the Russian Federation [...] has been characterized by a general disregard for the basic principles of distinction [of military and civilian targets], proportionality, and precautions set out by [international human rights conventions].«

These »may amount«, in the OSCE's very cautious judgment, »to war crimes and crimes against humanity.« The OSCE, of which Russia was a member, had to proceed diplomatically on these issues. The Russian government denied all allegations. But the evidence gathered by the international organizations made it clear that Russia was waging a war against the civilian population by deliberately demoralizing, terrorizing, and driving people to flee.

»Why?« I asked the army expert Sergei Krivenko with the Russian organization »Citizen. Army. Law«, who had to retreat abroad before the Russian authorities. Krivenko explained the »war crimes« by talking about the state of the Russian army. To him, the behavior was very reminiscent of the army's actions in Chechnya, where four main factors lead to criminal excesses. First, a tradition of impunity. Even in Chechnya, indiscipline and crimes against the civilian population were not prosecuted. Second, those in command neither paid attention to nor pursued such cases. Indeed, they not only tolerated them, but also participated in them. The NCO corps, in particular, was in a bad state. No one was held accountable for crimes, no one took responsibility for ensuring that such cases did not happen. Third, ordinary soldiers had no concept of the dignity or lack of dignity of their own actions. They were insulted and humiliated by their superiors across the board. And they treated war victims and prisoners in the same way. Krivenko does not believe there were specific orders for looting and rape. Rather, he says, they happen because of the absence of principles and orders to maintain discipline. Finally, he said, the whole operation was without a clear objective. The soldiers do not know exactly what they are fighting for in Ukraine. Are the Ukrainians now brothers, Nazis, or enemies in a civil war? Everything is unclear.

In the late summer of 2022, Russian deserters confirmed these assessments. The 33-year-old paratrooper Pavel Filatiev fought in Russian units that captured the Ukrainian city of Kherson at the beginning of the war. Filatiev wrote about and shared his experiences on social media. According to his accounts, the soldiers were very poorly equipped during the invasion of Ukraine. They lacked not only boots, but also functional weapons. The commanders and officers humiliated the rank-and-file with coarse language and nonsensical orders. As the Ukrainian resistance grew stronger and Russian losses increased, the »desire for revenge« awoke in some soldiers. Some tortured and mutilated captured Ukrainians, »cutting off their fingers and body parts,«

Filatiev wrote. Others went through the houses of Kherson and »hauled away computers and anything of value that could be found.« Another Russian soldier, 21-year-old Daniil Frolkin, fought in the Kyiv countryside with the 64th Motorized Rifle Brigade from Khabarovsk at the start of the war. He reported on social media about raids on residences, during which Russian soldiers stole alcohol, televisions, bicycles, and electronic equipment to later be sent back to Russia. He said that because the Russian army did not provide the teams with sufficient rations, the soldiers helped themselves in the homes of Ukrainians. After the shelling by Ukrainian fighters, retribution was taken against the civilian population; villagers were deliberately shot.

The framework for the brutality of the war was set by Vladimir Putin himself. The term »special military operation,« on the one hand, concealed the events and, on the other hand, announced worse things to come. Putin's ostensible war goal of »demilitarizing and denazifying« Ukraine and »bringing criminals to justice« showed that Ukraine was not a normal military campaign but a kind of final confrontation with Nazis and criminals. Putin did like to talk about Ukrainians as »brothers,« but only when they surrendered or declared themselves Russians. His talk of Nazis and criminals disfigured and dehumanized Ukrainian people, dehumanizing his enemy. Thus, it seemed that practically everything was permissible for the soldiers who would fight this end-of-times threat.

Many of the men who signed temporary contracts with the army are prone to indiscipline, Sergei Krivenko said. Many Russian soldiers come from small villages far from Moscow, where there are no opportunities for advancement and training is poor. The army is growing out of poverty. Across Russia, dilapidated towns where life hung on one factory are rich fields for the recruitment of commandos for the Russian army. When an assembly line shuts down, the young men find that enlistment into the army is an alternative that comes with social advancement. Soldiers receive a regular, livable salary and state-sponsored prestige in society. About one third of the young men choose to sign up for the army. Two thirds buy their way out, study, or work to avoid military service.

The area around Pskov, where I met the refugees from Ukraine, provides ample illustration. Parts of the Pskov region are among the poorest areas of Russia, despite their geographic proximity to the European Union. Pustoshka is a prime example of Russia's forgotten places, where depression is rampant. The town consists largely of peasant houses, many of which have no connection to the sewer system. A main street runs through the center of the town. There is a butcher, a small supermarket, several kiosks selling sweets and drinks, and a single run-down café. Young people pass the time on the street in front of the café because coffee and beer cost money. Anyone with a bit of income drives decked-out Ladas and leaves skid marks on the road—for fun. No sports club, no restaurant, no bar, and no recreational parks. The only small park is in front of the city hall and covered with plaques commemorating the Soviet era. Rightly so because nothing has happened in this little town since then. The last renovation of the town hall was under the Soviets. The railroad station has closed. The train from Moscow to Riga was canceled long ago. Pustoshka is a place where hardly any construction has been done since 1991, despite the oil and gas boom of the Putin era. One church was built with private money, nothing else. I met Alla Tafij, an administrative clerk at a kindergarten accessed by a steep, iron staircase. Jobs are rare in Pustoshka, she told me. Her husband was unemployed, and she earned the money in the family. She had sent her son to St Petersburg to study nuclear physics. »Men can sometimes work here in the old wood mill,« she said. Now that a new road was being built, »many people are helping with shovels and wheelbarrows,« she said. The salaries are low, 40,000 rubles, or the equivalent of about 600 euros a month. The armed forces have a magnetic effect on some men. In the Pskov region, the army advertised on posters that recruits receive one million rubles per six months deployment in Ukraine, which was about 16,000 euros. Some temporary soldiers had been here on leave to stay with their relatives and had come with money. Alla Tafij told me, »they left quickly.« Among them were soldiers of the airborne troops from Pskov.

The Pskov paratroopers, the 76th Airborne Division, are a unit renowned across Russia. They are sent on elite missions and are considered invincible until proven otherwise. In front of the barracks, there is a big poster and a gigantic monument. The poster depicts a paratrooper standing next to a tank under the caption, »Russia's borders end nowhere.« This is a Putin quote from 2016. The monument commemorates the greatest defeat of the 76th Airborne Division, when a detachment was ambushed by rebels in the Argun Gorge in Chechnya in March 2000. Dozens of soldiers died and were given mounds of medals to take to their graves. The division from Pskov is the pride of the Russian army. It fought in Chechnya as early as 1995 and in all of Putin's wars. The airborne troops have also been deployed in Ukraine. There, its soldiers were accused of crimes against humanity. The demand to join the airborne troops is low now. »Some time ago, the paratroopers were popular as an elite unit,« Alla Tafij said. »Today, it's war, and no one wants to go.« The campaign drags on, she said, and it becomes unpleasant. Many try to get into some school or go abroad to avoid being sent to Ukraine, she said. The news about the heavy losses in Ukraine spread among the population. The retreats of the Russian army from Kyiv and later from Kharkiv, called »regroupings« by the state truth-tellers, destroyed the myth of invincibility.

The state resorted to increasingly radical means. The newspaper *Pskovskaya Gubernia* reported in mid-August 2022, before the mobilization in September, that 20 prisoners from a penal colony had been sent to fight in Ukraine. And a Moscow human rights lawyer told me in August that the Russian army was going on a massive recruitment hunt specifically in penal colonies: murderers, bandits, and kidnappers were being called up. Later on, this became standard procedure. The Institute for the Study of War confirmed that National Guards and FSB agents were also being sent to the front lines to fight. But Vladimir Putin also targeted Russia's peripheries to fill the ranks from the ethnic republics. Buryats, Ingush, Dagestanis, and Chechens were fighting in Ukraine. Because too many Russians from the big cities avoided the army, the Russian ruler had men from the non-Russian republics fight, especially at the beginning of the war. Again, they came from impoverished towns and villages where the army offered itself as a last resort. This colonialist approach was strongly reminiscent of the Western colonial powers in World War I, when, for example, the British government used up recruits from the colonies on the front lines in the battles on the Somme in France and in Gallipoli in Turkey. In Ukraine, Buryats and Dagestanis died for Putin's colonization war against Ukraine. Funerals took place in gymnasiums and provincial cemeteries. Independent journalists were unwelcome and faced persecution from the secret service if they took pictures. The parents of the fallen were kept quiet with lots of money and medals for their deceased sons. A very successful Ukrainian offensive near Kharkiv in September became the turning point. Nationalists among the elite became agitated over a »special operation with the handbrake on.« Vladimir Putin imposed a »partial mobilization« of the entire country, what was really a staggered mobilization. Many young Russians received a draft notice. They had to fight side by side with Chechens, Dagestanis, Buryats, and foreign mercenaries from Syria against the Ukrainians.

    Russia is a multiethnic country. Traveling foreigners often do not stand out here; Ukrainians certainly do not. Ukrainian refugees from Mariupol could make fast progress on their trek. Oksana Merezhko and Oleg Fedorchuk continued their journey by train after the filtration camp in Taganrog. They always had their passports with them and could identify themselves anywhere to buy tickets. In the southern Russian city of Rostov-on-Don they bought train tickets to Moscow, from where they took the night train to Pskov. They found their way to the group that was being welcomed by the helpers at the station via Telegram.

Things did not go as smoothly for Pavel Krivonos. He started desperately looking for his passport at the Russian border. His wife, Yuliya, had her passport with her; his had been left somewhere in the burned-out apartment. But the Russian officials did not turn him away. They gave him a temporary travel document that allowed him to enter the country. »Welcome!« After the filtration camp, Pavel and Yuliya continued their journey by car.

»We mostly stayed in cheap motels,« Pavel said. »Many hotels do not accept Ukrainian refugees, so we had to spend the night in the forest.« They drove west in the old Nissan via Voronezh and Kursk. They were turned away at the Belarusian border. They tried the Latvian border next. Turned away again because he had no passport. Desperation grew until he came across the Russian helpers in Pskov via Telegram, who put them both up in a room in Pskov. There, Pavel and his wife decided to go their separate ways. She took her passport across the border to Estonia, then on to Latvia. He would see what worked. The parting broke his heart.

Russian aid networks are important for Ukrainian refugees. Most are private initiatives or church-based. One aid worker in Pskov told me that it is crucial to log on to the Telegram channels. After arriving in Pskov, the refugees drove in vans to a building in a backyard of the old Russian city. In a Protestant church, the helpers first explained the rest of the journey. Food was distributed, the refugees were taken to exchange currency, and they were assigned rooms for the night. Those who needed money received some assistance. The helpers made calls for them and prepared them in detail for the great journey west. Oksana Merezhko and Oleg Fedorchuk were excited. The very next morning, they were to head for the Latvian border, which was just over an hour away by car.

It is Russian soldiers who are shelling Ukrainian cities. It is Russian citizens who help the refugees. In Ukraine, Ukrainians are shot in the streets, while in Russia, Ukrainians are allowed to travel unmolested. The coexistence of destruction and care seems contradictory. Is this really fascism, as historian Timothy Snyder writes? I see significant differences. The Russian attackers did not operate industrially organized extermination camps like the Germans in World War II. Eastern European Jews could not have escaped, unmolested, from under the German reign of terror to England on trains through Germany. Nor could Poles, Belarussians, Ukrainians, and Russians have escaped the hell of German occupation via Germany during World War II. The Russian war is not directed against the Ukrainians as a »race« or as »subhuman« people. Unlike the German Nazis, the Russians in Ukraine today are not out to search and destroy the different. Instead, as contradictory as this may seem, they are shooting to ensure that Ukrainians remain as brothers and sisters, indistinguishable from Russians. Residents of the Donbas who submit and join Russia are very welcome. This is not reminiscent of Jews and Eastern Europeans under Nazi rule. Only when people insist on being different from Russians, that is, when they deny the assumed closeness and sameness, are they threatened with destruction and annihilation. This is the poisonous cocktail in Putin's speech about the united and indivisible people of Ukrainians and Russians, the endless siren song of »our brothers« and Kyiv as »a common cradle.« Because as an independent people, Ukrainians are worse than enemies: they are traitors! Russia wages war against brothers who don't want to be brothers and who have the courage to defend themselves. Thus, Ukraine must not be.

The Russian campaign against Ukraine cannot really be understood by recourse to Western European–style fascism. In fact, the brutality of warfare is a Russian and a Soviet tradition. In the 16th century, Ivan IV, called »the Terrible,« had the self-confident population of the trading city of Novgorod massacred because they wanted to be

»different,« namely Novgorodians. He doubted their unlimited loyalty. Then too, the alternatives were assimilation or annihilation. In the 18th and 19th centuries, Russian troops conquered the Caucasus in a merciless war. The Circassians, who did not want to be Russians, were driven out, starved, and murdered in an extermination campaign that lasted 100 years. Circassians in Turkey and other parts of the world still remember the genocide of their ancestors, during which up to 97 percent of the Circassian population had to leave or die. For Russian national-patriotic historians, however, it was merely a »migration« to the Ottoman Empire. Chechnya and other areas of the Caucasus were conquered in the 19th century by similar means: plunder, rape, and the expulsion, enslavement, and torture of villagers and burning of their homes.

The Russian colonial wars continued in a new form under Soviet rule. The conquest and domination of non-Russian territories of the Soviet Union often degenerated into merciless warfare against the civilian population. The Holodomor—a famine with millions of victims caused by the violent Soviet confiscation of grain and destruction of farms in Ukraine and the ban on migration from the famine areas accompanied by the systemic elimination of Ukrainian culture under Stalin—was an example of this. The Federal Parliament recognized the Holodomor as genocide in the fall of 2022. Kazakhstan and the southern regions of Russia experienced similar horrors. Stalin had the Chechen people deported to Central Asia in 1944. He also deported Crimean Tatars, Greeks, Armenians, Volga Germans, Kalmyks, and Balkans. From 1940, he conquered the Baltic states with the greatest brutality and sent considerable parts of the population to labor camps.

The modern Chechen war of Vladimir Putin stood in this dark tradition of Soviet and Russian colonial wars against the neighboring peoples. The crimes in Bucha and Irpin and the mass graves of Izium in 2022 were reminiscent of Putin's first war from 1999 on. At that time, the Russians spoke of »Bespredel.« The word originally referred to the collapse of state structures and lawlessness in the transition from the Soviet Union to Russia in 1991, but it was also a term to describe the nature of warfare in the Caucasus. Russian soldiers went into this war completely unprepared and encountered fierce resistance. The Russian army then unleashed a merciless war against the civilian population. Villages were razed. People were displaced. Russian forces besieged and bombed Grozny until not a single house or mosque was left standing.

Russia does not follow fascist models. It has its own colonial history. Unlike Western European powers, Russian leaders colonized neighbors and not distant lands. More than three decades after the opening of the archives and the reconsideration of the past at the end of the 1980s, the country shows itself incapable of breaking away from its historical path. Putin has cut off any critical examination of Russia's and the Soviet Union's history. The reappraisal of the darker sides of Russian and Soviet history, which began so promisingly under Mikhail Gorbachev and Boris Yeltsin, has been stifled by Putin in the spirit of the 1991 putschists, who did not like any of this. Today, the toxic legacy of the Russian-Soviet empire and its glorification by the regime threaten not only neighboring countries but also the remnant empire itself. Incapable of self-criticism, incapable of mourning, and incapable of self-correction, the Russian government, with the support of a considerable part of the population, is going down the path of annihilating a neighboring state, believing itself to be completely in the right.

Is it a genocide, as the Ukrainian foreign minister said? A study by the Raoul Wallenberg Centre for Human Rights and the New Lines Institute for Strategy & Policy found that Russian warfare bore the central characteristics of intentional genocide. Otto Luchterhandt, a Hamburg professor of Eastern law, examined the Russian conquest of Mariupol and concluded that the Russian attacks »fulfill the objective and also the subjective elements of the crime of genocide.« He pointed out that the Soviet Union had also acceded to the UN Convention on the Prevention and Punishment of the Crime of Genocide of December 1948. This convention protects the integrity of groups from destruction, whether national, ethnic, racial, or religious. The citizens of Mariupol are part of a group, Luchterhandt says, and it is precisely such groups that the convention targets.

On the one hand, Luchterhandt sees the destruction of Mariupol as genocide. The Russian government denied such accusations and insinuated that the Ukrainian side had perpetrated the attacks. Putin, on the other hand, accused Ukraine of genocide at every opportunity. He provided no conclusive evidence for any of these allegations. Many institutions are gathering evidence for the investigation of Russian war crimes. Ukrainian prosecutors, German lawyers, journalists and research teams, the International Criminal Court in The Hague, a joint investigative team of Ukraine, the Baltic states, Poland, and the prosecutor of the International Criminal Court as well as UN institutions are documenting the crimes. They are also looking at possible violations of international law by Ukrainian soldiers. This needs to be said because Russian diplomats accuse them of one-sidedness. This book was written while many crimes were taking place and investigations were ongoing. Russian tactics to make Ukrainian cities uninhabitable in an all-out air war by deliberately destroying water supplies, power plants, substations, and utility lines will also be examined in the context of attempted genocide. The verdict of the international investigations and tribunal on the Serbian capture of Srebrenica in 1995 were decisive in classifying it as genocide. Field research of this kind will also be relevant in the future evaluation of the crimes in Ukraine.

The refugees from Mariupol survived the extensive destruction of their city. Oksana Merezhko and Oleg Fedorchuk took a ferry from Riga to Travemünde a few days after our meeting. They wanted to build a new life in Germany. Pavel Krivonos was lucky. A neighbor found the missing passport in the ruins of his apartment and sent the document with a trustworthy fugitive across Russia to Pskov. It worked. With his passport, helpers were able to bring Pavel Krivonos to the border. At Estonian passport control, he was greeted by Russian-speaking helpers in Estonia who were also part of the network. Dazed by his unexpected happiness, Pavel left the country of tormentors and helpers. In Latvia, he reunited with his wife Yuliya again.

Of the half million people who lived in Mariupol in February 2022, only one in five remained.

# Planet Putin

# Russia seals itself off

It was the summer of great illusions. On a warm Sunday in Moscow in 2022, I saw the dancers. They were turning circles on the banks of the Moskva River. A small band played pop songs, and the couples twirled on a wooden parquet in Gorky Park. Many onlookers stood around. A ten-year-old girl in pink sneakers licked an ice cream. Her mother drank cappuccino, and her father carried her little brother on his shoulders. Children jumped through small fountains that shot out of the ground every minute. Benches invited people to linger. Cafés and restaurants beckoned. Young women in summer dresses sat on the riverbank, laughing loudly as they watched the party boats. On the red-painted path behind them, people in T-shirts rode into the sunset on bicycles, hoverboards, skateboards, and e-scooters. The city's magical silhouette glowed in garish colors from candy yellow to deep red. This is what Moscow, sanctioned by the West, looked like on a day of war in the late summer of 2022 in Gorky Park.

    I gazed at an exceptionally massive Stalin-era building on the other side of the Moskva River. In the Russian Ministry of Defense, orders were issued during those days to flatten the Ukrainian city of Lysychansk in a firestorm. The planners of the extermination worked right across the river from the dancers. Not 200 meters away. On our side of the river, four historic tanks formed a square. The T-34 models from World War II had been set up by the city government not to shoot but to be climbed. Children crawled over the old, iron monsters. In front of them, a new party boat was just leaving, and people were standing at the railing with their champagne flutes. Gloria Gaynor's »I Will Survive« sounded like mockery from the ship's loudspeakers.

These impressions stirred me every time I visited that summer. Gorky Park is the starting point of my bicycle trips along the Moskva River, and I live only five minutes away by bike. On this summer evening, I was perhaps a little too excited as I biked home from the park and encountered a neighbor in the lobby.

»Well, Mikhail, how are you?« She had just seen the television news on the state channel Rossiya 1 and greeted me excitedly. »It's good that these Nazis are being cleaned up now,« she said, nodding vigorously. Normally, I listen a lot during such conversations and let people talk. But today I didn't feel like listening; I felt like standing up to them.

»How do you know they're Nazis?« I asked.

»They've been committing genocide against Russians for seven years.«

»That's just made up. The Ukrainian president is Jewish himself, and some of his ancestors died in a real genocide, in the Holocaust.«

»Still, they're all Nazis!« she hurled back. »I come from southern Russia, and I know exactly what kind of bandits live across the border in Ukraine. Muggings, robberies, scams, murder!«

»But isn't that where the police have to step in—instead of the army?«

»Well, that's why this is a limited special operation! If only the West wouldn't arm the Nazis, then all this wouldn't take so long. That Biden, the old evil old man, is behind this!«

»Uh, it's probably the Russians who are waging war in Ukraine, not the Americans. The Americans had warned about war for a long time. And in the winter of 2021, no one believed them, not even the Ukrainians themselves.«

»This guy Biden needs to be careful he doesn't get a nuclear missile.«

»Then I guess Moscow would get one too,« I said, immediately biting my tongue.

Short pause. »Well, that's fate then. Putin always says that if Russia will cease to exist, then the world will cease to exist. Isn't he right?«

Completely unnerved, I wished her a nice evening watching TV and went to my apartment to simmer down. Gorky Park and my irritated neighbor, the two sides of Moscow within an hour, it was too much. But that's what Moscow was like in the summer of 2022: under the veneer of peacefulness, an aggravated aggressiveness suddenly lashed out.

The contradiction is not easy to explain. Russia also invaded itself with the war against Ukraine. Vladimir Putin initiated a new phase of self-pity, depression, and pathological aggressiveness. But this was hidden behind a grandiose staging of normality. Putin and the propagandists did a lot to rally people behind them and, at the same time, keep them quiet. From afar, they painted a picture of Russia's heroic struggle for survival against the West in Ukraine. In everyday life in Russia, the authorities pretended that the country was experiencing a period of unshakable peace. Thus, they insulated the country from reality while buying support for their brutal special operation. Putin tried to establish a hermetically sealed »information space.« He made an historic break with almost all European countries. There were no more flights to Russia from Europe, and only a handful of border crossings were still open. The country became increasingly isolated.

I would like to describe the contradictory life on Planet Putin from February 2022 to August 2022, the month before the great mobilization of men in September. What my neighbors, friends, and acquaintances thought. Where opposition flourished. What people were afraid of. How power intimidated them. How they denounced each other. Why they gave in to the illusion of peace and superficial Westernism and did not want to see reality. And how Putin tore apart this illusion when he threatened to lose the war.

There was less and less traffic coming out of Russia, but also less and less going in. Western tourists stayed away. Western foreigners, businesspeople, activists, and artists alike left the country. Others were expelled, especially diplomats and correspondents of Western media. Deutsche Welle was declared a foreign agent and had to close its Moscow office. Many English reporters and American journalists left the city forever. I myself lived in constant uncertainty about how long I would be tolerated in Russia. I felt harassed anyway. The new correspondent visas were only issued for three months instead of one year. Foreigners had to undergo regular health checks for tuberculosis, HIV, and leprosy if they stayed longer than a few months. I often did not even receive an answer to interview requests from Russians who I did not know from before. Muscovites no longer liked to talk to Westerners.

At first glance, Planet Putin looked quite normal and almost like Russia before the annexation of Crimea. There were many foreign car brands on the streets, especially German brands. Muscovites flocked to the shopping malls and populated the downtown cafes. Contrary to what some American newspapers said, the grocery stores were well stocked. The products came from Russia's regions, Turkey, the Caucasus, and Central Asia. The Moscow city government invested its rich budget in streets, historic lanterns, and sidewalks until everything shone. But the most important thing for people's sense of stability was that the ruble rose strongly against the euro and the dollar. The Russian government had taken the ruble off the world markets right after the war began and was now able to manipulate the inconvertible currency with impunity and without consequence. The central bank pulled the string from above to establish a bearish ruble exchange rate against the dollar, with which Putin wanted to send two signals to the people:

»We are winning!« and »We too can fight big wars without having to limit ourselves. Like America!«

In the first weeks of the war, I arranged to meet some old Moscow friends. After the joyful greeting, I began to ask them how they felt about the war. The Russian language offers an appealing menu of evocative euphemisms that can be translated as »events,« »incidents,« and »occurrences.« »Special operation« is another such word. I quickly agreed with almost all my friends that »war,« »attack,« and »raid« fit much better as descriptions of these incidents. With a friend who works for a raw materials company and does not want to see his name in print, I could not talk so straightforwardly. When we met in a nice café not far from the Cathedral of Christ the Savior, I asked him how he was doing. We talked about life for a long time. But when we got to talking about the »events,« he immediately went on the defensive. He could not understand why there were so many Nazis running around in Ukraine today and why the West was supporting them.

I asked him where the Nazis were. He told me that they were in the government and in the Azov regiment, which adorns itself with fascist symbols. I contradicted that there were no Nazis in the government and that the Azov regiment had separated itself from the political right-wing extremists since its affiliation with the Ministry of Interior

I had one question for him: »Why are Russian soldiers standing in an independent country that has never threatened anyone and whose population does not welcome these soldiers?« There is no real answer to this question in Russia. There are only excuses. And I heard them now from my acquaintance: Because Ukraine is ruled by Nazis. Because the West supplies weapons to the Nazis. Because Ukraine had committed genocide and many children had died. Because Ukraine wants to build nuclear bombs again. Because the Americans have turned Ukraine into an »anti-Russian project.«

I heard the entire program of Russian news broadcasts. It hurt. My acquaintance had been to Germany several times. He knew two foreign languages and had a good education. I asked him if he really believed all that. »It is being reported,« he said. Well, I could tell him about a few channels where things were told quite differently by Russian journalists I read and hear about on Telegram. They would report what was really happening without the Kremlin dictating the text. All he had to do was connect through a proxy server and he could read and listen to it on his cell phone. He raised his hand defensively. He knew all about them. They've run off to Riga, Vilnius, and Tbilisi and are now making anti-Russian propaganda. They were like the Ukrainians: »national traitors.« I kept silent. This was a label from the arsenal of the brutes. It comes from the Stalin era and was applied in the totalitarian dictatorship to any who were not toeing the party line. To be a national traitor is far more serious and terrible than being an »opponent« or »enemy.« These are people who are Russians or brothers or relatives, but who defect to the other side. I changed the subject and asked if he already had plans for summer vacation.

»The Crimea,« he said.

»What else,« I said. Then, as usual, we argued about who would pay the bill and said goodbye. We were to meet again.

Olaf Scholz said in August 2022, »It's Putin's war. It's not the Russians.« He may have meant that in a de-escalating and internationally understanding way, but he was still wrong. Russians supported this war, Russians like my friend who works for a raw materials company. If the official opinion polls of the summer months in 2022 are to be believed, it was even around 80 percent who supported their ruler and his campaign in Ukraine. And according to unofficial estimates, it was definitely a clear majority of Russians.

This also had to do with the summer illusion. Russia went through four phases of coping with the war in 2022. In the first days after the invasion, there was a mild state of shock. Hardly anyone had expected this war; almost all Russians to whom I spoke until early February 2022 said Putin would not go that far. After the first shock, people dared to take to the streets in Moscow and Russia's big cities during the second and short phase. They protested in small groups, shouting »No to war!« and holding up signs objecting to the war. This phase was resolved by a spreading paralysis from fear that ushered in a period of sustained repression. Most of the Russian population settled into the new conditions of sanctions, howls of war on television, and a normal life at home and on the streets, until mobilization came in September. Then everything changed.

Many people repressed the war as a distant, secondary reality. The campaign became a television event that was no more of a preoccupation than the war in Iraq was for the Americans in 2003. While the missiles were hitting Ukrainian city centers, Russia seemed protected and invulnerable. At least until explosions in Crimea in August 2022 destroyed aircraft, ammunition, and weapons, and the Ukrainian government scoffed that someone must have been smoking in the wrong place. But displacement from attention is not enthusiasm. Therein lies the big difference between the occupation of Crimea in 2014 and the invasion of Ukraine in 2022. »The invasion of Ukraine did not trigger patriotic euphoria among Russians,« Lev Gudkov of the independent polling institute Levada said in July 2022. While 51 percent of respondents felt »pride« over the Russian army's advance in Ukraine, almost as many, 47 percent, were »worried« because many civilians and soldiers died and there was a lot of destruction and suffering. Gudkov also noted that a large majority were in favor of the »special operation.« During the Crimean annexation in 2014, there was jubilation, whereas in 2022, fear dominated. In 2014, Russian »little green men« just walked in and took control, whereas in 2022, thousands of Russian soldiers died in a war of attrition. In 2022, Russian soldiers experienced all the bitterness of war in the capture of Ukrainian cities that mean little to most Russians.

In Moscow and St Petersburg, neither flags nor the operation symbols Z and V could be seen on balconies, cars, and houses. Even the millions of army T-shirts were sold mainly in smaller provincial towns and not in the big cities. Although the propagandists on state television shouted at people every day that Russia was now fighting for survival, no readiness for action could be detected. Everyone retreated into their own niches, and all forms of public discussion died out. The era of great silence began. This had two consequences.

On the one hand, the small cardboard »No to War« signs and the protests disappeared. On the other hand, even the hooting, flag-waving support was considered rather embarrassing in Moscow. The support for the war in Ukraine was more coerced than deeply felt among many big-city dwellers. Even my commodities trader acquaintance asked me not to mention his name. He felt that repeating the pre-punched formulas and his support for the »operation« was unimaginably embarrassing. Please no publicity!

This is exactly what a Russian, with whom I spoke at length in the early spring, asked me to do. He worked as a sound engineer and had lived abroad for several years. When we got to talking about the »incidents,« he turned out to be the counterpart of the raw materials man. »I am very worried because we have become hostages of a psychopath,« he told me. Vladimir Putin has grave issues: he is short and suffers from a Napoleon complex. In general, he said, the people in the Kremlin have a »huge inferiority complex« that was now the problem of the whole country. »They are lying to all of us.«

The sound technician had little use for the excuses I had heard from my commodity acquaintance. »We are the aggressor country, we have invaded a neighboring country,« he said. Ukraine is an independent state, he said, and it can go wherever it wants. It can also join any alliance it chooses for itself, he added. He thought nothing at all of the »paranoia« of the Russian elite to keep Ukraine from joining NATO. This war »is a crime against humanity.« There was no reason for it and no justification. Ukrainians, he said, were invaded in cold blood, and their cities are now being attacked with missiles and artillery. He said he was ashamed of this. »How can you even travel the world as a

Russian with this shame? I understand if Russians are now discriminated against in the West.«

The sound technician had a proxy server installed on his equipment. He did not watch state television, but he followed certain journalists and experts whom he trusted. BBC, Facebook, YouTube, and Telegram were his essential media, with which he broke through the »closed information space« of which the Russian government dreamed. He knew this put him in the minority: »I hear the conversations on the bus; people have become zombies.« By this, he meant people who supported the Z-symbol operation and believed what state radio served them. »Their consciousness is completely poisoned by propaganda,« the sound technician told me. »They should just turn off the TV for a month, then they will see the world with different eyes.« Russia had actually already lost the war, he said. But then power would take revenge on all those who opposed the war. »I'm afraid that at some point this country will face civil war; too much poison is accumulating.«

Neither the commodity man nor the sound engineer was a trained political analyst or professional Putin interpreter. They were characteristic representatives of the Russian middle class, and a rift divided them. The raw materials man considered people like the sound engineer to be »traitors,« and the sound engineer saw the other man as a »zombie.« Russia's superficial calm has a lot to do with the fact that they did not meet, talk, and argue in public. They did not want to be named. They disappeared, they said goodbye to the public, and they let the propagandists do the talking. This was deliberate. The state stopped not only anti-war demonstrations, but all rallies that were not initiated by them. Any free movement of the people was unwanted. Everyone knew that the regime had become a dictatorship and left its citizens no choice. The hybrid epoch of political semi-slavery between electoral autocracy and dictatorship of the past decade was finally over. Russia demanded unambiguity from the Russians. The special operation consumed its citizens.

I met Dmitri Trenin, the longtime director of the Carnegie Moscow Center think tank, in June 2022. He was someone who frequently spoke out in public. We had known each other well since the 1990s, and I always appreciated his astute analysis and global view. As a former officer in the Soviet army, he never lost sight of Russian interests. Especially after the annexation of Crimea in 2014, he held rather edgy patriotic views, but he soon after returned to a sober view of Russian politics. By June 2022, however, independence was over. The Ministry of Justice had ordered the closure of Carnegie Moscow. The Center was part of a whole series of nongovernmental organizations and think tanks that were closed down. Independent thinking was no longer in demand in Moscow. For Trenin, this marked the end of his life's work for now.

We sat in his office, located in an historic two-story building in the shadow of the huge Ministry of Foreign Affairs, a few days before his forced departure. »It's the time for big decisions,« Trenin told me. He, too, had to position himself as for or against Russia, he said. He could well understand when his colleagues at the institute had left the country. »I chose Russia,« he said. He said that he was a veteran officer, so »in this situation, I don't say or write anything that will harm the Russian army.« He hoped for some self-purification of Russia through the military operation. The country had suffered greatly from corruption and enrichment of the elites, he said. Now a great many would have to fight; the existence of the people and of Russia as a great power was at stake. This is the end of enrichment, he said. Trenin looked at me. »I have my life here, my apartment, my dacha.« He said he did not want to live abroad as an emigrant, where no one was waiting for him. »I'm needed here.«

Trenin stayed, and his much younger colleagues went to the West and continued working there. For them, there was nothing left to write about in Russia. With the surveillance and the trials against anyone who spoke of »war,« free, independent work was no longer possible. I felt this when I met with other political scientists and historians who were friends of mine and on whose judgment I had always relied. I was not allowed to quote anyone.

A Moscow political scientist told me that she observed self-censorship and opportunism among her colleagues. »Scientists are not revolutionaries,« she said, shrugging her shoulders. Although most are probably against the war, faculty retreated to the ivory tower to dodge the big issues and write about the innocuous. They provided the students with several theories or approaches to choose from and let them decide for themselves. They avoided contact with Western universities and stopped traveling. »I'm also just teaching and refraining from publishing currently.« A wave of synchronization rolled over Russia's universities and institutes starting in 2022. With dismissals and intimidation, teaching was switched from cognition to patriotism. Like many female professors, she feared being denounced at some point. Fear was rife at schools and universities. Denunciation was a new, popular sport in the summer of 2022. Such small but shocking reports accumulated in the local media:

- Irina Gen, an English teacher in Penza, was reported by her students for making critical remarks about the campaign in Ukraine. In the criminal proceedings, she faces a heavy fine or imprisonment for up to ten years.
- English teacher Marina Dubrova from Korsakov talked about the operation with a small circle of students after a school lesson. A student recorded her remarks on the phone and forwarded them to the police. She was fined 30,000 rubles (the equivalent of 500 euros) and faces prison if she repeats the offense.
- A Moscow woman denounced her husband because he told her in confidence that he planned to travel to Ukraine

and support the resistance there. She called the police. The man was picked up in his own apartment.
- A Moscow mother betrayed her 26-year-old son to the security services because he allegedly wanted to avoid military service. His business project, which he had given as the reason why he could not do military service, had failed, but the army knew nothing about it. His mother reported the failure to the Ministry of the Interior.
- A husband in the Gorky-10 settlement west of Moscow denounced his wife for making critical remarks about the Russian government and subverting their child. The police started an investigation.

Anyone who got caught up in the mills of the Russian prosecutors needed a good defense lawyer. Former journalist Maria Eismont, mentioned above, trained as a lawyer because it made her better able to protect the persecuted as what she had always been: a courageous defender of human rights. She did not hide her name. She fought very openly against the regime's violations that could be proven on the basis of Russian laws. In December 2021, she defended the human rights society Memorial against the liquidation ordered by the government. She was the lawyer for MP Elena Russakova, who was charged in April with violating censorship laws. The trial was open to Western journalists.

Russakova headed the Council of Deputies in the Gagarinsky district in Moscow and was a member of the liberal party, Yabloko. This party was no longer allowed to run in the nationwide Duma elections, but it was still allowed to operate at the municipal council level, until that too was revoked. What was Russakova accused of? A few days after the outbreak of war, on March 1, the municipal council under her leadership adopted an appeal. The council described the operation a »disaster for Russia« and called for peace negotiations. But it is not that easy to call for peace in Russia. Russakova was tried under the new censorship law, which criminalizes »false news« about the armed forces. She was ordered to pay the equivalent of 2,500 euros. Eismont defended her on appeal. The prosecutor presented the charges in a small courtroom. He accused liberal politician Russakova of violating the law combating extremism. Maria Eismont dismantled the indictment piece-by-piece. »Extremism« was not present in the case of her client. She had called for peace, she said. »Is that extremism?« Moreover, she had not been convicted of extremism at all. The prosecutor then began nervously searching through the files. »No,« Eismont continued, Russakova had been convicted of violating the censorship law. »But in doing so, law enforcement is breaking the law,« Eismont pointed out to them. For the appeal was dated March 1, but the censorship law was from March 4. And in the appeal, the armed forces were not mentioned at all. So Russakova could not have violated censorship. »There was no unlawful act,« Eismont concluded.

In any ordinary court in the world, Russakova would have been acquitted immediately had the investigation been so sloppy. Not in Russia. After the pleas, the judge retired for less than ten minutes to deliberate. Then she returned to the courtroom with a stack of files that had apparently been prepared earlier. From it, she read: »Elena Russakova is found guilty of violating the law on unlawful acts of discrimination against the Russian armed forces.«

The lesson of the trial: If the powers that be want a conviction, then the court will convict. And no higher appeal can save the defendant. In the past, Russian victims of justice could appeal to higher courts and, in the end, to the European Council. Today, this is not possible. Russia has not been a member of the European Council since March 2022 and refuses to implement international decisions. Planet Putin is outside any earthly jurisdiction.

The regime's totalitarian grip tightened as the war continued. In the summer of 2022, trials of female politicians, human rights activists, and journalists multiplied. In the northwestern Russian city of

Pskov, between two court dates, I met the respected Yabloko politician and human rights activist Lev Schlossberg. Of course, he was also concerned with »discrimination against the armed forces.« He had taken the liberty of commenting on YouTube about the Russian capture of Bucha in March 2022. He did not, however, say »crime,« nor did he attribute the acts to the Russian army. He only said: »These events change many things in the world.« That was already too much. The Defense Ministry and affiliated propaganda channels had an unrestricted monopoly in Russia on any commentary about Bucha. Investigators asked him, »Why are you talking about Bucha?« He had replied, »Because the whole world is talking about it.« This was also used against him. »You know what Russia's problem is? Our law and jurisprudence go in completely different directions,« he told me. His party, Yabloko, was the only anti-war party in Russia. But Yabloko is not allowed to speak out on the war: »We are still allowed as a party, but our positions are banned.«

Just as they did against the politician Schlossberg, the prosecutor's office initiated proceedings against the opposition politician and former mayor of Ekaterinburg, Yevgeny Roisman. Roisman was accused of violations of censorship laws. As the trials became more and more arbitrary, many Russians became frightened. The Moscow political scientist I reported on above decided not to say anything more about the operation for the time being. And she applied for a Schengen visa to be able to leave for Europe quickly just in case. Hundreds of thousands of Russians had left Planet Putin this way since March. They left out of horror at the government or fear of reprisals and forced recruitment. Among them were the mobile, free-thinking scientists, journalists, artists, and IT technicians. Such a decision is not easy, the political scientist told me. »My life here, my condo, my children, my pension.« But maybe at some point it will be necessary to leave.

The escape became more and more complicated for many male and female Russians. Putin had the borders closed against most men at the end of September 2022 because he needed manpower for the war against Ukraine. Some Russian regions banned all people from leaving the country after the introduction of martial law. Unfortunately, European states also worked diligently to close off Putin's empire. This began as early as March 2022, when EU states imposed airspace sanctions on Russia at the urging of East-Central European countries. Putin promptly imposed countersanctions and air traffic came to a standstill. Since then, Russians have only been able to fly out of Russia at very high cost via Istanbul, Dubai, or even more distant places. Or they came to Europe by land, via Estonia, Latvia, and Finland. The restrictions of eastern EU member states and the Russian government severely reduced or completely halted the issuance of visas to Russians at the end of August 2022. This affected the Russian opposition and many who, in case of doubt, could have quickly left the country with a Schengen visa. The EU increasingly barricaded itself against Russian citizens. »It's a disgrace that people are being excluded on the basis of citizenship, which you can't choose,« Maria Eismont grumbled to me. Forgotten were the Cold War lessons that the West leaves it to totalitarian regimes to imprison their citizens. Then, free Europe was open to Russians, Estonians, Latvians, Lithuanians, Poles, Ukrainians, and East Germans who had to flee from the totalitarian regime.

Nevertheless, Europe remained both a place of longing and an object of hatred in Russia. On the one hand, for the political scientist and the sound engineer, the EU was the last hope to escape possible arrest if need be. And despite all the mistakes made by European governments in the Putin era, they remained the bright shining alternative to the Russian dictatorship. My commodities acquaintance, on the other hand, seemed to hate Europe more and more. At a meeting in late summer, we were walking along a branch of the Moskva River and quietly arguing. I asked him if he thought the war was going on too long and claiming too many victims. His answer: »The operation was inevitable because Ukraine was about to attack Russia with Western help.« This is an important line of argument used by the Russian power to exonerate Putin, the central decisionmaker: war is not a decision but a fate, a providence, a visitation that cannot be escaped. »Putin himself has always said that war was coming,« the commodities trader said. He could not understand the »Russophobia« in Europe. What did he mean? In the West, he said, a campaign was underway against everything Russian, against the language, against the culture. The West is arming Ukraine, he said. »Why are the Germans supplying weapons to Nazis?« he snapped at me. »Haven't they learned the lesson of World War II?« He said he felt sorry for the many people who would have to die. Yes, I replied, when Russian artillery fires on residential areas. He replied that this was also a Russophobic prejudice of the West. »The fascists are shelling Russians and Ukrainians with Western weapons.« The West is waging war with sanctions. I was struck by the boundless self-pity: Russia invades Ukraine and Russian troops shell Ukrainian cities, but Russians are the victims. »The aggressor, it's the West, because the West is attacking Russia,« he said. The ready-made replies supplied by state propaganda enabled Russians like my acquaintance to end every conversation in a tightly wound, circular argument.

Russia's fractured relationship with the West became apparent in Moscow's cityscape over the course of 2022, and this became a problem for the regime's propagandistic message that the Ukraine campaign would not restrict the people. Under Putin, the capital in particular had become a catwalk for Western brands. Muscovites traveled in German limousines, wore Italian clothes, walked in English shoes, and dined in restaurants with French menus. The Western lifestyle that had been the privilege of the tsar's court in the 19th century was a matter of course in Russia of the past 20 years. Hence why the withdrawal of many Western companies in 2022 disturbed the façade of normalcy on Planet Putin and hit those Russians who had the money to afford this lifestyle especially hard. Russia reacted to the withdrawal of Western companies with defiance and a general effort to consume and use better Russian goods, Russian stores, and Russian technology. The money was there because oil revenues in 2022 exceeded all expectations. China and South Asia had increased imports of Russian raw materials. But China was not a »role model« in Russia's follow-up campaign, Europe and the US were. Vladimir Putin not only unceasingly spread hatred of the West, but also allowed unrestrained imitation of it. In July 2022, he praised Soviet agents who stole Western technology plans during the Cold War and businesses that tried to overtake the West with the knowledge they had stolen. Copying meant winning.

This began with fast-food restaurants to replace McDonald's. The opening of a McDonald's in Moscow's Pushkin Square in 1991 had been an iconic moment for the opening of the Soviet Union and a new lifestyle. Now McDonald's was gone.

»Vkusno i tochka« [»Tasty, period«] was the name of the new Russian fast-food chain. It sounds a bit like a command. The cheeseburger pretty much nailed the culinary secret of the McDonald's meat patty in a pillowy soft bun. The new branch on Moscow's Pushkin Square was super elegant with its façade of one-way glass and tropical plants in large flower tubs out front. Inside, there were large screens at eye level to order food by typing and swiping. You paid with the app, and the tray was already waiting at the counter. »We'll show *you*,« was the message the new fast-food chain sent to the West, which unfortunately didn't see it because Western tourists stopped coming. Soon after my visit, however, »Vkusno i tochka« fell into disrepute. Customers of the Russian fast-food chain complained about mold on their rolls on the Internet and Facebook. The web quickly laughed at the »MoldyBurger.« Others discovered cockroach and insect legs in the processed cheese.

Nevertheless, the chain was a trendsetter for how Russians dealt with Western brands that were no longer accessible. Starbucks was henceforth »Stars Coffee.« Coca-Cola also ended its production in Russia. The Russian answer: »Cool-Cola!« Fanta became »Fancy,« and Sprite became »Street.« Supermarkets were stocked with feta from Russia, parmesan from Belarus, and balsamic vinegar from the Moscow region. The markets had gone, but the attitude toward life was to remain. Still, the question remains: why didn't Planet Putin simply promote the Russian way of life, in the sense of »Drink more kvass!«? All these substitute products followed a Potemkin principle. Just as the conquistador Grigory Potemkin is said to have presented new settlements with a few inhabited houses to Tsarina Catherine I in the 18th century, these imitation products suggested westerness where there was none.

The spasmodic copying had a lot to do with how the Russian regime waged war. The soldiers were to shoot, conquer, and plunder such that the majority of the Russian population would notice as little as possible. They were not supposed to have to change their ways; instead, they had to maintain the Western lifestyle to which they had grown accustomed. The staging had its limits.

The withdrawal of Ikea came as a shock to Russian consumers. The giant markets on the outskirts of Russian cities were a destination for excursions, children's fun, and meatballs all at the same time. Before the closure, employees stormed their own store to get hold of the last goods. Ikea could not be replaced. Only aped. The Russian furniture company Lazurit from Kaliningrad, for example, placed furniture in its showrooms that resembled Ikea in its simplicity and modernity. Restaurants, children's playgrounds, and kitchenware were nowhere to be found. Instead, the model names were Western: the Lazurit table was called Dante, the divan was called Lisbon or Montana, the armchair was called Reims or Camelot. By local standards they were very minimalist, but they were also very Russian: too soft and too wide.

Putin's Russia repeated an age-old principle of the country: superficial westernization. Names, designs, and covers appeared Western, but the Russian facts remained hidden underneath. The Petrine reforms of the early 18th century were also partly concerned with externals, the cutting of beards and new dress codes, but Putin's Russia lacked Peter I's implementation of far-reaching reforms. Putin, who saw himself in the same league as Peter the Great, was content with mere appearances.

The Evropeysky shopping mall was Moscow's temple to façade. There, all the major European designers shone until the invasion of Ukraine. After February 2022, the mall bore internal scars from the crisis. Most of the stores were lit up, but a noticeable number were also closed. Some Western manufacturers declared on slips of paper stuck to the glass doors that they were closed »due to the circumstances« until further notice. But Russian brands are pushing forward, like the stores of St Petersburg fashion designer Alena Akhmadullina, or Snezhnaya Koroleva (the Snow Queen), a furrier who gained fame for winter fashion.

This was the challenge: create a Russian brand that did not immediately sully itself with mold and was a peer to Western brands, from a Russian point of view. For although Russia is a great power, many Russians carry a traditional inferiority complex about somehow not being up to Western standards. To prove the contrary, Vladimir Putin commissioned a luxury-class automobile to transport »the first figures of the state and other persons subject to the protection of the state« a decade ago: The »Aurus« was born.

There was a showroom for the car brand in a futuristic Moscow high-rise near the city center that had a specimen of this roadway boat, an Aurus Senat S600, in a two-tone paint scheme of Caspian blue and porcelain metallic. First impression from the outside: it looked like a Rolls-Royce Ghost. The massive chrome radiator, the taillights, the angular side rails, everything looked like it had been copied via 3-D printer from BMW's British premium brand.

Impression from the inside: It was like sitting in a tank, but on the finest beige leather and with a champagne fridge. The salesman rattled off the data: 598 hp engine with eight cylinders, weight of over three tonnes, fuel consumption of just under 20 liters per 100 kilometers. Putin himself rode around in an armored limousine version of the Aurus, for which there is no data. State secret. But I heard from the salesman that he was very proud of his patriotic premium vehicle. Besides this one, there were 27 other models driving around Russia in 2022. Could it be that a Russian car factory in Yelabuga produced a thoroughly Russian car in the super-luxury league with Rolls-Royce and Maybach?

Not quite. A German sports-car manufacturer had played a major role in the engine, and the on-board technology came from German suppliers. Consistently enforced sanctions could possibly put an end to such an Aurus. Or the carmakers in Yelabuga could produce a technically slimmed-down version that will look the same on the outside but be a vehicle from 20 years ago on the inside. The Aurus engine already did not meet the strict EU emissions requirements in the summer of 2022, so it could not be sold in the EU. There it was again: surface westernization.

Of course, Russian motorists are already noticing this. In the summer of 2022, there was a shortage of spare parts for Western cars everywhere. The factories of such Western companies as Volkswagen, Mercedes, and Renault were at a standstill. But even the production of Russian cars like the Lada stalled because the many Western ingredients that make the Lada a modern car were missing, like airbags, ESP systems, and ABS brakes. So, for the time being, there were no Ladas to buy until a model came onto the market that had made a technical journey 30 years back in time to the era of mechanical cars.

Resourceful propagandists organized an exhibition at the Moscow Museum of Contemporary History, where wounded patriotic pride in technology could be rebuilt in the summer of 2022, to ensure that there was no disquiet. »The Land of Achievements« presented groundbreaking inventions of the 19th and 20th centuries as purely Russian achievements that used a quote from Peter the Great as the headline: »Nature has given Russia only one thing: It has no rivals.« The exhibition showed that the light bulb was created not by the American Thomas Alva Edison, but by Russian electric pioneer Pavel Yablochkov. Liquid-fueled rockets were not the brainchild of German rocket designer Wernher von Braun or the two American rocket engineers Robert Goddard and John Whiteside Parsons but of Russian engineer Sergei Korolov. The exhibition concealed that Korolov only started working on the project in the 1950s because he had been in the Gulag. And the first airplane was launched by the Russian engineer Alexander Mozhaysky. Not a word about the pioneers Otto Lilienthal, the Wright brothers, or Louis Blériot. »The Land of Achievement« was a balm for the offended Russian soul. The exhibition was sponsored by Rossiya Segodnya, the Russian propaganda factory with Margarita Simonyan as its editor-in-chief.

The chief propagandist tried to console Russian viewers about the loss of the West in June 2022. Instead, she defined the cloistering of planet Putin: »Some people complain that now their children won't be able to study in the West, that they won't be able to tap into this brave new world, that they will live in a somewhat more closed space. I tell them: Listen, we should rejoice. Really rejoice. This brave new world is going to hell at high speed, so we'll be very thankful that our children didn't study there.« Some would ask when this estrangement from the West would end. »And I say, people, get used to it, it's forever!«

The propagandists and nationalists were already further ahead than the ruler in the summer of 2022. He hesitated. For all his radicalism, Vladimir Putin didn't want to worry the people too much. Hence the copies of Western culture, the museum's calming therapies, and the summertime staging of a normal, peaceful life. Hence the desperate appeals from the army to »please volunteer,« the comparatively good pay for the soldiers, and the recruitment drives in Dagestan, Buryatia, and, of course, in the prison camps. For a long time, Putin preferred to leave the »special operation« to the Wagner mercenaries, the non-Russian republics, and the poor regions of the country.

Vladimir Putin put together relief packages for the Russian population, subsidized certain foodstuffs, increased pensions, and strengthened the ruble with billions in foreign currency from the central bank. Moscow celebrated flower festivals in Manezhnaya Square at the Kremlin in the summer of 2022, while bombs rained down on Ukrainian cities. Stability in Russia; operation in Ukraine: »everything is going according to plan,« was a phrase repeated like a mantra on a prayer wheel. Kremlin-affiliated political pundit Sergei Markov summed it up: »Putin wants to leave people alone. […] Ideally, they should not even notice the military operation. It should not affect their lives.« Instead of a national mobilization of soldiers, the Russian population had experienced an unprecedented chloroforming and depoliticization by August 2022. Anyone—like my acquaintance in the raw materials business or my neighbor—who wanted to, could have their thinking taken over. The independent Russian political scientist Lev Gudkov called the combination of agitprop, fear, and games the »totalitarian consensus.« It lasted as long as Putin shied away from general mobilization.

His hesitation also had to do with his pains from the past. Putin remembered the uprisings against his return to the presidency in 2012, which he had dismissed as American-secret-service rummaging. He could still feel the people's resentment over his 2018 pension reform in his bones. It had primarily affected his resentment-laden older clientele and, in the end, him, because his popularity abruptly slipped. He could tell from the low numbers of volunteers and the growing disinterest of the Russian population in the »special operation« that it was not as popular as the annexation of Crimea in 2014. Few wanted to go to war, especially once they realized that Ukraine was a strong opponent. Big-city dwellers in Moscow, St Petersburg, and Yekaterinburg have long lived in the post-heroic age. What was not apparent from the telephone polls was how they did not trust their ruler and how he distrusted them.

For in spite of all the fear, not all Russians allowed themselves to be cut off. They had not completely lost their own way of thinking or their sense of right and wrong, arbitrariness, and freedom. When Russian troops in Ukraine were forced to retreat in September 2022, a group of local parliamentarians in Moscow called on Putin to resign because his »model of government was hopelessly outdated« and hindered the »development of Russia and its human potential.« They demanded he be tried for treason. Shortly thereafter, Russian pop idol Alla Pugacheva addressed the public. In a tweet, she sarcastically asked the Justice Ministry to »add me to the ranks of foreign agents of my beloved country.« She declared solidarity with her husband, who had openly opposed the war and left Russia. She herself was in Moscow and called her husband a »true patriot of Russia« who wished that »our boys no longer have to die for illusory goals that make our country a pariah and make life difficult for its citizens.«

I myself experienced an iconic moment of civilian courage in Moscow when an abusive police officer was put in his place. I was riding my bike past the Oktyabrskaya metro stop, where the Russian Ministry of the Interior is located, on my way home from an evening meal. A remarkable car crossed my path, a GAZ 21 Volga, built in 1968. It was clanking and loud and smelly, but it was rolling just fine. The driver, a young guy with a goatee and a bright orange hoodie, had worked on his car with a grinder. The result was a Beuys-like work of art made of chrome, rubber, rust, and a touch of residual blue. »Beautiful machine,« I thought to myself, and two women of around 30 who stood next to me at the traffic light, each with a bottle of beer in her hand, probably thought so too. We marveled at the vehicle as it drove by and said »kruto,« which in this context means something like »cool.« But then, the same thing that always happens whenever someone in Putin's Moscow drives »kruto« through the area, happened. The unavoidable police officer stationed at every intersection raised his baton and waved the Volga and its driver over. The Western limousines drove through, and the driver of the patriotic GAZ 21 Volga was frisked. I was as outraged as the two women, but unlike me, they took action. They walked straight up to the police officer, beer bottles at the ready, and confronted him. What did he want from the driver? This was not the way to do the job. Any mafioso could drive through here, but regular people were harassed. He should let the Volga driver go immediately. The cop was quite surprised, but he hardly got a chance to speak before he was immediately interrupted by the larger of the resolute women. He decided it might be wise to forgo the usual invented excuses and let the man drive on. Silently, the police officer handed the papers back to the driver. The Volga began to jolt and stutter down the road, the police officer stared at the ground, and the women went on their way.

By the end of the summer of 2022, unrest and nervousness were growing among the chloroformed population. Warning signs that the contradiction of flower festivals here and bombs raining down there would break open increased. The war could no longer be fought on the periphery, especially as the Ukrainian troops were now advancing. Putin's course of soporific depoliticization had become untenable. The grand illusion of that spooky summer collapsed when Ukrainian troops overran Russian lines near Kharkiv in mid-September to regain more territory in a week than the Russians had conquered in the previous five months. The Russian troops were running as an army advanced against them, an army that Russian propagandists described as a force of »drug addicts, opportunists, and Nazis.« Nothing, but nothing, went »according to plan.« Putin remained silent for two weeks. Then he launched a major strike—against his own population.

# Empire of Fear

## The mobilization of the people

An old acquaintance told me not to miss it. The Russian foreign policy elite wanted to talk about the Cuban Missile Crisis of 1962 at a conference. The diplomatic academy on Moscow's Krymskiy Bridge was only a ten-minute walk from my apartment. In late September 2022, Russian Deputy Foreign Minister Sergei Ryabkov consulted with geostrategists there about the nuclear threat, and I was the only foreign correspondent present. The hall was almost full and had high stucco ceilings but no air conditioning such that it soon got stuffy. Some participants had nodded off until this sentence was uttered: »We need the return of fear!« So said a geostrategist who was claiming that the »world rests on fear.« When fear disappears, he said, danger looms. This is apparent in the West, which is arming Ukraine as a beachhead against Russia. The West does not respect Russia enough: »We need fear so that they finally fear us again.« Silence in the room. Everyone looked at each other. Then applause and shouts of approval broke out. Everyone celebrated the speaker. »Страх!« pronounced »strakh« means fear or terror in English; it made sense to everyone. »Страх« is the key to Russia's greatness.

Vladimir Putin's prefers fear as the cement of his empire. He has used it in recent years to systematically silence many people and drive them out of the country. But Russians didn't really know what fear was until September 2022. It took a change in policy unlike any other since Vladimir Putin took office to change life in Russia. The turnaround cannot be understood without considering the extensive withdrawals of the Russian army, which was overrun by Ukrainian forces in the

Kharkiv region and had to leave behind many tanks and howitzers, and much of its ammunition. Russia became Ukraine's largest arms supplier in one fell swoop, and Putin suddenly found himself with his back against the wall in September 2022. The war he had started was backfiring on his troops. The principle of fear had failed in Ukraine.

After a week of silence, Putin appeared on television on the morning of September 21, 2022, with a punitive speech against the US and Europe. He wanted to instill fear and caution in the West with the nuclear threat, but then, and this was the policy shift, he announced a »partial mobilization« with which he terrified his people. The »part« soon became a large whole. Putin sent hundreds of thousands of men to fight in Ukraine. This was Putin's second major escalation after February 24. This time, in addition to Ukraine, it shook Russia itself, which plunged into a new era. Now the mobilization commandos were hunting down Russian men between 18 and 60. The war came home to Russia. And with it, fear.

Putin reacted to the humiliating series of defeats in Ukraine with a leap forward: he expected his people and the world to experience an immense acceleration of the war. A few days after holding sham referendums in the occupied territories, on September 30, 2022, he had ministers and deputies, as well as national bloggers and actors, gather in the Kremlin's George Hall. He was talking again. This time, he accused the West of »satanism,« »evil manipulation,« and »perversion,« along with the supposedly intended annihilation of Russia. What he actually wanted was to annex four Ukrainian regions, which happened next in a pompous ceremony and was celebrated afterwards on the Red Square.

I rode my bicycle around the Kremlin and Red Square that day and heard only the cheers. Onlookers were lined up along the Moskva River such that it was almost impossible to get through. The square itself was reserved for invited citizens. The buses they had been carted in on were everywhere in the center. I was able to follow what was happening on Red Square with the other Muscovites on screens. After his annexation speech in the Kremlin, Putin stood on a red, white, and blue decorated stage in front of St Basil's Cathedral and whipped up the people: »One, two, three!« They thanked him with cheers and choruses of »Rossiya.« A Russian actor called for a holy »people's war« against the powers of the West, and the popular nationalist blogger Vladlen Tatarsky, invited by the Kremlin, shouted in all seriousness: »We will conquer everyone, we will kill everyone, we will plunder everyone—just as we please.«

The summer of partying was definitely over. It rained for weeks. Moscow seemed subdued, quieter and emptier than usual. In September, I met my friend who had sent his son to Turkey because he was a top candidate for mobilization. He had successfully persuaded his son to leave the country just before Putin's annexation speech, as I described in the first chapter. The son had said goodbye to his life in Russia, to his family, to his job, to his country. After arriving in Istanbul, he called his father and told him that the plane was full of Russian men who had cried the whole flight. He was one of them.

Russia wrote many of these stories of anguish at crowded airports, in the traffic lineups at the borders, and in the mountains of the Caucasus. The FSB domestic intelligence agency reported that at least 260,000 men had fled by September; Russian independent newspapers in exile cited far higher numbers. In other words, more men had fled than Putin wanted to mobilize in the first wave, which amounted to a mass conscientious objection. Meanwhile, for the men in Russia, draft orders came from the janitor, from the police officer around the corner, and from the pizza delivery man. Military police broke open apartments to draft civilians who had never held a weapon. Even blind men received draft notices. They took the men out of hotels, hospitals, houses, broom closets, and airplanes that were already taxiing on the runway. There were shootings in district military offices, scuffles in the streets, and crying children and women saying goodbye to their fathers and husbands. In Moscow, buses drove through the city to round people up. At a recruitment point next to the Belorusskiy Railway Station in Moscow, I saw men with draft notices being shouted at and kicked by uniformed men. The few who dared to protest in Moscow in the first few days were given conscription orders, as were 180 men who tried to cross the border into Georgia at the Kazbegi–Verkhnii Lars crossing. Military police were waiting for them instead of border guards.

The fear was justified. The reports were frightening. In a training center in Sverdlovsk Oblast, three draftees died while preparing for the mission. One collapsed with a heart attack, one committed suicide, and the third was sent home, where he died of cirrhosis of the liver, a condition he had before he was drafted. On a base near Moscow, fierce brawls broke out between soldiers who had been serving for some time and those who had just been drafted. The veterans demanded the jackets and cell phones that the new recruits had brought with them. Mobilized recruits told social media that they had only received one day of training, after which they had gone to the front. They said the instructor's advice had been: Pack your own sleeping bags, medicines, and bandages, as well as sanitary napkins and tampons that they could then apply to their wounds. Upon arrival in the occupied areas, mobilized people filmed themselves spending the night in the field without shelter and warming food they had brought with them over campfires. Others showed the rusted rifles they were handed. At a training ground near the Ukrainian border in mid-October, a shootout broke out between Muslim soldiers and Christian Orthodox superiors that resulted in a dozen dead. At the same time, the army admitted that quite a few of the mobilized men had died shortly after arriving at the front. What all the stories have in common is that things did not go according to plan for Putin. As before, the mobilization was a dilettante effort. This had consequences for the man in power.

With the mobilization, Vladimir Putin broke with his own policy of the past two decades. The president had obtained a kind of general power of attorney from the people for his foreign policy adventures and, in return, he kept his subjects quiet with benefits from the oil and gas coffers. Meanwhile, Putin waged his wars in Chechnya, Georgia, Syria, Libya, West Africa and, above all, Ukraine with mercenaries. Meanwhile, the Russians went to work, to restaurants, and on vacation. That was the deal up until the summer of war in 2022. Putin's troops devastated Mariupol and the suburbs of Kyiv, and they bombed Ukrainian cities. Muscovites danced to live music on the Moskva River and rode the Ferris wheel. Putin tore up this social contract with his people. »On Sept. 21, Russians understood what had happened on Feb. 24,« said liberal politician Lev Schlossberg. The war, which had been a never-ending television series for them, became a deadly reality show for able-bodied men. With the social contract, however, went Putin's »plan.« Until then, he had been telling his people that Ukraine was undergoing a »special operation,« well-planned and running like clockwork. This illusion could no longer be maintained. With the arrival of autumn in Russian, the flower festivals disappeared, and the fireworks in the Moscow sky went out. A new reality seeped into the people's consciousness. Vladimir Putin took from the Russians what was by far the most important achievement of the era of Mikhail Gorbachev and Boris Yeltsin: the freedom to travel. Henceforth, men of military age were only allowed to leave the country in exceptional circumstances. The country's borders closed. And fear moved into every home.

For Putin in the Kremlin bunker, this was not all that bad. He himself traveled to friendly regimes, to Minsk, to Beijing, to Damascus, and that was enough for him. He had seen and experienced everything. Putin looked like a very old man. The Russian anthropologist Alexandra Arkhipova provided an apt outline of the ruler in the autumn. She felt that his speeches reminded her of an »old woman in a third-class carriage on the Russian state railroads« who annoyed the passengers sitting around her with tirades about the evil West, sex changes, gays, liberals, and youth without manners. The ruler spoke of the old people's fear of change and the future. Young Russians were now allowed to die for his entry in the history books.

The last time there was a mobilization like Putin's was the Great Patriotic War against Hitler's Germany. After six months of war against Ukraine, military losses were several times higher than in the decade of war in Afghanistan beginning in 1979. For Russia, a national tragedy loomed in the fall, the greatest since World War II. Only this tragedy was provoked by its leader, who had maneuvered his country into a hopeless situation with a series of inconceivable mistakes. In the War-in-Sight crisis of January 2022, he chose to invade despite all warnings. During the invasion, he chose the disastrous march on Kyiv. He chose to lie about a »special operation« that would not affect the people. As his troops retreated, he opted for the great mobilization. And he still did not call it war. Putin, who for more than 20 years had grown accustomed to winning in controllable campaigns, in 2022 failed every step of the way in his first real major war against a neighboring country.

Political scientist Tatyana Stanovaya pointed out how Putin had voluntarily left a sovereign situation with many options and entered a very vulnerable situation. Many would just be amazed, Stanovaya said: »His Ukrainian obsession was never shared to the same extent by most of the Russian elite. His willingness to sacrifice thousands of Russian lives is not shared by most of his voters. He seems to be pursuing a scenario in which he is the only one willing to pay any price and fight under a banner of 'all or nothing.' The president's maniacal course has the bitter taste of suicidal desperation.«

People's doubts about the ruler's wisdom grew in the autumn of 2022. Putin's popularity sank, but could the polls be trusted? It was more by the empiricism of chance that I found out for myself that support for this war and Putin's obsession was waning. In late September, I went to the »Chistye Prudy« metro station in Moscow, where a demonstration had been announced via a Telegram news channel. It was a farce. Armies of police and journalists waited in the drizzle for the demonstrators, who never came. A little later, in a side street not far from the metro station, I met a woman who was quietly ranting to herself. She was the mother of two sons eligible for the draft. »They lied to us,« she said. They had said no war, no casualties, no prolonged conflict. »All lies!« Now Putin was talking about »partial mobilization,« but they would grab anyone they could. »For what?« she asked. »Back in 1941, we were invaded by the Germans, but now we have attacked another country. And are failing at it.« That's how many talked when they thought the powers that be could not hear them. In October 2022, I sat down to dinner with a Russian diplomat, his wife, and a Moscow artist. To protect the latter, I won't mention names. It all began with the Russian diplomat's wife sighing loudly: »Oh, why this attack on Ukraine? We had such a nice life before!« The diplomat explained to her and the artist at length why the attack had been inevitable. He told her about how Putin could no longer tolerate people dying in the Donbas and how the West had not listened and was now fomenting war with weapons—Putin's narrative.

The artist interrupted him, »I come from the Donbas.« Nothing was inevitable, he said. »There is no evidence for these stories of shelling and genocide of the people of Donbas.« In fact, he said, there had been a tense calm. Ukraine had not wanted war, but the Russian government had. It was a raid, not an operation, the artist said. It just bubbled out of him. At some point, the diplomat fell silent. His wife kept sighing.

The doubts could not be ignored. No celebration, no speech, no ceremony could dispel them. The jubilation over the annexation lasted barely more than a day. The Ukrainian armed forces simply continued advancing on their territory. And Putin's spokesperson had to admit publicly that he himself did not know exactly where the borders of the annexed territories were. The government's helplessness was obvious. To protect Putin, the propaganda army switched into repair mode. But where to start? Rossiya Segodnya editor-in-chief Margarita Simonyan warned that »many mistakes are being made in mobilization.« This must be corrected urgently, she said. Putin's radical pundit Vladimir Solovyov suggested in his broadcast that »dishonest mobilization officers« in recruiting centers be »shot.« These incantations calmed no one. The authorities tried to dampen the unrest among the population by informing men via text message on their cell phones that they were »deferred« from military service. Even I, a German, received such a message on my Russian number. It did not let me sleep any easier. Finally, Putin allowed his army to be tarnished to avoid responsibility for the campaign.

It began with an event in October 2022, when a hitherto little-known deputy head of the Russian occupation authority in Kherson was allowed to comment on the Russian army's withdrawals in Ukraine: »A defense minister who allows this should shoot himself.« Under Russian censorship laws, »disparagement« of the armed forces is punishable by up to 15 years in camps.

Kirill Stremoussov, however, did not get an arrest warrant. He got applause from Moscow. In the Duma, an influential deputy from Putin's party asked where the kits had gone for 1.5 million soldiers. On television, the propagandists and liars of the trade shouted at the army leadership, »Stop lying!« No one was threatened with punishment.

Putin allowed the army to be shot down by shady politicians and propagandists to save himself. The armed forces were suddenly condemned in October 2022 for the abandonment of thousands of square kilometers of land and the loss of tanks and ammunition. They were blamed for the failed defense of the bridge from the Russian mainland to Crimea that in September was still Putin's construction for the ages and by October had been severely damaged by an attack. The criticism from two of the Russian ruler's minions was particularly striking. As commanders in their own right, they had built up entire private armies. Ramzan Kadyrov, the head of Chechnya and a notorious militia leader, called the Russian commanders in Ukraine »incompetent.« Yet Kadyrov's troops had fought in the march on Kyiv in the spring of 2022, for example, and did so very brutally but not successfully. Kadyrov found an ally in Yevgeny Prigozhin, founder and leader of the Wagner militia, which staged a mutiny in 2023. Prigozhin's mercenary force had been fighting in Africa, Syria, and Ukraine for years and is accused of numerous war crimes. Prigozhin had been filmed in a prison camp in the late summer of 2022, recruiting murderers and sex offenders for the war, saying, »Those who retreat, surrender, drink, rape, will die. We are very accurate in sexual offenses, but mistakes can happen. All right? Sign up there.« In Prigozhin's opinion, the Russian army fought »old-fashioned« and »ineffectively.« He himself was in competition with the armed forces for imprisoned criminals. Both the army and the Wagner militia recruited volunteers from the penal camps of the Putin Archipelago. The army lured with pardons, and Prigozhin with a promise: »You can do whatever you want with the Ukrainians.«

Kadyrov and Prigozhin stood for the Russian party of total war. What was striking about their criticism of the army was how they gave a wide berth to the man who had started the war without need or cause, who had been responsible for the failed attack on Kyiv, and who had micro-managed the campaign in a way that was most embarrassing for everyone: Vladimir Putin. This was a central motive of the massive criticism of the army and the general staff: divert all doubts from the greatest commander of all time to the incompetent generals and the defense minister. They had allegedly deceived the leader. For the time being, Putin gave free rein to the mercenary leaders and allowed them to disparage the Army. It was not until almost a year later, during the mutiny of the mercenary chief Prigozhin, that he realized how dangerous this could be for him.

Rumors spread in Moscow that Putin was increasingly interested in alternative fighting units beyond the regular army. Putin's state broadcasters reinforced this impression. In mid-October 2022, Dmitry Kiselyov's agitprop newsreel »Vesti nedeli« on Rossiya 1 showed a long report on a parade of Kadyrov militia troops in Grozny. Reporters panned their cameras past the neatly lined-up regiments of soldiers with long beards. The Rossiya 1 correspondent effusively praised the discipline and fighting spirit of the troops. A decorated Kadyrov was allowed to say smugly into the camera, »Our boys no longer want to see the state in danger. We will come back with victory.«

Such promises were direct attacks on the Russian Ministry of Defense located on the Frunzenskaya embankment of the Moskva river. Obscured by its thick walls, Sergei Shoigu, who for a long time was Putin's closest confidant, was actually picking mushrooms and sitting around a campfire in the taiga. The defense minister and his chief-of-staff, Valery Gerasimov, went into hiding. They were not heard from, but they needed to endure, not talk. Their function was to act as living shields to intercept all criticism of the failed operation such that none of it hit Putin. After all, the ruler provided Shoigu with temporary relief. The Ukraine operation got a new commander-in-chief, General Sergei Surovikin, who was considered brutal and unrestrained. He had already made a name for himself at the age of 24 when he commanded the tank that simply ran over three demonstrators in Moscow's Arbat district during the 1991 coup attempt. Surovikin served in the wars in Chechnya and Syria, where he was involved in the cover-up of chemical weapons operations and in the destruction of Aleppo, a city of millions. He is also not new to Ukraine; he had been in charge of the southern front from April to October 2022. Moscow media reported unanimously about Surovikin's dreaded »performance reviews« of the Staff. One of his subordinates felt compelled to take up arms and shoot himself. Sergei Surovikin, also called »General Armageddon,« would solve the problems of the operation from now on.

A concrete example of Russian-style problem solving is the uninhibited bombardment of Ukrainian cities with cruise missiles and long-range bombers. Kadyrov, whom Putin had appointed colonel general of the »Russian Guard« in October, was delighted and wrote on Twitter that he was »one hundred percent satisfied.« Propaganda channels celebrated the attacks like New Year's Eve fireworks; one presenter filmed himself dancing on his balcony, wearing a baseball cap and pajamas with the inscription »Army of Russia.« Even Kherson's ill-tempered satrap, Kirill Stremoussov, said, »Now we start talking like adults to those who don't want to listen to us.« The armed forces used not only very expensive cruise missiles, but also old Soviet explosive devices that often missed the target for this »adult talk.« What was good for Ukrainian soldiers on the front lines became a disaster for civilians in the densely built-up cities. Here, a change in strategy by the Russian attackers became apparent in the fall of 2022. Soberly, they realized that they had little chance of conquering all of Ukraine, but they were now able to rely on the mass of mobilized troops.

The Russian air force destroyed the infrastructure of the Ukrainian cities because the Russians no longer expected to take them over in the foreseeable future. The new strategy was described by ex-general and deputy of Putin's United Russia party Andrei Gurulyov in October 2022 as follows: »If they have no water, no sewage system, no electricity, and no money, they cannot buy food, cannot cook, cannot work, cannot live. A wave of refugees will go to the West.« Russian propagandists were tasked with broadcasting images of misery from Ukraine and providing Moscow's rulers with a new narrative: as long as Ukrainians were even worse off than Russians, a protracted war could be endured. Chaos was victory.

In Russia, Vladimir Putin focused on blaming everyone else for his personal mistakes. No one could be sure anymore that they wouldn't be next. He expanded the rule of fear: Repression of people who rallied in the streets; arrest of opponents of the war; detention of nationalist bloggers who, in the Kremlin's view, exaggerated with overly platitudinous demands for the destruction of Ukraine; and a peppering of nationalist politicians who supported Putin's course. Censorship laws were selectively applied, and nationalist firebrands were sent to the front. Stremoussov died in an ominous car accident. Constant uncertainty about one's fate was to become the norm in Putin's war of attrition against Ukraine, the West, and his own people. Throughout the country, the administration was placed under the control of emergency committees, industry was converted to a war economy, and martial law was introduced in many provinces. In the Russian south, Putin had trenches dug in the cities because of the alleged threat of an invasion by Ukraine. What began as his personal war was now to become the »People's War« against the Western enemy.

Putin risked everything he had achieved in the prior 22 years. He looked like a delusional entrepreneur who had a very successful business model for a long time, and who, at the end of his career, goes to the casino to gamble away his pension and his children's inheritance. His stake was the political, economic, and cultural stability of Russia, of which he was once so proud. A national tragedy was brewing that Russia could bear for generations to come. At least, it could be for those Russians who stayed; millions of young people with a good education had left the country. Putin declared the »People's War« and took revenge against Ukraine, which did not surrender as he had expected, and against his own army, which did not fight as heroically as he wished, with the young Russian men who now had to sacrifice their lives on the altar of Russian greatness. It was not clear whether he would crush only his successes, or his rule, or the entire country.

On August 30, Mikhail Sergeyevich Gorbachev, the last Communist Party general secretary and Soviet president whom Putin accused of destroying the Soviet Union, died. Putin did not attend his predecessor's funeral. Unlike thousands of people who made the pilgrimage to Gorbachev's coffin laid out in the columned hall of the legendary Trade Union House next to the parliament. They stood in line with flowers for many hours to say goodbye. And they came back and stood for a long time at the Novodevichy cemetery to say goodbye once again. Mikhail Gorbachev's mortal remains sank in a sea of flowers. If Putin had donated a memorial, it was no longer to be seen. Instead, the card of an unknown mourning Muscovite stood out, a rectangular white sheet lying on red carnations and roses. He had written in blue ink on the card in beautiful Cyrillic letters: »I thank you, Mikhail Sergeyevich, for freedom, for hope, and a life without fear.«

# Rebels
—resistance from the right

»Prigozhin is dead, long live Prigozhin.« After the fall of the Russian mercenary leader on August 24, 2023, spontaneous shrines to Yevgeny Prigozhin were erected in many places in Russia: mountains of red carnations, Prigozhin photos and drawings, candles, and even the occasional mock-up of a sledgehammer. The man had deserters beaten to death with a real one. People mourned a murderer in droves. Forty days after Prigozhin's death, I visited his grave at the Porokhovskoye cemetery north of St Petersburg. The mercenary leader has no place of honor in this cemetery. He lies between densely packed graves next to his father. A large maple tree towers behind him. Prigozhin's final resting place offered little room for the thousands of flowers that adorned his grave at the time of my visit. Among the blooms were red glasses with candles, pictures of Prigozhin' in gold frames, a teddy bear, and small notes saying, »Thank you!«, »You are our hero forever!«, and »Just the way we love it!«

In October 2023, forty days after his death, many in Russia commemorated the man who crashed a plane with the rest of Wagner's management team on August 23. Vladimir Putin spoke about this at a meeting of international political scientists and experts in Sochi at the time. He claimed that remnants of shrapnel had been found in the bodies, and drugs had been seized in the Wagner offices. In other words: first, the Wagner leadership got high, then they scuffled, and finally one of them set off a hand grenade. You never know with these rough lads. A dubious 'version of events from one who could have ordered the plane crash.

Putin's explanation was not really convincing. Many people were not discouraged by the ruler's character assassination campaign and came to the grave anyway. They mourned and were annoyed by the way the government either suppressed or dismissed Prigozhin's crash as an unfortunate but not very important accident. The crucial question for Putin, however, was whether anger and grief would eventually turn into rage. Anger could become dangerous for the Russian ruler.

Both Vladimir Putin and us in the West have a vested interest in this situation because the growing anger of the people opens up all kinds of possibilities for change. Anger can force Putin's hand. It can cause panic among the elites and, in the most extreme case, provoke a change of power, either through a rebellion, as Prigozhin tried on June 24, 2023, or simply through chaos. Such turmoil is Putin's nightmare. It would increase the chances of an end to the war or at least a ceasefire, and not for the first time in Russian history, as he well knows. There were uprisings against the government in the war against Japan in 1905. The revolution of 1917 shattered the Tsarist Empire and ended the war against Germany. But after the death of Yevgeny Prigozhin, Vladimir Putin, who teetered over the edge of the abyss on June 24, could breathe more freely again, if only for the time being. The rebellion had exposed the cracks in his apparatus and his own insecurity.

Putin had never looked so deeply into the abyss in the many years of his rule. For twenty-three hours, the Wagner mutiny was probably the most dangerous crisis of his time in office, more threatening to him personally than the war against Ukraine, more provocative than all the demonstrations against power during his time in office, and potentially more dangerous than such political opponents as Aleksei Navalny with his anti-corruption films. Putin understood this very well on the day of the rebellion when he noticeably gasped for air during a speech to the people. He was uncharacteristically restless during his dramatic speech, as if searching for the emergency exit. It didn't come to that because Prigozhin eventually called off his »March on Moscow« of his own accord, partly from lacking the courage of his own convictions.

Nevertheless, the Wagner revolt of June 24 was a loss of face for Putin that can no longer be erased from the history books. The mercenaries entered Russian territory with surprising ease, reached the city of Rostov with its millions of inhabitants, marched straight to the army headquarters, and from there commanded their march on the capital, Moscow. They are said to have shot dead more than a dozen Russian uniformed personnel and knocked a military plane out of the sky. Prigozhin apparently had some, although not enough, patrons in key positions in the Russian defense forces. Security forces worked against each other. The FSB secret service and military intelligence failed. And to Putin's horror, parts of the population of Rostov applauded and greeted the Wagner mercenaries as liberators.

This mutiny did not require a Western conspiracy. Neither the CIA nor MI-6 nor former US Secretary of State Hillary Clinton (whom Putin usually likes to suspect) had a hand in it. It was an uprising from within Russia. Prigozhin was entirely Putin's creature: his cook, his mercenary boss, his man for the heavy lifting. The Wagner group was only able to come into being because Putin had deliberately smashed the Russian state's monopoly on the use of force. In 2014, he unleashed armed criminal gangs as »insurgents« against the Ukrainian Donbas. He sent Prigozhin's mercenaries to Africa and, in 2022, the Chechen battalions to Kyiv. On June 24, 2023, the mercenaries suddenly turned against their own government.

Even if the plane crash of Prigozhin and the entire Wagner leadership finally suffocated this concrete threat, the mutiny has exposed a lie of the regime: Putin is not the guarantor of stability but the source of the spreading destabilization. The pyramid-like dictatorship built around him is, in reality, an unstable edifice without the structurally necessary counterweights, no opposition, and no possible alternatives to Putin. It is highly unlikely that the politically weak figure of the prime minister would automatically succeed Putin in the event of his departure, as is provided for in the constitution. By comparison, the Soviet Union with its Politburo and Central Committee was an almost orderly system in which the collective produced the successor in good time in a mostly regulated process. Russia is dominated by the unpredictable chaos of a personalized, arbitrary rule that has sealed itself off from the outside world. It is not the West or Ukraine that can destabilize Russia. Putin has already done that himself by unleashing nationalism in his country.

Prigozhin is the representative of this strong political current in Russia, the roots of which go back to the 19th century and which experienced a renaissance in the 1990s. It has grown under Putin and has now been elevated to the status of a state ideology: nationalism in its extreme form. After returning to the presidency in 2012, Putin declared his support for nationalism; he made pacts with nationalists and instrumentalized nationalists. The operetta nationalist Vladimir Zhirinovsky, who died in 2022 after a protracted Covid infection, was a dazzling example. He was allowed to rant because he was a political actor one hundred percent loyal to Putin. Other nationalists were more headstrong, hence why Putin repeatedly tried to rein them in when they slipped out of his control. Prigozhin is a particularly overt example of how nationalist movements can take on a life of their own and ultimately threaten Putin's power. Over the past decade, Putin has repeatedly had to deal with smaller-scale outrage, unrest, and resistance from the nationalist camp. These nationalists were often more educated, more elitist, and more cautious than the popular, impulsive, risk-taking Prigozhin.

Aleksandr Dugin is a very well-known example of these nationalist thinkers. His international fame grew in the summer of 2022 when his then-29-year-old daughter, Daria Dugina, was killed by a car bomb suspected to have been planted by Ukrainian services and intended for him.

At his daughter's funeral service, Aleksandr Dugin explained in a trembling voice that his »Orthodox« girl's first words« were »Russia,« »our people,« and »our empire.« Daria Dugina and Mother Russia as victims of the same attack—that is the message. Dugina was a reporter for the nationalist station Tsargrad and state channels. She reported from the Ukrainian Donbas and the long-embattled Azovstal factory in Mariupol. Putin calls her a »philosopher and war correspondent.« Above all, however, Daria was Dugin's favorite child, his learned student and heiress. She wanted to »continue his ideas and his struggle.«

Aleksandr Dugin is a leading ideologue of Russian imperial nationalism. Much can be learned from Dugin's positions on the radicalization of nationalism in Russia and why Russia invaded Ukraine. Together with other writers, journalists, and philosophers, Dugin brought nationalist ideology from the margins to the center of society. He is a man of his time—but not an unconditional or loyal fan of Putin.

I met Aleksandr Dugin in Kazan in the 1990s at a conference on federalism and Russia's multi-ethnicity. Even then, Dugin struck me as a character straight out of a Dostoyevsky novel: lean, bearded, obsessed. After the conference, three of us sat down together around a bottle of vodka: Dugin, the English American political scientist Fiona Hill, and me. Dugin talked about the many peoples of Eurasia, including the Ukrainians, who were all fated to belong together, and explained why the Russian world was the only possible template for this. He talked like the Eurasian ideologues of the early 20th century. Then he quoted Hegel and the heartland and Lebensraum thinkers Halford Mackinder and Karl Haushofer. Fiona Hill and I enjoyed Dr. Dugin's hot-air geopolitical theories washed down with vodka.

This was when what was then his most influential book was published: »*Foundations of Geopolitics*,« later shortened to »*Geopolitika*« for an abridged popular edition. Members of parliament and political technologists devoured the work. Dugin's imperial nationalism sees

Russia as the Eurasian leader of many nations. It will »either be great or nothing at all.« The philosopher is the mastermind of an »eternal opposition« between East and West. His system of coordinates sets Russia against America, Eurasia against the Atlantic world, the land powers against the sea powers, and the holy procession of the cross of the Orthodox Church against the scandal-ridden Love Parades in the West. There is no bridge between these rival identities, for Dugin believes in a »conflict of eternal values.«

In the late 2000s, Dugin traveled a lot and made contacts with like-minded people. He was a popular guest at the Lega Nord in Italy and the Front National in Paris. I met him again at a dubious conference in Istanbul, where Turkish ultra-nationalists, retro-Ottomanists, and Eurasianists were conspiring against the West. He was also in contact with the AfD.

In 2014, I met a proud Dugin for an interview at Lomonosov University in Moscow. He was no longer an errant prophet and now a full professor. Crimea had been occupied, and Russian troops were advancing in the Donbas. But Dugin grumbled. He felt that Moscow was not helping the oppressed brothers in »New Russia« enough. There was a lack of military support. Was that criticism of Putin? He didn't mean it that way. »That's down to the sixth column.« That's what Dugin called the circle around Putin, the political technologists and economic liberals. Like Dugin, other radical nationalists also lashed out at the Kremlin administration and called for a major offensive against Kyiv. They were breathing heavily down Putin's neck. When dozens were killed in clashes between pro-Russian and pro-Ukrainian activists in Odessa in 2014, Dugin shouted: »I think you have to kill, kill, kill. I say this as a professor.« That was too much even for Putin. Out of nowhere and with the Kremlin's blessing, a movement emerged with more than 10,000 signatures demanding his dismissal. Dugin lost his job but was allowed to continue lecturing in private.

In the summer of 2014, I also visited the editorial office of *Zavtra*, a nationalist newspaper that I had first become acquainted with in the 1990s. At the time, it seemed to me to be an offbeat paper published by marginal nationalists; after the annexation of Crimea, it could be described as a mainstream media outlet. Their offices sat on the Frunzenskaya embankment, right next to the Ministry of Defense building.

I was greeted by Andrei Fefelov, the deputy editor-in-chief of *Zavtra*. Its circulation was one hundred thousand, he claimed, and the editorial office was in a small, dark, nondescript first-floor unit. We spoke in the office of editor-in-chief Aleksandr Prokhanov. I couldn't tear my eyes away from a half-height cupboard that was arranged like an altar. On top, Soviet stars shone next to Orthodox crosses and models of tanks, and in the middle sat a large, Byzantine double-headed eagle made of porcelain. Two ornate spouts for the vodka in its belly grew from the eagle's neck. A red banderole bearing »J. V. Stalin« hung around its wings. The altar showed the world view of Russian nationalists: Christian Orthodox Stalinism. What to the untrained Western eye does not fit together forms a flourishing symbiosis in today's Moscow: red and white Russia, Stalinism and tsarist glory, socialism and orthodoxy. Everything that makes Russia look great fits together—or is made to fit.

What fascinated him about the Soviet Union was the ascetic modesty of life, Fefelov explained: »It had that in common with Orthodoxy.« The Soviet Union was also against the »pomp and circumstance« that unfortunately prevails in Russia today. Russia is far too dependent on international capitalism—and therefore on the USA, which dictates the conditions everywhere. Putin is moving in the right direction, but there is still an absence of a party that fights corruption as hard as Stalin once did.

The imperial nationalists were the masterminds behind the great war of aggression against Ukraine. Andrei Fefelov knew them all. They had gone to universities together and marched across battlefields. With a former separatist commander from Donetsk, the legendary Igor Girkin, alias Strelkov, Fefelov drove through the devastated Chechen capital, Grozny, in a jeep in 2000. »He knew every stone there.«

Strelkov is a military historian. In the 1990s, these nationalists, mostly writers, directors, and philosophers, warmed up to the idea of re-enacting historical battles and modern wars. Some of them fought in Bosnia, Serbia, and Chechnya. In Russia, many of them were on the side of the opposition to President Yeltsin in the bloody battle for parliament in 1993. Many of them wrote in *Zavtra* or on websites with a similar orientation. They used to be considered eccentric and extreme. But then, under Putin, Soviet nostalgia and a longing for global greatness returned. Since 2014, the intellectual nationalists have been the cheerleaders and firebrands in the never-ending war against Ukraine. They are fighting for a country they call »Novorossiya« (New Russia).

They also challenged Vladimir Putin with their exuberant enthusiasm. Field commander Girkin grew up to become a national hero in Russia in 2014. He fought in Donetsk under fire from the Ukrainians while Putin, assisted by a zookeeper, stroked leopard cubs for the evening news. Putin invented drama. Girkin lived it. To the nationalist audience, he came across as more authentic than the Russian leadership.

Sincerity and authenticity are the means to be close to the people, said the nationalist writer Sergei Shargunov. I met him in a literary café in downtown Moscow that looked like a yellowed postcard from the late Stalin era: dark wood, worn parquet flooring, beige lampshades with tassels, waitresses with white aprons and lace bonnets over their pinned-up hair. Shargunov had visited Donetsk several times with Andrei Fefelov and other enthusiasts and had spoken to Russian fighters there. »These people have what the Russian bureaucrats don't have: Convictions.« railed Shargunov. »New Russia« is a testing ground for new ideas »against the injustice of bureaucracy, against dependence on the outside and on the oligarchs.« Shargunov called it the »Russian Spring,« another nationalist movement. »We are leading an uprising against Ukraine, the West, Russian officials, and all the corruption at the same time.« The Russian Spring unites left and right, Stalinists, Orthodox Christians, Russians, and allied Ukrainians. It is a radical opposition that is rebelling against two governments: directly against the one in Kyiv and indirectly against Kremlin officials. Their battalions are in Ukraine, and their ideas are on the Internet, where commentators often rant and rave about the Third World War.

For Putin, these people are, on the one hand, basically likeminded people, but, on the other hand, are quarrelsome competitors who exert annoying pressure on him. They are difficult to control in their nationalist fury, a Girkin just as much so as a Dugin. Both were sidelined after 2014. Dugin lost his chair at Lomonosov University, and Girkin was ostracized, isolated, and left in severe financial difficulties. Only since Putin's second major invasion of Ukraine in 2022 have these nationalists, with imperial dreams, ideas of New Russia, and Russian Spring fever, almost reconciled with power again. Almost. Since 2022, a younger generation of war correspondents and military bloggers have also been living out their bloody dreams of great power, especially on social media. They engaged in a radical competition to outdo each other in describing how Ukraine could be conquered even more brutally. One of them, the popular blogger Vladlen Tatarsky, was later killed in an assassination attempt. He had made a name for himself when he recorded and uploaded footage of himself in the Kremlin calling for »everyone in Ukraine and Europe to be killed and plundered, just as we please.« The military bloggers were conspicuously unrestrained in their criticism of the Russian defense minister and general staff. After the withdrawal of Russian troops from Kharkiv and Kherson in the late summer of 2022, they slammed the »corrupt bureaucracy«

and the accursed defense minister. Sergei Shoigu was their favorite enemy, and Yevgeny Prigozhin and his Wagner mercenaries had been adored heroes since the costly capture of Bakhmut (Russian: Artemivisk). Prigozhin spoke to the soul of these people in his videos. His words resonated with many Russians who vote for Putin but distrusted the bureaucracy. Prigozhin was far too popular for Putin.

With the crash of Prigozhin's plane en route to St Petersburg in August 2023, Putin got rid of one of his worst opponents. Prigozhin was someone who broke out of Putin's system of loyalty., who did not stick to agreements, and who attacked regardless of losses. He did not adhere to Putin's mafia-like code of honor: »I cover your crimes, and you don't talk about my mistakes and villainy.« Worst of all, his breaches of Russian etiquette made Prigozhin popular. Others were now in free fall too. Putin was once again settling accounts with the Russian nationalists. Igor Girkin, who now operates as the chairperson of the »Club of Angry Patriots,« was in prison on extremism charges. The Wagner Group was literally decapitated by the crash of the Embraer private jet because, in addition to Prigozhin, Wagner founder Dmitry Utkin and senior Wagner troop leaders were also on the plane. Their property was distributed. Their mercenaries were largely absorbed by the Ministry of Defense, of all things.

This does not mean that criticism from the right has been overcome. The silent protest, perhaps even silent resistance, is expressed today in the commemoration of Prigozhin. Parts of the movement have found a martyr to whom they now pay homage with red carnations and lots of photos and candles. Wagner fans, nationalists, and also many rather apolitical citizens erected memorial corners and lavish Prigozhin shrines in many Russian cities after the death of the mercenary leader, but especially in St Petersburg, Prigozhin's hometown.

Prigozhin's former bar, where the military blogger Tatarsky was blown up with a bomb, is located on the banks of the Neva. Flowers with pictures of Prigozhin and Tatarsky lay at the entrance to the bar, which has probably been permanently closed, when I visited in October 2023. Two steps further on, I was already at the Hotel Trezzini Palace, also part of the Prigozhin estate, where I ordered a favorite Wagner dish in the restaurant: buttered dumplings with bear meat and sour cream. Outside the city center, an impromptu memorial had been set up in front of 'the glass business center formerly owned by Prigozhin. There were photos, candles, and wreaths in the greenery along the street. Prigozhin's grave at the Porokhovskoye cemetery became a real meeting place. Many people gathered there: Prigozhin admirers, Putin supporters, and even opponents of the war. There, people talked openly in a way you rarely hear on the street in Russia.

A cabinetmaker in a cognac-colored leather jacket with an old leather bag was among the admirers. Arkady (who didn't want to give his surname) still couldn't quite believe that Prigozhin was really dead: »There's a tiny chance that he's still alive after all.« Maybe that was just a wish, he said, but it all seemed a bit too simple to him. Did Prigozhin really get on a plane with the entire Wagner management? That would be too perfect, so doubts remained. Even if the powers that be wanted to oust Prigozhin, he would not be forgotten because he had many followers. Arkady pointed to the grave and shouted: »This was a man who sincerely wanted Russia to finally rise up!«

A woman joined our small group. She called herself Sonja. She was in her mid-forties, an artist from Moscow, and made a point of keeping her surname to herself. Sonja compared Prigozhin to the mythical Russian figure Ivan the Idiot. He was not stupid per se, but he was so straightforward and honest that he always said what he thought. And meant what he said. Arkady nods. Prigozhin spoke honestly, and that's why the people liked him, Arkady added.

»Prigozhin was sometimes very tough,« said Sonja. »But life is brutal. In this world, being tough is part of it. Sometimes you even have to be tough in the family when everyone is talking out of turn. Prigozhin was surrounded by bureaucrats in the Kremlin, by oligarchs and traitors. And yet he achieved a great deal for his country. Toughness was necessary.«

Then Arkady unpacked his worries. »The main problem is Shoigu!« The Minister of Defense and Prigozhin's favorite enemy has »'been all talk and no action. They moved the Black Sea Fleet from Crimea to Novorossiysk so that missiles wouldn't hit it. Although we're only dealing with the Ukrainians. What if it was NATO? Do they want to bury the ships then?« Nobody understands all this, he grumbles. »We need a spirit like in 1941, like in the Great Patriotic War, when the huge country rose up!«

'Arkady's outburst of anger attracted Leonid, a 67-year-old man with a peaked cap, mirrored round sunglasses, and a light blue anorak. He contradicts Arkadi: »If we don't leave Ukraine, the Ukrainians will never leave us alone and will attack us again and again.« A very revealing little argument followed that provides an insight into what is fomenting beneath the smooth surface of the dictatorship in Russia.

Arkady said, »We have to finish the job.«

Leonid: »No, we have to leave and give back everything we've conquered.«

Arkady: »What will happen in our country then?«

Leonid: »Well, what already?«

Arkady: »Are we supposed to fall to our knees now? We could finish all this in a year if we do it right.«

Leonid: »And what are we fighting with?«

Arkady: »Listen, we're Russians, we can also fight with clubs.«

Leonid: »No, it's hard to fight HIMARS missiles with clubs.«

Arkady: »But the West started it!«

Leonid: »No, this is Putin's war. He absolutely wanted it. A bad peace is better than an eternal struggle. It will all end very bitterly for Putin. Putin's power depends on war. That's why it has to end.«

Arkady: »Let's talk honestly about the operation in Donbas. A friend told me that our people stole everything there. The military bureaucracy is enriching itself. The consequences are felt by the ordinary soldiers who don't have enough ammunition at the front.«

Leonid: »Yes, I believe that Prigozhin was not the last rebel in Russia.«

Arkady: »Definitely not, it's just a question of time. But if we lose against Ukraine, there will be a revolution here all the more.«

Leonid: »That wouldn't be bad at all, would it?«

Arkady: »It may be necessary. I see things differently now. I used to watch TV and vote for Putin. Now I keep myself informed through other channels. Forgive my thoughts! Sometimes it gets to me.«

Leonid: »Well, in conflict, the truth is illuminated.«

Arkady nodded and said goodbye. He took a deep breath, bowed before the grave, and crossed himself. »Well, Yevgeny Viktorovich, rest in peace!«

In contrast to the dead at the Porokhovskoye cemetery, Putin's Russia is unlikely to rest in peace.

# Holy War

## Putin's Revenge on the West

It was always their fault. In the 1990s, hardly anyone noticed him, not even when the unassuming man was head of the powerful Russian secret service. His appointment as prime minister in August 1999 was a surprise to many. As president, he proposed a joint anti-terror alliance to the West to justify his war against Chechnya—but the US declined with thanks. He felt duped by the US intervention in Iraq; and although he was by no means the only one, he kept it to himself. Later, a US president called his great nuclear-armed Russia a »regional power.« When Russians protested against his rule, he blamed it on the Americans. His attempt to conquer and abolish Ukraine was met by the West with arms shipments to the »invented country.« When he wanted to offer condolences to the British King Charles III on the death of his mother Elizabeth II in 2022, he was not even invited to the funeral because of the invasion of Ukraine. And the whole world was there. His highly emotional speech on the annexation of further Ukrainian territories at the end of September 2022 was a bitter indictment against the West, the shouted psychogram of a deeply offended person. Indignation is a main trait of the Russian ruler, and his often-imagined motives were part of the essential influence of the West on Vladimir Putin.

Apart from that, it is difficult to influence the man. He sits in his castles of isolation in Moscow and on the Black Sea. Since the pandemic, all roads to him have narrowed even further. Visitors must undergo embarrassing tests and sometimes a prolonged quarantine. When I saw him from a distance on a grandstand in Red Square at the

May 2022 parade, I had taken three PCR tests on the three consecutive days prior and was wearing a mask. In the stands, he kept a safe distance from his generals and ministers. His food is checked by food chemists, and he gets his information presorted for him. Former confidants told me he likes to watch state television, rarely uses a smartphone, and hardly ever surfs the Internet. In 2022, he would still speak on the phone occasionally with Chancellor Olaf Scholz or President Emmanuel Macron. He declines those calls more often now, especially the ones from Paris. He is a man who for years has resided in seclusion, sometimes in Moscow, sometimes in Sochi, sometimes in his dacha. Putin lives in a hermetically sealed world.

Some in the West believe that Putin's campaign is a regional war of no major significance for the world. He simply wants to annex Ukraine, which is already within Russia's sphere of influence and was dominated by Moscow until 1991—as if that were not bad enough. But precisely this attribution of a limited goal is a dangerous error that leads to an underestimation of Putin once again. He is concerned with much more. He has been pursuing the central political project of his term in office in his confrontation with the West since his return to the presidency in 2012: revenge and the seizure of power.

Putin revealed his essential drive on the world stage back in March 2018. In a speech to the nation in the Moscow Manege next to the Kremlin, he accused the United States and the entire West of trying to contain Russia with armaments and sanctions. That attempt failed, he said. »Nobody wanted to talk to us. They didn't listen to us. Then let them listen now!« Putin shouted, and then let video footage of an armada of new hypersonic intercontinental and cruise missiles drone over the audience. The assembled members of parliament, state and church leaders, and representatives thanked him with great applause. The West has no defense against Russia's new weapons, the ruler triumphed.

Putin was ostensibly seeking revenge for the many imaginary insults, but the long-standing demand for equal footing turned into a claim to superiority during his fourth term in office. He now wanted to enforce this claim in a hybrid war. Addressing the leaders of parliamentary factions on July 7, 2022, Putin said, »If the West wanted to provoke a conflict in order to enter a new stage of struggle and deterrence against Russia, this is it. The war has been unleashed.« Putin, Russia's supreme revanchist, dared the West into the final showdown in 2022. He waged his long-planned confrontation, aiming for nothing less than world supremacy. He wanted, just as First Secretary of the Communist Party of the Soviet Union Nikita Khrushchev dreamed as early as 1956, to bury the West. But because Putin had set his sights so high, his and his regime's survival was at stake. In front of the passing nuclear warheads and armored troops in Red Square, Putin said on May 9, 2022: »The defense of our Motherland when its destiny was at stake has always been sacred!« Thus, he outlined the metaphysical dimension of the struggle against the West. How did Putin wage this war of all wars?

Putin used the security of his country to justify the unprovoked invasion of Ukraine. He had launched a »preemptive strike« against an imminent attack, he said in Red Square on May 9, 2022: »An invasion of our historic lands, including Crimea, was openly in the making.« He had merely preempted the West before it could attack Russia over Ukraine. The beginning of Putin's attack was in December 2021, when the Russian ruler had presented an ultimatum, demanding the end of NATO's expansion, the dismantling of NATO infrastructure installed in Europe over the past 25 years, the withdrawal of US nuclear weapons from Ukraine, and no further military exercises in Russia's vicinity, by which he also meant Ukraine and other »Russian« countries. In his annual press conference at the end of December 2021, Putin told Moscow journalists that NATO was advancing: »True, there are military bases all around us. To the east and to the south, and the north of Russia, new military systems have been installed.« A look at the map does not confirm that claim. The last NATO expansion to the east was almost 18 years ago. Of the 57,680 kilometers of its external borders in 2022, Russia shared a good 800 kilometers with NATO members Norway, Estonia, and Latvia. Poland and Lithuania border the exclave of Kaliningrad for around 400 kilometers. Finland's accession to NATO, with its 1,300 kilometer border with Russia, only came after the invasion of Ukraine. »Encirclement« looks different.

Vladimir Putin is deliberately feeding a Western misconception about Russia to the outside world. Many believe that Putin is only reacting to the US and NATO. If only the West behaved differently, showed more understanding, and responded to Putin's concerns and needs, then he would act very differently. If NATO countries did not support Ukraine, Putin would immediately stop his fight against the West and start supplying natural gas again. This is a false assumption and, moreover, it makes Russia seem small and underestimates it. Russia is a world power, sovereign and large enough not to react to others but to act on its own initiative. That is exactly what Putin is doing.

Putin's personal radicalization is not a reaction to an external development, but to the threat to his power within Russia. His path to the new nationalism began after the demonstrations against his return to the Kremlin in 2011/12, which shocked him. The occupation of Crimea and parts of the Donbas took place in 2014/15, after the Ukrainians got rid of their authoritarian, corrupt ruler and wanted to democratize the country, which was a dangerous model for Russia. But the Crimean euphoria had faded years later. Putin's popularity has plummeted since 2018. He was in search of a new narrative. He discovered one in the eternal struggle against the West, the struggle for world domination. But the impetus for this came from within.

Putin's confrontation with the West is part of a profound upheaval in Russia that he initiated 20 years ago. He was helped by the security services, the armed forces, and the propaganda machine.

Together, they instigated a revolt against the 1990s and everything that was created and adopted then. It is a revolt against an open Russia with reasonably free elections that committed itself in treaties to peaceful coexistence and respect for the borders in Europe. Putin and his comrades-in-arms took revenge for what they saw as undesirable developments. They first turned their country inside out. They tested and crossed borders, first internally, then externally. And because Putin rules a nuclear superpower, he is now shaking Europe and the world that had felt safe for three decades.

Putin showed how deep his dislike for this world runs when he met the last president of the Soviet Union. When détente hero Mikhail Gorbachev died at the end of August 2022, Putin did not attend his predecessor's funeral service or burial. His condolence message was reminiscent of a wretched apprentice's report card, essentially, »Always tried hard.« Putin embodied the security establishment's contempt for the man of openness and disarmament treaties. He also took revenge on him. Gorbachev had criticized Putin for not stepping down after two terms in accordance with the constitution. Putin's spokesperson Dmitry Peskov responded by mocking Gorbachev, who was revered in the West: »So, a former head of state who dismantled a giant country is recommending that the man who saved Russia from this fate resign?« Putin had the newspaper *Novaya Gazeta*, which Gorbachev co-founded and in which he also held shares, closed down in Russia. He accused the Soviet leader of gambling away the empire and betraying the state.

What Putin and his elite found most disturbing about the 1991 coup against Gorbachev was that it could not stop the opening of Russia: free discussion, the rise of liberal politicians in government, the emergence of a vibrant civil society and entrepreneurship independent of the state still happened. In a press briefing in 2017, Putin himself described the 1990s as a »murky puddle« in which »the oligarchs were allowed to catch their goldfish.«

Russia has become a different country under Putin. The various waves of repression have affected many professions. Anyone who is politically active is threatened with being branded as a foreign agent or immediately condemned as a terrorist or extremist. Political opponents are banished to penal colonies. The organizations of civil society are either controlled by the state or destroyed. These are not »internal affairs.« The president himself revealed the interplay of internal and external at his annual press conference in December 2021, when Memorial was put on trial. Russia is threatened, Putin said, but it »cannot be defeated, but can only be [...] dismantled from within.« He believed he had averted the internal danger by the end of 2021. Since then, he began his vendetta against the outside.

Putin's perception of a weak, decaying West was crucial to his path to war. He felt strengthened by the »consolidated society« under a dictatorial regime, whereas the West was breaking down due to interstate competition, social struggles, gender decadence, and immigration. Putin wanted to lead Russia's steel-armed unity into the field against the West's vulnerable diversity. He had been preparing this for years. Russian elites had long feasted on the shocks of the West. The Trump era, the yellow vest movement in France, the mavericks and Putin brigades in Germany, and the rise of nationalists and populists in many EU countries gave Moscow hope and satisfaction. Putin himself seemed to have been in a good mood since the Geneva summit with US President Joe Biden in June 2021 and to have been convinced that he was the mentally and physically stronger leader. In 2021, Biden seemed to be going downhill: a fractured party, faltering reforms, the disastrous withdrawal from Afghanistan in August 2021. The chaotic end of the 20-year NATO intervention in Afghanistan seemed to show, in Putin's view, that the West was no longer capable of serious military operations. His attack was not a reaction to Western actions but the logical consequence of his assessment that the time was ripe to strike.

Europe and its paralyzing polyphony hardly took Putin seriously anymore. Since the departure of Angela Merkel, who led the EU in joint sanctions against Russia in the 2014 Crimea crisis, the EU seemed leaderless. The new German chancellor, Olaf Scholz, was laughed at in Moscow as a »clown« who could not keep his wide-spread coalition in check. Moscow elites watched with satisfaction as French President Emmanuel Macron, opposed by left and right, was re-elected by a shockingly small margin over his challenger (and Putin's friend), Marine Le Pen. He lost his majority in parliament to boot. Putin knew that many countries in Europe depended on Russian natural gas. He knew that more than half of Germany's imports and more than a third of Italy's imports came from Russia. These countries, he thought, would offer little resistance to Russian encroachment.

Putin's revolt against the order of the 1990s swept across Europe, which he wanted to free from American tutelage and subject to Russian leadership. Konstantin Kosachev, a foreign policy expert and chairperson of the Federation Council Committee on International Affairs, said in January 2021 that Europe had been taken over by a »foreign will [...and ] is also our continent, and they want to take it away from us. We, of all people, are the model for the future of Europe—a united, sovereign continent from Lisbon to Vladivostok.« Russian claims matched this. Putin's demand for the withdrawal of US nuclear weapons would do nothing other than end the commitment to nuclear protection. The demand for a halt to NATO enlargement was directed not so much against Ukraine, which had little prospect of joining, but against the freedom of action of the European states. The irony is that Putin achieved the opposite by invading Ukraine: Finland and Sweden applied for NATO membership soon after. But Moscow's clamor over NATO's eastward expansion was only a pretext for bigger plans anyway. In Putin's new order, the US would find no place at all in a weak Europe dependent on Russia. Russia laid claim to unrestricted leadership on the continent.

Putin did not want to return to the Cold War with its firm alliances and agreements. He was striving forward into the 21st century, when military strength and national unity were to count above all. »We are proud of our strong country, which is sovereign and self-sufficient,« the president used to say. He wanted to keep the West under permanent pressure with military extortion, cyberattacks, and a commodity price war. In the chronic tension, Putin intended to dictate the international agenda. With this tactic, he followed a rule of thumb that is widespread in Russia: »Whoever fears us also respects us.« At the outbreak of the war, 86 percent of all Russians, according to a survey by the Public Opinion Foundation, believed that Russia was »feared« in the world. Almost three quarters said it was »respected.« Admiration and trust, however, are hardly considered desirable in Russia. Fear is a constant source of power for the Russian leadership. Putin is also relying on it in the battle for Europe.

The Russian ruler felt that the 1990 Charter of Paris and the numerous treaties on the inviolability of borders and security in Europe were intolerable, and Russia had signed two of them with Ukraine in exchange for its nuclear weapons. Putin decided that all these agreements were concessions by predecessors in moments of historical weakness and prepared for the rematch. Back in 2016, he uttered a memorable sentence at the Russian Geographical Society: »Russia's borders do not end anywhere.«

By fighting the West, Putin mobilized his people in two ways. On the one hand, he could explain why he had no choice but to invade Ukraine, which the West was using as an »anti-Russian« project. On the other hand, he recalled all the old Soviet resentments against liberal capitalism and an open society. Most Russians could better understand the national self-assertion against the US and its allies than the quite contradictory fight against the imaginary »fascists« in the Ukrainian brother nation. In the face of the many setbacks over the summer of 2022, the faltering »special military operation« needed ever new explanations. Six months after the invasion, Russian forces had not gotten far. There were major losses, embarrassing »regroupings,« changes of command, and abrupt strategy shifts. The longer the war against Ukraine lasted, the less the ruler spoke of Ukraine in his speeches, and the more he spoke of the »collective West« and the »NATO bloc.« The real enemy was in the West: he had no face, no brain, no heart, only four bloodless letters. An anonymous monster, a powerful adversary threatened Russia. This was Putin's narrative.

Things came to a head in September 2022 after Russian troops fled the Kharkiv region following the Ukrainian army's strikes. When parts of the Luhansk district were also lost again, and later Kherson, so many things had not gone »according to plan« as Putin had promised. Under the tremendous pressure of these events, he had to order the mobilization. His campaign changed from a distant war of mercenaries and contract soldiers to a people's war to which anyone could be drafted. This needed a completely new justification.

Putin suddenly spoke of a »battle for life and death.« In his mobilization speech on September 21, 2022, he asserted, »The goal of [...] the West's is to weaken, divide and ultimately destroy our country.« Putin was leading his people into the ultimate struggle for survival. For now, he said, the theater is still Ukraine. Still, »They used indiscriminate Russophobia as a weapon [...] primarily in Ukraine, which was designed to become an anti-Russian bridgehead. They turned the Ukrainian people into cannon fodder and pushed them into a war with Russia.«

In 2022, an exhibition entitled »NATO: A Chronicle of Cruelty« at the Museum of Contemporary History of Russian near Moscow's Pushkin Square brought these messages to the people in an exemplary manner. In showcases and on panels, the exhibition organizers claimed, against all historical truth, that NATO invaded Vietnam, intervened in Panama and Grenada, and executed a coup d'état in Chile. The exhibition even claimed that NATO had detonated the atomic bomb in Hiroshima, four years before its foundation. The exhibition was organized by state institutions, MGIMO University, the TASS and Rossiya Segodnya news agencies, the Russian Historical Society, and the Ministry of Defense. In the Museum, I saw children with their parents, who obviously enjoyed spending their weekends in front of such display cases and panels. Schoolchildren and students, veterans, and visitors from China and Africa stood around an antitank missile from Western arsenals, supposedly looted by Russian troops in Ukraine. The missile was supposed to prove that Russia was waging war not against Ukraine, but actually against the four letters. A display case with war trophies was supposed to show how »NATO,« Nazis, and Ukraine fit together. The evidence was scanty. A black motorcycle helmet on which someone had painted SS runes was on display alongside a Ukrainian license plate that read »Azov,« the name of the regiment, dominated until 2016 by right-wing extremists, that had fought in the battle for Mariupol and held out at a contested steel mill. Next to the license plate, a Ukrainian flag and a US flag were lain disjointedly. »Ukraine is NATO's anti-Russian project,« an exhibition guide explained to children and parents. Prior projects, he said, included the Kosovo War in 1999, the US invasion of Iraq in 2003, and the French and British intervention in Libya in 2011. Now, he said, Ukraine is the West's staging area. In this narrative, the Ukrainians figure as NATO's remote-controlled combat robots, instead of citizens with their own state and self-determination. Here, after months of failed warfare in Ukraine, the shift in the Russian narrative was audible. From the summer of 2022, it was no longer imaginary Ukrainian »Nazis« who were the main enemy, but NATO. In his speech on the mobilization of the Russian population on September 21, 2022, Putin ignored the fighting strength and motivation of the Ukrainians in the fight against the Russian attackers as well as their successful tactics. His false claim that Russia was fighting against all of NATO in Ukraine was meant to explain Russia's bouts of weakness.

NATO was a perfect enemy for Putin. True to his spirit, the exhibition provided explanations for all generations and tastes. For young Russians, NATO is a sinister organization that wreaked havoc on the world since before they were born. For older Russians, NATO is the familiar enemy against which the Soviet Union lost the Cold War, and which has been expanding like an octopus ever since. For left-wing Westerners, NATO is the instrument with which the United States dominates the world. And for the Global South, NATO exists as a military bloc that prolongs Western colonialism into the future in a supposed delirium of freedom.

In August 2022, the independent opinion research institute Levada asked the Russian population who was to blame for the war: more than 70 percent named the US and NATO, 17 percent identified Ukraine, and only 7 percent said Russia. The brainwashing worked. At the same time, the formerly bright image of Germany collapsed. After many years of being one of the most popular countries in Russia, Germany was suddenly considered an enemy. According to a June 2022 Levada survey, 37 percent of respondents rated Germany as a »very hostile country.« Whereas in August 2019, 61 percent of respondents said Russia had »good relations with Germany,« by May 2022, 66 percent said relations were »bad.« And the trend continues. The once-good relationship with Germany is among the major collateral damages of the war. Crucially, the rapid deterioration of Germany's reputation in Russia has less to do with the actual feelings of the population than with the deliberate condemnations of politicians and propagandists. The Vice-Chairman of the Security Council and former President Medvedev was particularly prominent in this regard. He insinuated that the German government had a quasi-colonial interest in Ukraine when he remarked sarcastically in May 2022 that »toward the end of the 1930s, someone had already calculated like this.« In September 2022, Medvedev accused Germany of »waging a hybrid war against Russia« by supplying Ukraine with lethal weapons. »Germany is acting as an enemy state,« Medvedev told Berlin.

I noticed that this remark was coordinated across the government spectrum while surfing through the Russian TV channels in the evening in Moscow. The director of Rossiya Segodnya, Kiselyov, loved quick montages of Ukrainian Azov fighters, German SS soldiers in World War II, and Olaf Scholz giving a speech to Bundeswehr soldiers. TV propagandist Vladimir Solovyov said in late July 2022 that Foreign Minister »Annalena Baerbock would fit into a Nazi uniform very well« and that Chancellor Olaf Scholz was proving himself »a worthy successor to the Nazis.« A scene in which Scholz, dressed in a suit and leather shoes, clumsily climbed onto a cheetah tank was a ready meal for Solovyov: »Herr Scholz is not such a small leader,« Solovyov sneered with an affected German accent in his broadcast. »Now Scholz has gone completely nuts,« he commented about photos of the chancellor on the anti-aircraft tank. Then he showed black-and-white pictures of Adolf Hitler standing on a tank: »Here he is emulating his mustachioed idol!« Scholz was training »Banderovites,« a Russian epithet for Ukrainian nationalist bogeymen.

The message of the cheap propaganda was immediately clear to every Russian: The Germans were arming Ukrainian fascists and behaving just as they had in the Great Patriotic War of 1941 to 1945. They had learned nothing from the past. The effect was tremendous. Talking to Muscovites on the street in the second half of 2022, I heard the same complaint over and over again as soon as I identified myself as a German: »How can you give weapons to the fascists?« In a Solovyov broadcast in mid-September, Duma Deputy and former tank division commander Andrei Gurulyov of Putin's party proposed wiping out Berlin with a nuclear strike. This no longer outraged anyone. Solovyov, Kiselyov, and their consorts had reprogrammed the people's minds. The propagandists secured Putin's wars among the population. And sowed hatred among nations.

Some German interpreters of the Russian reality from a distance, who were already conspicuous for their excessive sympathy for Putin before the war, viewed the Russian government's aggressive stance as a consequence of Berlin's support for Ukraine. This is a dangerous misunderstanding. The hybrid war against Europe, and especially against Germany, did not begin in 2022. In April 2015, a hacker collective from the Russian intelligence service GRU attacked the Bundestag and targeted the office of German Chancellor Angela Merkel. In February 2018, there was a massive cyberattack on the German Foreign Office in Berlin. Russian hacker collectives also targeted German companies and utilities. They interfered in the French election campaign to support nationalist Marine Le Pen. Russian intelligence had opponents of the regime shot in Berlin. Putin invested a lot of money to promote nationalist parties that divide and disintegrate. The most obvious example of Russia's hybrid war is the gas supply.

Putin's gas war against Germany and Europe and the subsequent price shocks in the summer of 2022 have a long history. It began with the targeted purchase of Germany's largest gas storage facilities by Gazprom in 2015, a transaction approved by SPD Economics Minister Sigmar Gabriel. Russian energy companies bought up strategic German energy infrastructure, pipelines and distribution stations, utilities, and the large refinery in Schwedt that supplies much of eastern Germany with gasoline. The aim was to extend Russian influence over Germany and, in the event of conflict, to have ample leverage against the largest EU state. The Russian government used the narrative, also spread by German politicians and energy managers, of Russia's alleged reliability as a gas supplier to get this done. In 2021, barely a year before the Russian invasion of Ukraine, Putin let the trap snap shut. Gazprom began limiting supplies to the European market after the cold and snowy winter of 2020/21. Demand was high. Gazprom would have made a lot of money if it had supplied more gas, but that was not politically desirable in the Kremlin. The artificial shortage led to a noticeable increase in gas prices in Europe as early as 2021. The nasty surprise came in the fall. Germany's largest gas storage facility in Lower Saxony, owned by Gazprom, had a fill level of only 18 percent at the beginning of winter 2021. The other gas storage facilities owned by the Russian state monopolist were also almost empty because Gazprom was already cutting supplies sharply in 2021 and withholding urgently needed gas. This happened long before the Russian invasion of Ukraine. Putin's long-term policy of shortages escalated in the summer of 2022, when he first demanded, in violation of the contract, that gas bills be paid in rubles. Then he had the deliveries by the numerous pipelines cut off.

He played a cat-and-mouse game with Germany over allegedly non-functioning turbines, constant maintenance failures, and a lack of documents for the re-import of an overhauled turbine into Russia. Starting in September, Putin imposed a de facto gas embargo on Germany, as he had previously done to other EU countries. In late September, attacks ruptured three of the four strands of the two Nord Stream pipelines. Putin was not responding to arms deliveries from the West but continuing his longstanding policy. This was openly discussed In Russia, but the news did not really reach Germany. On Russian television, Kremlin advisers and commentators had long been advising that Europe should be punished for its »obedience to America.« Before the 2022 attack on Ukraine, military commentator Igor Korotchenko had urged the Russian government to »grab Europe by the udder.« Then he specified, »They should feel our firm hand, and we their anxious pulse.« This is exactly what happened in the late summer of 2022, when panic broke out among some business leaders, politicians, and citizens in Germany in the face of skyrocketing gas prices and high inflation. Putin and his propagandists were delighted. They enjoyed showing on television how industry would move out of Germany, how unemployment, devaluation of currency, and the freezing of living quarters would drive people to despair.

Vladimir Putin claimed in almost every one of his speeches that he would be fighting against the United States and its »obsolete claim to world supremacy.« But the US could only be affected to a limited extent because the US itself exports gas, has nuclear weapons, and its armed forces are ready for action anywhere in the world. No more than cyber warfare and interference in the American election campaigns was possible, so Putin concentrated his attacks mainly on the EU and especially on Germany. The European continent became his battlefield, with soldiers and weapons against Ukraine and with hybrid means against the EU for the time being. Since the summer of 2022 at the latest, the Russian ruler has been trying to destroy Europe: its peaceful coexistence, its standard of living, and its attitude to life. Putin's speeches are full of hatred for Europe's freedom and lifestyle. In March 2022, he accused Russians who have a European attitude of a »slave mentality.« They could »no longer live without foie gras, oysters, and gender freedoms,« Putin sneered. »They apparently consider themselves members of a higher caste and higher race.« He agitated Russian resentment and fueled cultural hatred of Europe.

Putin has distanced Russia from Europe like no Russian leader before him. He is entering new historical territory. In the past, Russia was often at loggerheads or at war with other European states. But it always had allies in Europe, it always remained part of the continent. Tsar Peter I fought against Sweden for decades, but he had Denmark, Saxony, and Poland on his side in the Northern War from 1700 to 1721. Alexander I fought Napoleon until 1815 and was temporarily allied with England and, in the War of the Sixth Coalition, with Prussia and Austria against France. Nicholas II waged war against Germany in 1914 alongside France and England. Stalin defended himself against Germany's attack in World War II in the anti-Hitler coalition with Great Britain and the United States. And the Soviet Union was allied with half of Europe in the Warsaw Pact. Today, by contrast, Russia stands alone in Europe, if one disregards the Belarusian dictator Alexander

Lukashenko who sought refuge with Putin out of fear of his own people. Russia has never been so isolated from Europe in its history. This is Putin's doing.

And the isolation will not be limited to the regime and politics. A new Iron Curtain is descending on Europe's external borders with Russia. Putin's empire will hardly be visited by Europeans in the future, neither by tourists nor artists nor by representatives of civil society. Russians will hardly be able to travel to the EU after the de facto Russian exit ban for many and the tightening of EU visa rules that leave only a few exceptions for those with relatives in the EU or a compelling humanitarian reason. The borders are closing. Russia's exchanges with Europe are likely to largely collapse. No planes have flown since the war broke out. There will be no more trains, trucks, or passenger cars. The exchange of goods will shrink to a minimum. Museums will no longer be able to exchange works of art. Hardly any musicians will perform on the other side of the curtain. Europeans will no longer get to know Moscow and St Petersburg. As long as Putin's regime of revenge remains in power, Europe for Russians will consist only of photos of Rome, Paris, Barcelona, or Berlin on the Internet, of paintings by European artists in Russian galleries, of images of Western European architecture in Russian cities, and of the travel memories of parents and grandparents. The ruling Russian elite defines its country in sharp distinction to all European countries except Belarus. Vladimir Putin is forcing his entire country to say goodbye to Europe, to which Russia had belonged for centuries.

Instead, Putin and his spin doctors are now praising a joint alliance with China. The Russian armed forces regularly hold joint military exercises with the Chinese army. In September 2022, they even invited India, a rival of China, to an exercise in the Far East. In Russia's big cities, an openness toward China is being demonstrated almost frantically. In restaurants, menus are printed in Chinese. In the car showrooms, Chinese luxury limousines are increasingly filling in the vacuum left by German brands. At airports, there are announcements in Russian, English, and Chinese; the only thing missing is Chinese people to hear them. At the September 2022 meeting of the Shanghai Cooperation Organization in Uzbekistan, Putin praised China for its »balanced attitude« in the world. Back home in Moscow, spin doctors cheered. »We are dealing with a West that is furiously running against the loss of its positions,« triumphed Kremlin-affiliated whisperer Sergei Karaganov. The »new Cold War« is winnable, he said: »China is on Russia's side. The Russian people are fed up, and Russia owns the truth vis-à-vis a morally discredited West.«

The decline of the West was Putin's main theme in his speech on the annexation of the occupied territories in Ukraine on September 30. It was not a solemn speech, but pure condemnation, the furious punitive speech of a man possessed. Putin accused the West of forced »gender operations« and rituals of »perversion« and »Satanism« that lead to »degradation« and »extinction.« He spoke of »human test subjects« in Ukraine. Up to that point, it was his most ideologically charged hate speech against Europe and the West. Putin went on for minutes with half-truths and complete lies about colonial history. With the posture of a left-wing colonial critic, he claimed that today, »The West is ready to cross every line to preserve the neo-colonial system which allows it to live off the world, to plunder it thanks to the domination of the dollar and technology. [...] Its primary source of unearned prosperity [is] the rent paid to the hegemon.« he said. »[The West does] not want to see us a free society, but a mass of soulless slaves,« Putin said. In other words, he addressed China and Asia, Africa, and Latin America at the same time. With the misleading claim that »in the 20th century [Russia] led the anti-colonial movement,« he recommended himself as an ally and leader of the Global South.

Indeed, Russia succeeded at getting the point across in many countries in Asia and Africa. Iran supplied Russia with drones and other missiles at discount prices for the terrorist war against Ukrainian cities. Putin's arms purchase conflated the wars and trouble spots of Eastern Europe with those of the Middle East. The rampant distrust of the West, the reawakened memory of colonial rule in the southern hemisphere, and China's rivalry with the US made Russia's point of view seem less far-fetched in a number of countries than it did in the West. I felt this also in the »NATO: A Chronicle of Cruelty« exhibition. Around the display cases with Azov relics and US flags stood Chinese, Uzbeks, and four officers from Mali. They were all studying at the Moscow Frunze Military Academy, the famous school of the Ministry of Defense. I met the Malian officers as they looked closely at the captured Western anti-tank missile. A 33-year-old officer from Bamako read the placards about the »NATO wars« in Iraq and Afghanistan. He felt reminded of the French. »That's exactly what they're doing here!« he complained. He found what NATO was doing in Ukraine »not at all wise.« Above all, he categorically denounced Western arms deliveries to the Ukrainian armed forces. »The French and Americans are interfering everywhere.« After all, he said, this is about a geopolitical struggle in the Russian sphere of influence. The Americans want to dispute Ukraine with Russia.

Zones of influence, Americans, Russians, world domination: the bombed Ukrainians and their wishes do not feature in this worldview. Putin's narrative is thus quite relatable in a world free of empathy. Many people do not notice the contradictions. Today, Putin is damning Lenin's Soviet Union as a multi-ethnic state and emulating Stalin's imperial-nationalist Soviet Russia. He subscribes to anti-colonialism with Indians and Africans, but he is waging a colonial war against Ukraine with the help of a colonial army of Buryats, Chechens, Tuvans, and Dagestanis. What they all have in common is their dislike of Europe and their hatred of the West. For many Africans and Arabs, the antipathy is rooted in colonial history and the succession of Western interventions, especially by the United States, Britain, and France. This explanation alone would not work for Russia, itself a colonial power. Therefore, the metaphysical dimension is added: the holy war.

Putin proclaimed this holy war himself on Red Square on May 9, 2022, when he called the defense of the motherland a »sacred« cause. At the annexation ceremony held at the same place on September 30, 2022, speakers whom he appointed called for the »holy war« against the West. This is also how Josef Stalin spoke during World War II, when the »holy war« was celebrated in a popular song. This is how Tsar Nicholas I described the Crimean War of the 19th century against the British and the French. And that's how the authorities talk in Putin's Russia. Orthodox Patriarch Kirill prayed for »Russian power« on Victory Day in the Cathedral of Christ the Savior. Russia has »never invaded anyone else,« the patriarch by Putin's grace said in all seriousness. May God protect the »sacred Russian borders« from »those of a different origin.« After Putin's mobilization, Kirill urged Russians to not fear death: »Sacrificing oneself purifies the soul from all the sins of life.« One of Putin's spin doctors who set the tone among the elite, duma Deputy Vyacheslav Nikonov, defined the character of the showdown with NATO as a metaphysical struggle between good and evil. »We are fighting a holy war here, which we must win.«

Now only the people had to be convinced of the message of the apocalyptic final battle. In his annexation speech at the end of September 2022, Putin said that the Americans had set themselves the goal not only of containing Russia but also of »dismembering and wiping out our country.« Ramzan Kadyrov called for the »de-Satanization« of the West. On state television, propagandists prepared viewers for the worst. Putin's star presenter Olga Skabeyeva said on her »60 Minutes« program: »A real war has broken out, the third world war. We are now forced to demilitarize not only Ukraine, but also the whole North Atlantic Alliance.« Putin called for Russia to fight together with China, India, and the rest of the world to destroy the »dictates and despotism« of the West. He claimed that the US has clawed its way onto the sun deck of the world, but its world order is already a thing of the past: »The ongoing collapse of Western hegemony is irreversible.« The US should finally step down from the world stage.

In the fall of 2022, such demands seemed grotesque at least in view of the ineffectiveness of Russian forces in the war against Ukraine so far. Therefore, the question remained: What if the US does not want this? What if the motivation and will of Ukrainians to assert themselves are stronger than any Russian attempts to destroy them? And what if the weapons supplied by the West enable the Ukrainians to push back or hold at bay Russia's troops? If so, Russia was always going to increase the pressure. Putin repeatedly threatened the West with the use of nuclear weapons during the course of the war against Ukraine. As early as 2018, he said, half-jokingly, that in the event of a nuclear war, Russians »will go to paradise as martyrs, but they (in the West) will simply die.« A remark Putin dropped in 2018 in a conversation with liberal opposition politician Grigory Yavlinsky is passed around Moscow. Yavlinsky confirmed to me that he had asked the president at the time if he knew that his foreign policy could lead to nuclear war. »Yes,« Putin replied flippantly, »and we will win it.« All that remains for the final chapter is the ultimate question: does he really mean it?

# Triumph or Armageddon

## His endgame

The outcome of the biggest global crisis since the Second World War depends above all on one man. Vladimir Putin boasts that he alone decided on the occupation of Crimea in 2014. In February 2022, he ordered the invasion of Ukraine by more than a hundred thousand Russian soldiers. He threatens the West with the use of nuclear weapons. Everything, including the survival of humanity, is in his hands.

In 2022, Vladimir Putin played wantonly with the weapons that had served as the ultimate deterrent since the Cold War, that no one could seriously imagine using unless the same were used against them. Putin's irresponsible rhetoric and his threats of using nuclear weapons for the first time refute an old assumption often heard in Germany: Putin is better than an unknown successor who is possibly even more radical. This is wrong. Vladimir Putin is not the better alternative to an even worse ruler. He himself is the radical alternative, the worst-case scenario. The assumption that Putin takes a moderate position in the Russian spectrum has for many years led to his misinterpretation and underestimation everywhere in the West but especially in Germany. He has adopted the radical positions of nationalists and warlords like Ramzan Kadyrov. Instead of pursuing policies aimed at unification and economic well-being, Putin has systematically and purposefully plunged Russia and the world into the greatest crisis in decades. Europe is experiencing the worst military confrontation since World War II. In this book, I have traced his main stages in this war:

Vladimir Putin has misled Germany and many gullible politicians. He has continued the legacy of the 1991 coup against Mikhail

Gorbachev and destroyed the democratic institutions of the 1990s. He has used the Chechen dictatorship as a blueprint for all of Russia. He has allied himself with nationalists and dictators around the world. He exposes his population to daily brainwashing by propaganda that turns the Russian people against themselves and the whole world. He has revived the Soviet system of law enforcement and prison camps. He has turned his country into a dictatorship with totalitarian features and a leader cult. He abuses the Russian past to poison the country and justify a war of aggression. He has waged a campaign of extermination against a neighboring country. He is sealing off his country from the world and reality and shattering the future of all Russians. He is declaring a holy war against the West and threatening the entire world with nuclear doom if things don't go his way. Taken together, this is enough to unleash the greatest catastrophe in human history. Putin's rule continues to radicalize. It is the most threatening regime in the world.

Today, the Russian president appears as a tough ideologue, but his world view is borrowed. As a nationalist by choice, he acquired his ideology at the advanced age of 60; he plays with it and varies it at will so as not to be falsifiable. He wants to build a state on the model of the Soviet Union, but only in its imperial outlines and not in the formation of society. A hermetic, socialist, world-gratification model would be dangerous for him because it could always prove contradictory, as happened in the late Soviet Union when socialist dreams and existing dictatorial leadership no longer fit together. Putin stays flexible. He represents ethno-nationalist and imperial-nationalist ideas at the same time; he presents himself as not only a Great Russian, but also pro-Islamic. He invokes family values, but he never appears with his partner or children; his own daughters have disowned him. He preaches hatred of the West and the EU, but he clings curiously to Europe and hesitates to clearly commit his country to the Asian future of which he and his comrades-in-arms speak. What connects all these contradictions is an aggression that has grown out of deep resentment.

For Russians, a question will arise in the not-too-distant future about what legacy the 71-year-old ruler will leave. For the masses, a certain degree of prosperity and, above all, political stability would have been an answer in 2021. But Putin's stabilization of the past 24 years, which he was able to provide largely thanks to high oil and gas prices, has collapsed because he is undoing his own successes. The start of the war in February, the mobilization, and the annexation of the occupied Ukrainian territories in September were turning points. Putin is sending a whole generation of young Russians to their deaths for a senseless war. Putin is destroying Russian society and rebuilding Russian industry for purely military reasons. He plunders the once-full state coffers. He is setting the country back years, if not decades. He is ruining everything for his Ukraine adventure.

Putin is too old to build anything new again. Unlike Peter I, who founded and reformed the Russian empire, unlike Catherine II, who extended the empire to the Black Sea and turned Russia into a country of immigration, unlike Alexander II, who abolished serfdom, and unlike Stalin, who left behind Soviet industrialization as well as mass crimes and millions of victims, Putin's legacy is likely to be primarily demolition and ashes. His chronic resentment and desire for revenge are blocking Russia's internal development. The attempted annihilation in Ukraine will backfire also in Russia, and the consequences of the vendetta will be catastrophic. Putin lacks a truly positive agenda, or even a noble goal, let alone a utopia worth fighting for.

Will the Russians overthrow him for this? The revolutions of January 1905 and February 1917 erupted when Russia was about to lose major wars. There was no sign of a broad popular uprising in Putin's Russia, only a mutiny of mercenaries when Russian troops came under pressure at the front in Ukraine in 2023. But can Putin be toppled from the throne without a revolution? Russia has no real tradition of army coup or coup d'état. The 1991 security services coup was the disintegration of the Soviet Union. The assassination of Tsar Peter III in 1762 and the deposition of party leader Nikita Khrushchev in 1964 took place under conditions that did not resemble Putin's situation in any way. The small demonstrations against mobilization in late September 2022 were stifled by a superior force of police. There were no symptoms of state decline, no elite opposition to Putin, no oligarch conspiracy, and no significant independent forces in society that could revolt against him. One exception was the mutiny of Yevgeny Prigozhin's Wagner brigades in June 2023, although according to Wagner's slogans, this was primarily directed against the Ministry of Defense rather than Putin as a person. It is doubtful whether Prigozhin ever intended to replace Putin. The nationalists, who took over the discourse in the media during the war, called for more bombs and more brutality but never questioned the ruler. Putin's hold on power was not threatened. The only thing that threatened him was himself.

Putin wanted to take his place between Peter the Great and Joseph Stalin in the eternal portrait gallery of Russian leaders. With the conquest of Crimea, he had already booked himself a niche in the hypostyle hall of immortality. But since the invasion of Ukraine in 2022, his political legacy has been suddenly at stake. Putin has unleashed a war that in its course and scope has slipped out of his control. Even if he serves this narrative to the people, it is not a defensive war as it was under Stalin, whose Soviet Union defended itself against Hitler's invasion in 1941. It is a war of aggression of his choice. Putin has taken total responsibility for it. He had the decision for the invasion staged on television. On February 21, Putin lectured to his closest aides, the intelligence directors, the security council chief, and the defense minister. He publicly paraded them around to commit them to his decision to go to war and to engage in co-liability. He made the decisions, and they had to implement them. In the war of aggression against Ukraine, Putin initially assumed the role of commander-in-chief. The commanders changed, as did the war tactics. In the »special operation,« Putin partly engaged in micromanagement; the big war against the West was all his own thing anyway. Only when the Russian army suffered defeat after defeat in Ukraine did Putin appoint a visible commander-in-chief for the operation, General Sergei Surovikin. He was to bear responsibility for the setbacks, including the inglorious withdrawal from Kherson in November 2022, only to be replaced again in 2023. Putin planned to take the cheers for any of the hoped-for victories.

The Russian people were not to have any other Putins besides Putin. The personalization of the regime gave him a pharaoh-like fullness of power; he became master of war or peace, of life or death over his citizens. But since everyone knew about this delimitation of power, he could no longer shift responsibility. All violence emanated from Putin. »If there is no Putin, there is no Russia,« one of his political lackeys once said. It was almost a caricature of dictatorship, but it contained a kernel of truth. If the Stabilocrat Putin falls, Russia's pyramidal architecture will be shaken. Changes in personnel are likely to cause shocks that would affect only the apparatus, but changes in elites could possibly shake up the whole society. The stakes are higher than ever before. That's why Putin cannot afford to do things by halfmeasures: no compromises, no concessions, no defeats. Others lose. In the eyes of the people, he must win.

Putin tried to turn the tide on his army's retreats in the Ukraine war by mobilizing the male population of Russia in September 2022. He adopted the old Russian approach of using a sheer mass of bodies to fight an adversary with technically superior weapons. Putin also bombed Ukraine and wreaked enormous destruction in major cities. Russia put its industry behind large quantities of weapons and ammunition, and Iran supplied drones. Until early 2024, it seemed at least possible that this war tactic could succeed in the long run.

Putin's second major front was against the West. He speculated that Western governments would either collapse under the pressure of unaffordable energy prices, runaway inflation, popular protests, and the rise of right-wing populist forces or turn to pro-Russian policies. He was betting on the return of Donald Trump or the seizure of power by a Trump copy from the Republican ranks in the US. He hoped for a policy turnaround in Eastern Europe and a resulting halt in arms deliveries to Ukraine. A Putin victory had always been possible. A defeat, however, was just as conceivable after the Kharkiv and Kherson retreats.

Those who repeat like a mantra that the great power that is Russia cannot lose are mistaken. History is full of examples of great powers that lost to supposedly inferior opponents. The Persian Empire against the Greek city-states, the Roman Empire against the Germanic tribes invading from the north, the Ottoman Empire against the rebelling peoples of Southeastern Europe, the Russian Empire against Japan in 1905, the US against Vietnam. Both nuclear powers, the Soviet Union and the United States, suffered defeats in Afghanistan, the mausoleum of the great powers.

So Putin could lose the war. Ukraine built the second-strongest army in Europe to defend against Russia. Volodymyr Zelensky mobilized his country at the very beginning of the war and sent a trained army of several hundred thousand soldiers into the field. In 2022, this force had managed to recapture several territories in eastern and southern Ukraine, even if the Ukrainian counter-offensive in 2023, like the Russian offensives before it, made little progress. Putin nurtured a formidable opponent. In contrast to the Russian army, the Ukrainian armed forces were highly motivated and mobilized and, in some cases, equipped with high-tech equipment.

Putin set two monstrous threats, the atomic bomb and the energy war, against his possible defeat in the war. He sharpened the nuclear threat in his mobilization speech of September 21, 2022. He went far beyond the Russian nuclear doctrine that envisions the use of such weapons in the event of a threat to Russia's existence. Putin threatened to use nuclear weapons in the event of a »threat to the territorial integrity of our country« when he declared, »To defend Russia and our people, we will certainly make use of all weapon systems available to us.« He then boasted that Russia had »more modern« nuclear weapons than NATO. »This is not a bluff.« Putin shortly thereafter had the occupied territories of Ukraine annexed in a pompous ceremony. Any attack from then on could be seen as an attack on Russian territory. In this way, he tried to deter Ukraine from reconquering and the West from further arms deliveries. What is worse, he upped the ante and blocked his own way out of the escalation. This was unusual for Putin, who used to like to keep multiple options open. The man drove himself to radicalization.

Putin and Security Council Vice-Chairman Medvedev used the Armageddon threat in 2022 in an almost inflationary manner. In Moscow, not a week went by without Putin or appointed politicians, talk show hosts, propagandists, and political technologists predicting the nuclear pulverization of London, Washington DC, or Berlin. This was part of the psychological warfare. It was intended, above all, to wear down the Germans by leveraging their tradition of nuclear apocalypticism and make them rebel against their government. This same stratagem was behind the talk of »dirty bombs« and the shelling adjacent to Ukrainian nuclear power plants. Russian forces staged battles around nuclear facilities and repeatedly fired on or around these sites to make it clear to Europe that it would be 5 seconds to midnight on the Doomsday Clock if the EU states did not stop supplying weapons very quickly.

But was Putin really ready for the fallout from a nuclear strike? In the spring of 2022, he had raised the level of combat readiness of the Russian nuclear forces to level two (out of four). After that, he refrained from a further increase in operational readiness. In the interim, he even had his spokesperson say that people should not keep talking about nuclear weapons. Was that a sign? In fact, the use of tactical nuclear weapons in Ukraine made little sense, because they are suitable for attacks on large targets like an entire army group or a major city. Ukraine's armed forces, however, are decentralized. Wiping out an entire city in Ukraine by nuclear strike could easily spread fallout over the Russian population. Russian soldiers would then have to capture such a city, and radiation would weaken their fighting strength. Another argument against a tactical nuclear strike was that in the event of a nuclear attack on the West, Putin would have to reckon with a counterattack on his country. Putin is not a suicidal man per se. His biographer, Fiona Hill, described him as a »survivalist,« someone who fights stubbornly to save his own skin. He wants to secure a prominent place in Russian history. A ruler who wantonly starts a nuclear war may still get to peel potatoes with Hitler in the kitchen of Hades, but he will certainly not get a place of honor in the pantheon of human history. Putin's nightmare is his political end, the timing and circumstances of which he does not determine for himself. For him, the ultimate weapon also provided a measure of self-deterrence because its use would lead to the same result, only faster.

But there is unfortunately also something to be said for the use of nukes. Whoever constantly threatens the nuclear option but never exercises it may, sooner or later, have to carry out the threat to maintain credibility and the usefulness of the weapons as a deterrent. Whoever keeps talking about nuclear weapons and lets others talk about them lowers the threshold for deployment and increases the risk of an accidental launch of a nuclear missile. Since Putin declared the possibility of defending the territories annexed in Ukraine with nuclear weapons, the stakes have risen dramatically for everyone. In the recent past, he has confirmed his preference for the most radical option. Was Putin talking himself into using the ultimate weapon? Putin fights hardest for his own survival, but what does that mean for the

71-year-old ruler in his nuclear bunker? If he were ever to use nuclear weapons, it might be in a situation where his personal fate was at stake. It is hard to predict what he will choose.

Since he could not effectively hit the US, Putin carried out the second threat in the summer of 2022 with an energy war against Europe. Before the EU's painstakingly coordinated and long-term sanctions plan against Russian energy supplies could take effect, Putin simply cut off Europe's gas. He did not need a majority vote to do so; he is the majority in his country. He predicted that before the Western sanctions took full effect in Russia, the EU would collapse under high gas prices, inflation, and riots. Europe, especially Germany, would be the main theater of Russia's hybrid war against the West. But would this calculation work out? Putin had so often been mistaken about Europe's weakness and had repeatedly underestimated the EU. He did not count on the European sanctions in 2014/15. He did not count on the failure of his support for far-right parties in Europe. He did not count on determined EU support for Ukraine in the war. Of course, it is quite possible that Europe will sink into a deep economic crisis with dramatic political consequences in the coming years. But it may just as well be that Putin is wrong again about Europe's self-assertiveness. His influence on the European continent has shrunk enormously as a result of the war.

Putin is now exchanging interdependence with Europe for dependence on China. In the relationship with Europe, he used to have a lot of leverage, but not so with China. Putin's influence on Chinese domestic politics is nil. But because he is ostracized by the West and other parts of the world, China remains his only recourse. Increasing dependence on its dominance in high-tech goods, financial and foreign exchange transactions, and gas exports will severely restrict Russia's freedom of movement. At the Shanghai Cooperation Organization summit in September 2022, Chinese leadership made their superiority felt. Russia still has an advantage in nuclear armaments, but

China will catch up within a few years. Putin's bitterest pill to swallow will be the prices dictated to Moscow by Beijing as the main buyer of Russian gas. The dystopia that Russian writer Vladimir Sorokin drew up in *Day of the Oprichnik* (2010) is on the horizon: a Russia that lives as a backward quasi-colony run by a dictatorial clique entirely on Chinese technology and Chinese consumer goods. As a satellite of China, Planet Putin would lose its sovereignty.

Moreover, the structural weaknesses in the Russian army exposed in Ukraine have reduced Russia's strategic importance throughout Asia. This became apparent in October 2022, for example, when Putin had to endure a punishing speech from the Tajik president at a post-Soviet summit in Astana. Kazakhstan, Azerbaijan, Armenia, and other states also distanced themselves. Respect and fear for Russia plummeted in Central Asia. It was hard to imagine that Putin could still resolve conflicts in the post-Soviet space in a few days, as he once did by sending in a few paratroopers. In the neighboring countries, doubts grew about the man fixated on military power. He lost his sparkle as a result of the war.

But for now, Putin is left with the vast wealth of fossil fuels that he is using against the West and the world. Putin is linked to these fuels like no Russian leader before him. He owes his career as ruler to the oil and gas resources. Putin's rise began in the early 2000s, when OPEC agreed on a set minimum price for a barrel of oil after chronically low commodity prices in the 1990s. Commodity prices rose to record highs during his tenure and financed the prosperity he sold to the people as his own achievement. Export pipelines to Europe were of considerable importance. Oil and gas helped him expand his power despite many setbacks. Oil and gas enabled him to finance the war in the first half of 2022 and to cushion the sanctions imposed by the West. Putin believes he can use these fuels to force the West to back down. Here, too, he could be wrong. There is much more to suggest that the commodity war is Putin's last stand and one that he will lose.

Putin's gas embargo against Germany and most EU states in 2022 ended Russia's lengthy period of petro-fortune. Europe was not only the largest buyer of Russian gas, but also the natural customer for Russia's largest gas reserves, which lie in western Siberia. Europe imported about fifteen times as much Russian gas as China until the Russian gas embargo. But since 2022, the numerous pipelines to Europe have lain idle. What is more, the attacks on three strands of the ultramodern Nord Stream pipelines shattered the prospects of supplying large quantities of hydrogen to Europe in a post-gas future. Only the pipelines to Turkey still supplied fuel to southeastern Europe. Revenues from the export of raw materials fell. The surplus gas burned in huge flares over northern Russia and entered the atmosphere to heat up the world. For his hybrid war against the EU, Putin sacrificed both climate goals and Gazprom, the nation's fossil-fuel flagship and a source of pride. The Russian gas industry had no real alternative to its European customers. There is a pipeline to China, but it has less capacity than Nord-Stream 1 alone. And even this pipeline was not at full capacity in 2022 due to a lack of gas resources in East Siberia. To fill the pipeline completely, it would have to be connected to the gas fields in Western Siberia, which Russia lacks the money to do during the war. Were China to foot the bill and lay another gas pipeline from Western Siberia to China, it would take at least twelve years to complete, according to independent energy experts. The rapid expansion of gas liquefaction plants for LNG exports is being delayed or prevented by Western sanctions. Many of the supporters of this technology are based in the West.

Putin could use the gas as a weapon against Europe only once. America could never be directly hit. His former major customers, on the one hand, have long since reoriented themselves. Germany gets its gas mainly from Norway, America, and, in the future, perhaps also from Africa and the Gulf states. Putin, on the other hand, is setting back his heavily sanctioned gas industry by many years with the war.

The big business of the coming period will be done by others: the Gulf States, the US, Canada, Australia, and new suppliers from Africa. While Russia should have been upgrading technology to expand equally in the global gas market, other suppliers will have already divided it up. Western industrialized countries are also increasing their investments in renewable and sustainable energy production as a result of the war. Russia, unlike the Gulf States, is barely investing in hydrogen production. The post-fossil age is emerging. Oil and gas will be in less demand in the future than they are today.

Putin said in May 2022 that he was waging a preemptive war because NATO wanted to attack Russia. That was a lie, of course, because NATO was planning nothing of the sort. But he is, in fact, waging a kind of preemptive war—before Russia's inevitable disempowerment in the future. Putin's campaign against the loss of significance is probably the last war that the country can wage while fully exploiting its oil and gas reserves. Its exports have already shrunk sharply. Russia had to sell crude oil to Asian countries at fire-sale prices. It burned the surplus gas production and warmed the atmosphere. What else does Russia have to offer? The future of the world is not fossil fuels, and the future does not belong to Russia if it only offers itself as the last fossil fuel giant for the international community.

It was impossible to predict how the war and the world's most threatening regime would develop when this book was completed. There was constant speculation about an uprising against Putin and a quick end to the war. The Wagner rebellion of summer 2023 demonstrated the simmering discontent in nationalist circles and the potential explosive power. But 'Prigozhin's rapid failure also showed that Putin had secured his power well; he was difficult to challenge. A major hot war against the West was possible at any time, but Putin would be at a disadvantage entering an even larger military conflict while his army was engaged in intense fighting in Ukraine. The most likely outcome was a war of attrition, with bombs and artillery against Ukraine and with hybrid, digital, and energy weapons deployed against the West.

There is much to suggest that the attack on Ukraine and the West may be Putin's last great war. He has torn up the social contract with his people and is burning through the petro-prosperity of the last two decades. In its place, he has built a reign of fear. The best and brightest of his people are leaving the country. Real innovations and discoveries have not come out of Russia for some time. Large parts of Russian industry are groaning under the conditions of the war economy, which is poised for a hard landing once the war will be over. The end of the fossil-fuel era is approaching and, as a result, Russia's revenues will shrink. The country is drifting into dependence on China. The campaign against the Ukrainian people threatens to be a draining endeavor in which Ukraine is destroyed and Russia is cannibalized for its ruler's obsessive war. Hundreds of thousands of people have already died for this obsession with vengeance, and many more may die. With the mobilization of Russian men, he is, in effect, waging war against his own people. A severe demographic crisis, caused by emigration, insecurity, excessively high mortality, and the massive losses at the front, will affect the Russian population. Putin has destroyed his life's work of »stabilizing« Russia. His unbridled destructiveness is now hitting Ukraine, his own country, and possibly the world.

This does not mean that Russia will disappear from the map, as Putin himself murmurs apocalyptically, in the event of defeat. Nor is there much to suggest at present that the country could disintegrate. Putin's great hope is that the torn and confused West will defeat itself. Yet the age of revenge is entering a finale, the duration and drama of which are difficult to predict. The lengthy decline of Putin's regime has begun with this war. Putin can now rely on only one thing. His prominent place in history is assured—as the most bloodthirsty ruler Russia has seen since Joseph Stalin.

# Further Reading

**Attack**—Russia is out for revenge
- Brackvogel, Thomas, Michael Thumann, and Christian Schmidt-Häuer. 1999. »Da wird kein Krieg geführt. Wladimir Putin über Tschetschenien, Korruption und die Wirtschaftslage.« *Die Zeit.* November 18.
- Thumann, Michael. 2016. »'Vielen Dank, meine Herren!' So höflich ging Russlands neuer Präsident 1999 mit Journalisten.« *Die Zeit.* February 15.
- Bush, George W. »Flashback: President Bush on Putin's 'soul'« NBC News. https://www.nbcnews.com/video/flashback-president-bush-on-putin-soul-208352323648
- Medvedev, Dmitry. 2022. »August 9.« VKontakte. https://vk.com/wall53083705_54582
- Winkler, Heinrich August. 2022. »Die Legende von der versäumten Chance« *International Politics* June 27. https://internationalepolitik.de/de/die-legende-von-der-versaeumtenchance

**Misguided**—How German Politicians Helped Putin
- Adler, Sabine. 2022. *Die Ukraine und wir. Deutschlands Versagen und die Lehren für die Zukunft.* Berlin. [English edition 2023: *Ukraine and Its Western Allies.* Stuttgart: ibidem-Verlag].
- Fleischhauer, Ingeborg. 2006. »Rathenau in Rapallo, eine notwendige Korrektur des Forschungsstandes.« *Vierteljahreshefte für Zeitgeschichte,* Jahrgang 54(3): 365-415.
- Schieder, Theodor. 1967. »Die Entstehungsgeschichte des Rapallo-Vertrags.« *Historische Zeitschrift* 204(1).
- Thumann, Michael. 2022. »Ein verhängnisvolles Abkommen. Der Vertrag von Rapallo festigte vor 100 Jahren Deutschlands heikles Verhältnis zu Russland – mit Nachwirkungen bis heute.« *Die Zeit.* April 15.

- Krupa, Matthias, and Michael Thumann. 2018. »Rohrkrepierer. Polen motzt, Amerika wütet, die EU fremdelt. Wie die Gaspipeline Nordstream 2 für Deutschland zum Debakel wurde.« *Die Zeit*. October 3.
- Die Zeit. 2022. »Wenn der Gasmann zweimal klingelt: Wie sich ein Netzwerk sozialdemokratischer Politiker von Putin und dem russischen Erdgas verführen ließ – und so Deutschland erpressbar machte.« *Die Zeit*. February 10.
- Thumann, Michael. 2022. »Fatale Geschäfte mit Erpressern. Der Gaskonzern Uniper hat Deutschlands Abhängigkeit von Russland vorangetrieben und Alternativen ignoriert. Die Steuerzahler werden das wohl teuer bezahlen müssen.« *Zeit Online*. July 8. https://www.zeit.de/wirtschaft/2022-07/uniper-eon-russland-gas-abhaengigkeit-5vor8
- Klingst, Martin. »›Nordstream 2 war ein Fehler. Und auf die Osteuropäer haben wir schlicht nicht gehört.‹ Ein Interview mit dem Vorsitzenden der Atlantik-Brücke, Sigmar Gabriel.« Atlantic Bruecke. https://www.atlantikbruecke.org/nord-stream-2-war-ein-fehler-und-auf-die-osteuropaeerhaben-wir-schlicht-nicht-gehoert/
- Dornblüth, Gesine, and Thomas Franke. 2022. *Ruhmlose Helden. Ein Flugzeugabsturz und die Tücken deutsch-russischer Verständigung*. Berlin.

**Gallery of Ancestors**—Why the 1991 Putschists have Won Today
- Plokhy, Serhii. 2014. *The Last Empire. The Final Days of the Soviet Union*. New York.
- Thumann, Michael. 2021. »'Papa, steh auf, ein Umsturz!' Im August 1991 greifen KGB und Militär in Moskau nach der Macht. Der Putsch scheitert an Boris Jelzins Widerstand – und wird doch zur Geburtsstunde des heutigen Russland.« *Die Zeit*. August 20.
- Zubok, Vladislav M. 2021. *Collapse. The Fall of the Soviet Union*. New Haven: Yale University Press.

**Exercises in Democracy**—The Hopes of the 1990s
- Alexievich, Svetlana. 2015. *Secondhand Time: The Last of The Soviets*. New York.
- Gessen, Mascha. 2017. *The Future is History. How Totalitarianism Reclaimed Russia*. New York: Riverhead Books.
- Siegert, Jens. 2021. *Im Prinzip Russland. Eine Begegnung in 22 Begriffen*. Hamburg.
- Thumann, Michael. 2016. »Prost! Auf den Untergang! Am 8. Dezember 1991 löste Boris Jelzin in einem abgelegenen Jagdpalais die Sowjetunion auf. Eine Rekonstruktion des dramatischen Tages.« *Die Zeit*. December 8.

**Rogue Republic**—The Chechen Model
- de Waal, Thomas, and Carlotta Gall. 1997. *Chechnya. A Small Victorious War*. London.
- Politkovskaya, Anna. 2002. *Tschetschnja. Tschuschaja wojna ili schisn sa schlagbaumom*. Moscow: n. p.
- Thumann, Michael. 2002: *Das Lied von der Russischen Erde. Moskaus Ringen um Einheit und Größe*. Stuttgart/Munich.
- Dubnov, Vadim. 2016. »Chechnya's New Contract With the Kremlin.« Carnegie Moscow Center. https://carnegiemoscow.org/2016/10/27/chechnya-s-new-contract-with-kremlin-pub-64955

**Nationalists by choice**—Putin's good friends in the world
- The opening quote from Putin comes from the film »World Order« by Vladimir Solovyov, which was published online on March 7, 2018 [video now private and unavailable]: https://www.youtube.com/watch?v=uC2bWSbZdQ4
- Interview. 1999. »Da wird kein Krieg geführt. Wladimir Putin über Tschetschenien, Korruption und die Wirtschaftslage.« *Die Zeit*. November 18.
- Lendvai, Paul. 2021. *Orbáns Ungarn*. Vienna.

- Thumann, Michael. 2020. »Der Neue Nationalismus. Wiederkehr einer totgeglaubten Ideologie.« Die Andere Bibliothek vol. 430. Berlin.
- Putin, Vladimir. 2012. »Russia—The Ethnicity Issue.« *Nezavisimaya Gazeta*. January 23. http://archive.premier.gov.ru/eng/events/news/17831/

**Information war**—How the Russians are incited
- Pomerantsev, Peter. 2014. *Nothing Is True and Everything Is Possible. The Surreal Heart of the New Russia*. New York.
- The business connections between Margarita Simonyan and her husband as well as her sister Alissa were highlighted by the BBC's Russian service on November 7, 2018: https://sova.news/2018/11/07/1053-1072-1082-1086-1084-1077-1076-1080-1102-1050-1088-1099-1084-1089-1082-1080-1081-1084-1086-1089-1090-1076-1072-1083-1080-1076-1077-1085-1100-1075-1080-1073-1077-1079-1082-1086-1085-1082-1091-1088/
- Aleksei Navalny's research team has also comprehensively described Margarita Simonyan's network: https://snob.ru/society/fbk-rasskazal-o-sotnyah-millionov-rublej-kotoryj-zarabotali-margarita-simonyan-i-ee-muzh-na-kontraktah-s-aeroflotom/
- Atai, Golineh. 2019. *Die Wahrheit ist der Feind. Warum Russland so anders ist*.« Berlin.
- Thumann, Michael. 2015. »Und… Action. Früher waren die Sowjets hochgerüstet, heute streben die Russen nach Dominanz im digitalen Informationskrieg.« *Die Zeit*. August 9.
- Spahn, Susanne. 2016. *Das Ukrainebild in Deutschland. Die Rolle der russischen Medien. Wie Russland die deutsche Öffentlichkeit beeinflusst*. Hamburg.

**The Putin Archipelago**—Russia's system of penal camps
- Merridale, Catherine. 2001. *Night of Stone. Death and Memory in Twentieth-Century Russia*. New York.
- Solzhenitsyn, Aleksander. 1974. *The Gulag Archipelago*. Paris.

- Thumann, Michael. 2021. »Mit ihren Regeln machen sie ein Tier aus dir.« *Die Zeit*. April 28.
- Applebaum, Anne. 2004. *Gulag. A History*. New York.

**Elections without choice**—Descent into dictatorship
- Belton, Catherine. 2022. *Putins Netz. Wie sich der KGB Russland zurückholte und dann den Westen ins Auge fasste*.« Hamburg.
- Bota, Alice. 2021. *Die Frauen von Belarus. Von Revolution, Mut und dem Drang nach Freiheit*. Berlin.
- Thumann, Michael. 2022. »Habe ich Angst? Schritt für Schritt hat Putin in Russland eine Meinungsdiktatur errichtet, die ihre Gegner wegsperrt oder ermordet.« *Zeit-Geschichte*. July 18.
- Kolesnikov, Andrei. 2022. »Putin Has Moved from Authoritarianism to Hybrid Totalitarianism.« Carnegie Endowment. https://carnegieendowment.org/2022/04/19/putin-s-war-has-movedrussia-from-authoritarianism-to-hybrid-totalitarianism-pub-86921
- Snyder, Timothy. 2022. »We Should Say It. Russia Is Fascist.« *New York Times*. May 19. https://www.nytimes.com/2022/05/19/opinion/russia-fascism-ukraine-putin.html

**Executor of History**—Putin's abuse of the past
- Adomeit, Hannes. 2018. »Nato-Erweiterung. Gab es westliche Garantien?« *Bundesakademie für Sicherheitspolitik, Arbeitspaper Sicherheitspolitik* 3. https://www.baks.bund.de/de/arbeitspapiere/2018/natoosterweiterung-gab-es-westliche-garantien
- Creuzberger, Stefan. 2015. »Die Legende vom Wortbruch. Russland, der Westen und die Nato-Osterweiterung.« *Osteuropa* 3: 95–108
- Sarotte, Mary. 2021. *Not One Inch. America, Russia and the Making of the Post-Cold War Stalemate*. Yale.
- Savranskaya, Svetlana, and Tom Blanton. 2017. »What Gorbachev Heard.« National Security Archive. December 12. https://nsarchive.gwu.edu/briefing-book/russia-programs/2017-12-12/nato-expansion-what-gorbachev-heard-western-leaders-early

- Teltschik, Horst. 2019. »Die Legende vom gebrochenen Versprechen.« *Die Zeit*. July 10.
- Thumann, Michael. 2022. »Der Geschichtsvollzieher. Warum Putins Erzählung von den gebrochenen Versprechen nicht stimmt.« *Die Zeit*. February 24.
- Thumann, Michael. 2022. »Der Mythos vom falschen Versprechen.« *Zeit Online*. January 21. https://www.zeit.de/politik/ausland/2022-01/ukraine-konflikt-nato-osterweiterung-russland
- Wiegrefe, Klaus. 2022. »Genscher-Vertrauter widerspricht Putin im Streit über Nato-Osterweiterung. Genschers Spitzendiplomat Frank Elbe schildert, wie er die Gespräche erlebt hat.« *Der Spiegel*. February 25.
- Kappeler, Andreas. 2019. *Kleine Geschichte der Ukraine*. Munich:
- Putin, Vladimir. 2022. »Address by the President of the Russian Federation 21 February, 2022.« The Kremlin. http://www.en.kremlin.ru/events/president/transcripts/67828
- Putin, Vladimir. 2021. »On the historical unity of Russians and Ukrainians.« The Kremlin. http://en.kremlin.ru/events/president/news/66181

**Special Operation—How to wipe out Ukraine**
- Sasse, Gwendolyn. 2022. *Der Krieg gegen die Ukraine. Hintergründe, Ereignisse, Folgen*. Munich: C.H.Beck.
- Eigendorf, Katrin. 2022. *Putins Krieg. Wie die Menschen in der Ukraine für unsere Freiheit kämpfen*. Frankfurt.
- von Fritsch, Rüdiger. 2022. *Zeitenwende. Putins Krieg und die Folgen*. Berlin.
- Quiring, Manfred. 2022. *Russland – Ukrainekrieg und Weltmachtträume*. Berlin.
- Plokhy, Serhii. 2022. *Die Frontlinie. Wie die Ukraine zum Schauplatz eines neuen Ost-West-Konflikts wurde*. Hamburg: Rowohlt 2023.

- Shekhovtsov, Anton. 2022. »Das Asow-Regiment ist keine extremistische Organisation« *Die Zeit*. May 7.
- Jeska, Andrea, and Michael Thumann. 2022. »500 000 Ukrainer sollen nach Russland verschleppt worden sein. Stimmt das? Oder sind es Flüchtlinge? Eine Spurensuche« *Die Zeit*. June 5.
- New Lines Institute. 2022. »An Independent Legal Analysis of the Russian Federation's Breaches of the Genocide Convention in Ukraine and the Duty to Prevent.« New Lines Institute. https://newlinesinstitute.org/wp-content/uploads/An-Independent-Legal-Analysis-of-the-Russian-Federations-Breaches-of-the-Genocide-Convention-in-Ukraine-andthe-Duty-to-Prevent-1-2.pdf
- Luchterhandt, Otto. 2022. »Völkermord in Mariupol. Russlands Kriegsführung in der Ukraine« *Osteuropa* 72: 65–85.
- Quote from Iryna Veretschuk in: Gnauck, Gerhard. 2022. »Russland stiehlt Kinder, um sie adoptieren zu lassen.« *Frankfurter Allgemeine Zeitung*. August 12.

**Planet Putin**—Russia seals itself off
- Ganijewa, Alissa. 2022. »Die Anbetung der Stärke. Warum Putin in Russland so populär ist.« *Frankfurter Allgemeine Zeitung*. May 13.
- Schumatzky, Boris. 2022. »Die russische Schuld. Ein Vernichtungskrieg wie in der Ukraine ist aus einem Wahn gewachsen. Und ob ich es will oder nicht – ich steckte mitten drin.« *Frankfurter Allgemeine Zeitung*. May 29.
- Thumann, Michael. 2022. » Wir zeigen es Euch! Ob McDonald's, Coca-Cola oder Ikea – nach dem Rückzug westlicher Firmen werden deren Produkte in Russland imitiert.« *Die Zeit*. June 20.

**Empire of Fear**—The mobilization of the people
- Thumann, Michael. 2022. »Moskaus Partysommer ist vorbei. Mit der Mobilmachung hat Wladimir Putin den Krieg ins eigene Land getragen. Nun könnte ihm die Kontrolle entgleiten.« *Die Zeit*. September 28.

- Putin, Vladimir. 2022. »Address by the President of the Russian Federation« [speech on »partial mobilization,« September 21]. The Kremlin. http://en.kremlin.ru/events/president/news/69390
- Stanovaya, Tatiana. 2022 »Putin's Apocalyptic End Game in Ukraine. Annexation and Mobilization Make Nuclear War More Likely.« *Foreign Affairs* October 6.
- Thumann, Michael. 2022. »Die geprügelte Armee. Putins Truppe wird neuerdings auch in Russland kritisiert – warum sind die Streitkräfte in so einem maroden Zustand.« *Die Zeit*. October 15.

**Holy War**—Putin's Revenge on the West

- Putin, Vladimir. 2018. »Speech to the Federal Assembly.« The Kremlin. March 1. http://kremlin.ru/events/president/news/56957
- Levada Institute. 2022. »Survey on German–Russian relations.« Levada Institute. June. https://www.levada.ru/2022/06/15/mezhdunarodnye-otnosheniya7/
- Thumann, Michael. 2022. »Im Westen nichts Gutes. Feindbild Nato. Eine Ausstellung in Moskau unterstützt Putins Ukraine-Krieg ideologisch.« *Die Zeit*. May 13.
- Patriarch Kirill. On the Holy War. http://www.patriarchia.ru/db/text/5922848.html
- Putin, Vladimir. 2022. »Signing of treaties on accession of Donetsk and Lugansk people's republics and Zaporozhye and Kherson regions to Russia [speech on annexation of occupied territories of Ukraine].« The Kremlin. September 30. http://en.kremlin.ru/events/president/news/69465

**Triumph or Armageddon**—His endgame

- Hill, Fiona, and Clifford G. Gaddy. 2015. *Mr. Putin. Operative in the Kremlin*. Washington, DC: Brookings Institution.
- Radchenko, Sergey. 2022. »Coups in the Kremlin. What the History of Russia's Power Struggles Says about Putin's Future.«

*Foreign Affairs*. September 22. https://www.foreignaffairs.com/russian-federation/coups-kremlin
- Sorokin, Vladimir. 2022. *Der Tag des Opritschniks*. Cologne.

# Thanks

The idea for this book was born a few weeks after the Russian invasion of Ukraine, when it became clear that Europe and the world had slipped irreversibly into a new age. I wrote the manuscript mainly in the summer and early fall of 2022, when I was in Moscow, watching with bated breath as the Russians settled into the double world of the war in Ukraine and the almost carefree life at home.

I am grateful to many who helped me write this book.

My long stays in Moscow had to be endured by my wife, Susanne Landwehr, and my children, Nikolaus Thumann and Konstantin Thumann. They also put up with me and spurred me on when I retreated to my desk during my visits to Berlin. Without the firm support of my family, I would not have been able to write.

*Zeit*'s longtime editorial assistant in Moscow, Lena Sambuk, and journalist Alexander Sambuk helped me understand and penetrate Russian politics and society as much as possible. Alexander and Lena Sambuk tirelessly proofread my manuscript at all hours of the day and night, giving me crucial tips and making important corrections. Without them, the writing would not have been possible.

During the writing process, it was very important for me to have a productive exchange with my editor at Verlag C.H. Beck, Matthias Hansl, without whose attentive eye and farsighted advice I would be lost. Before I started working with C.H. Beck, I was helped in the preparations for the book by fruitful exchange with the Mercator Foundation, especially with Florian Christ and Anne Duncker.

The editor-in-chief of *Die Zeit*, Giovanni di Lorenzo, and the head of the politics department, Heinrich Wefing, sent me to Russia two years ago, after I had already worked there as a *Zeit* correspondent from 1996 to 2001 and from 2014 to 2015. The editorial team provided me with close and attentive support during the difficult weeks and months of 2022. In Russia, I was able to gather the experience and perspective that have gone into this book.

Many conversations in Moscow and Berlin about Russian politics and German Ostpolitik accompanied the book and its preparation. I regularly exchanged ideas not only with my colleagues in the politics department of *Die Zeit*, but also outside the editorial office. The discussions with Thomas Bagger, Falk Bomsdorf, Markus Ederer, Sabine Fischer, Rüdiger Freiherr von Fritsch, Géza Andreas von Geyr, Tim Guldimann, Jochen Hellbeck, Christoph Heusgen, Fiona Hill, Christiane Hoffmann, Manfred Huterer, Thomas Kleine-Brockhoff, Andrea von Knoop, Andrej Kolesnikow, Andrej Kortunow, Anna Kuchenbecker, Nico Lange, Andreas Nick, Jurij Piwowarow, Ruprecht Polenz, Manfred Quiring, Boris Ruge, Ina Ruck, Gwendolyn Sasse, Wolfgang Silbermann, Frank-Walter Steinmeier, Constanze Stelzenmüller, Angela Stent, Karl Schlögel, Martin Schulze Wessel, Alexander Tschepurenko, Tobias Tunkel, and Markus Ziener were so important. I would not want to have missed out on the thoughts and suggestions from all of you.

I would like to express my sincere thanks to all of the above.

*ibidem*.eu